William Henry Simcox

The Revelation of Saint John the Divine

With Notes and Introduction

William Henry Simcox

The Revelation of Saint John the Divine
With Notes and Introduction

ISBN/EAN: 9783337779870

Printed in Europe, USA, Canada, Australia, Japan

Cover: Foto ©Lupo / pixelio.de

More available books at **www.hansebooks.com**

The Cambridge Bible for Schools and Colleges.

GENERAL EDITOR:—J. J. S. PEROWNE, D.D.
DEAN OF PETERBOROUGH.

THE REVELATION

OF

S. JOHN THE DIVINE.

WITH NOTES AND INTRODUCTION

BY THE LATE

REV. WILLIAM HENRY SIMCOX, M.A.

RECTOR OF HARLAXTON.

EDITED FOR THE SYNDICS OF THE UNIVERSITY PRESS.

CAMBRIDGE:
AT THE UNIVERSITY PRESS.
1890

PREFACE
BY THE GENERAL EDITOR.

THE General Editor of *The Cambridge Bible for Schools* thinks it right to say that he does not hold himself responsible either for the interpretation of particular passages which the Editors of the several Books have adopted, or for any opinion on points of doctrine that they may have expressed. In the New Testament more especially questions arise of the deepest theological import, on which the ablest and most conscientious interpreters have differed and always will differ. His aim has been in all such cases to leave each Contributor to the unfettered exercise of his own judgment, only taking care that mere controversy should as far as possible be avoided. He has contented himself chiefly with a careful revision of the notes, with pointing out omissions, with

PREFACE.

suggesting occasionally a reconsideration of some question, or a fuller treatment of difficult passages, and the like.

Beyond this he has not attempted to interfere, feeling it better that each Commentary should have its own individual character, and being convinced that freshness and variety of treatment are more than a compensation for any lack of uniformity in the Series.

DEANERY, PETERBOROUGH.

PREFACE.

THE MS. of the Commentary as well as a Transcript of the Text for the Cambridge Greek Testament were substantially completed in 1883, so that in the first draught of his work my brother could not make use of the Revised Version; and though the MS. was subsequently carefully revised as to substance he did not insert systematic references. These have now been generally supplied. The third Appendix is from a paper read by request before a society of theological students at Oxford, which accounts for a somewhat personal tone. The substance would probably have been embodied in the Introduction if the writer had lived. I am responsible for the summary of Völter's Analysis, which was not required by the audience, and for some additions to the First Excursus, of which I failed to discover a completed MS.

G. A. SIMCOX.

CONTENTS.

		PAGES
I. INTRODUCTION.		
Chapter I.	Authorship and Canonicity of the Revelation	ix—xxxii
Chapter II.	Date and Place of Composition	xxxii—xli
Chapter III.	Principles of Interpretation	xli—lviii
Chapter IV.	Analysis	lviii—lx
II. TEXT AND NOTES		1—146
III. APPENDIX.		
Excursus I.	The Angels of the Churches: Elemental Angels: the living creatures	147—151
Excursus II.	On the Heresies controverted in the Revelation	151—155
Excursus III.	On the supposed Jewish origin of the Revelation of St John	155—174

⁎ The Text adopted in this Edition is that of Dr Scrivener's *Cambridge Paragraph Bible*. A few variations from the ordinary Text, chiefly in the spelling of certain words, and in the use of italics, will be noticed. For the principles adopted by Dr Scrivener as regards the printing of the Text see his Introduction to the *Paragraph Bible*, published by the Cambridge University Press.

Much he ask'd in loving wonder,
  On Thy bosom leaning, Lord!
In that secret place of thunder,
  Answer kind didst thou accord,
Wisdom for Thy Church to ponder
  Till the day of dread award.

Lo! Heaven's doors lift up, revealing
  How Thy judgments earthward move;
Scrolls unfolded, trumpets pealing,
  Wine-cups from the wrath above,
Yet o'er all a soft Voice stealing—
  "Little children, trust and love!"

KEBLE.

INTRODUCTION.

CHAPTER I.

AUTHORSHIP AND CANONICITY OF THE REVELATION.

IN the case of some of the books of Scripture, the questions of their authorship and of their canonical authority are quite independent of one another. Many books[1] are anonymous, many have their authors known only by a post-canonical tradition[2]; and the rejection, in any case where it may be called for, of this tradition need not and ought not to involve a denial of the divine authority of the book. Even in cases where the supposed author is named or unmistakeably indicated in the book itself, it does not always follow that the book must either be written by him, or can owe none of its inspiration to the Spirit of truth: the person of the professed author may be assumed dramatically without any *mala fides*[3]. On the other hand, there are books which plainly exclude any such hypothesis, and must either be forgeries, more or less excusable but hardly consistent with divine direction, or else must be accepted as genuine and inspired works of their professed authors.

The case of the Revelation may be regarded as intermediate between the two last-named classes. The author gives his name as "John," but gives no *unmistakeable* token, in this

---

[1] e.g. Judges, Kings, and Chronicles; and in the N.T., Hebrews.
[2] e.g. the Synoptical Gospels.
[3] As is certainly the case with the apocryphal Wisdom of Solomon, and almost certainly with Ecclesiastes. It is conceivable that the case of the Pastoral Epistles of St Paul might be similar.

book itself, to identify him with St John the Apostle: and hence the opinion is rationally tenable, that the Revelation is the work of a person named John, writing what he *bonâ fide* regarded as a supernatural vision, but not having more claim on the reverence of the Church than his work can command on its own merits. On the other hand, we shall find that the book was so early and so widely received as the work of the Apostle, that it may well be suspected that, if not really his, it was falsely put forward as his, and intended by the real author to be received as his: so that the hypothesis of fraudulent forgery, if not necessary, can hardly be considered gratuitous.

It thus will be convenient to discuss the two questions of *authorship* and of *canonical authority* in connexion with one another, though remembering that the determination of one does not (except in one case) necessarily involve that of the other. The book may be either (1) the genuine and inspired work of St John the Apostle; or (2) a forgery in the name of St John the Apostle; or (3) it may be the genuine and inspired work of another John; or (4) a *bonâ fide* but uninspired work of another John. We may fairly set aside the logically conceivable cases, of the Apostle writing *not* under divine inspiration, or of a person writing indeed fraudulently, but not intending to personate the Apostle. Let us examine the evidence, external and internal, for each of these views:—

I. The external attestation of St John's authorship is extremely strong: it happens to be quoted, with the author's name, earlier than any other book of the New Testament, with the one exception of St Paul's First Epistle to the Corinthians. Justin Martyr, in his *Dialogue with Trypho the Jew*, says expressly, "There was with us a man named *John, one of the Apostles of Christ*, who in the Revelation made to him"—says, in substance, what is said in Rev. xx. 3—6. The date of this *Dialogue* is variously fixed from A.D. 135 to 148: the scene is laid at Ephesus, where surely, if anywhere, the true authorship of the Revelation must have been known. The same writer in his First *Apology*, which was written not later than A.D. 160, refers unmistakeably to Rev. xii. or xx. 2: but this is only evidence to the authority, not to the authorship.

We may regard as practically contemporary with this the evidence afforded by Papias, bishop of Hierapolis, near Laodicea, who acknowledged the Apocalypse, as is stated by Andrew, bishop (in the fifth century?) of Caesarea, in Cappadocia, in the prologue to his Commentary on the book. Papias's evidence, if we had it at first hand, would be even more convincing than Justin's: for not only did he belong to the district where the Revelation was first circulated[1], but he is said to have been a hearer of St John himself—he certainly was a zealous collector of traditions relating to him. But Papias's own works are lost, and though Andrew was doubtless acquainted with them, his testimony is not quite decisive. Eusebius professes (*H. E.* III. iii. 2), in his account of early divines, to state whenever they quote as Scripture books of which the canonicity was disputed: and he does thus note the passage of Justin already cited. In his account of Papias (*ib.* xxxix. 13), he tells us that he quoted the First Epistle of St Peter, and that of St John, though, as the canonicity of these books was *not* disputed, he was not bound to note the fact. If then Papias had quoted the book about which there was the keenest dispute of all, Eusebius would surely have told us so; especially as he actually founded a conjecture as to its authorship (see p. xxii) on a passage in Papias. Thus the argument from the silence of Eusebius, which is worth very little as evidence that Papias did not know St John's Gospel, is, as regards the Revelation, as strong as an argument from silence can be.

Moreover, he enables us to account for Andrew's assuming that Papias knew the book, without his having expressly cited it. Papias certainly held the doctrine of a Millennium, which is not, even apparently, taught in any canonical book but the Apocalypse. Andrew may therefore have taken for granted that he derived the doctrine from it, while in reality he may have had no authority but the general belief of the Church. The only passage in the extant fragments of Papias bearing on

---

[1] It has been observed that, while the Churches of Laodicea and Sardis must have known the facts about the origin of the Apocalypse, they had every interest in discrediting its authority, if they honestly could.

the subject seems to be derived by tradition from the Book of Enoch. If he had read the passage of that book, which he seems to be reproducing, he could not have put the rather silly description of the ideal bliss which it contains into the mouth of our Lord.

But, even if Papias did not expressly quote the Revelation, it does not follow that he was not acquainted with it: and in fact we find it unhesitatingly received by the Churches of Asia during the second century. Of the many Christian writers of that age and country, almost all the works are lost: but we have catalogues of those of Melito, bishop of Sardis, the ablest, most learned, and most critical among them, who flourished in the reign of M. Aurelius, A.D. 161—180. He not only acknowledged "the Revelation of John," but wrote a commentary upon it.

A colony from the Churches of Asia appears to have been established about this time, or earlier, at Lyons, in Gaul. In A.D. 177, they and their neighbours of Vienne were exposed to a savage persecution, of which a detailed account, addressed to their Asiatic kinsmen, was written by a surviving brother: and considerable fragments of this are preserved by Eusebius (*H. E.* v. i—iv.). In this, the Revelation (xxii. 11) is expressly quoted as "the Scripture." Besides this, we have constant evidence of the writer's familiarity with the thoughts, images, and phrases of this book: he speaks of Christ as "the faithful and true Witness" (Rev. iii. 14), and of "the heavenly fountain of the water of life" (vii. 17, xxii. 1). The Church is personified as a Virgin Mother (c. xii.): the Martyrs in their spiritual beauty and exultation are compared to a "bride adorned in embroidered robes of gold" (xxi. 2): and throughout we have constant references, not only to the expected persecution of Antichrist, but to the imagery of the Dragon and the Beast.

Pothinus, the aged bishop of Lyons, who died in this persecution, was succeeded by Irenaeus. The latter was certainly a native of Asia, probably of Smyrna: and, though his works belong to a later date than Justin's or the other writers we have named, he is not practically more remote from the source of authentic tradition. For in his boyhood he had known and heard St Polycarp, bishop of Smyrna, and remembered the account he gave of his personal intercourse with St John (*Ep. ad Flor.*, *ap.* Eus. *H. E.* V. xx. 8, 9). Now St Polycarp was burnt A.D. 155, and had then been a Christian 86 years: his conversion therefore, or birth in a Christian family, must have taken place A.D. 69 or 70. And St Irenaeus states (*Adv. Haer.* III. iii. 3) that both his conversion and his appointment as bishop, was the act of "Apostles," the latter can hardly have been the act of any other Apostle than St John, who (according to Irenaeus) "lived till the time of Trajan," i.e. at least to A.D. 98. At that time Polycarp may have been from 30 to 40 years old; thus it appears that he had been the personal disciple of St John from early childhood to full maturity. His traditions therefore about the Apostle must have been absolutely authentic, and they must have served as a check on the circulation in Asia of spurious ones, at least among those who knew Polycarp personally. It thus appears that Irenaeus received authentic traditions about St John, passing through but one intermediate step; now Irenaeus' testimony to the authorship of the Apocalypse is even more definite than any that we have yet met with. He not only everywhere ascribes it to the Apostle, but states (*Adv. Haer.* V. xxx. 1) that "it was seen not long ago, but almost in our own generation, near the end of the reign of Domitian" (i.e. A.D. 95—6). And he tells us that this statement rests on the authority of persons who had seen St John—possibly therefore of Polycarp, or at least of Papias.

Shortly before the date of the martyrdoms of Lyons arose the fanatical heresy of the Montanists, on the borders of Mysia and Phrygia. Their wild beliefs on the subject of the New Jerusalem would tend rather to discredit than to support the authority of the book they appealed to as teaching the like: but the fact that their opponents in Asia accepted it as a common ground for discussion proves how unanimous was the tradition respecting it. The Martyrs of Lyons themselves wrote on the controversy, which in their days had not amounted to an actual schism: one of their own number was a rather prominent member of the Montanist party. On the other hand,

Apollonius, who is said to have been an Ephesian, wrote after the controversy had grown very bitter: but we are told that he quoted the Revelation as authoritative, and apparently as the work of St John.

Tertullian, who wrote in Africa at the very end of the second century and in the early part of the third, constantly quotes the book as St John's, and seems to know nothing of any doubts about it, except on the part of heretics. His testimony is however the less valuable, as he admitted the Book of Enoch: he became a Montanist in later life, and his quotations from the Revelation seem all to be in works written after his fall into heresy. Still it is probable that this is due to a change of temper, rather than to a change of opinion: for everything indicates that the orthodox Church of Africa accepted the book without hesitation. It certainly did so in the next generation, as we know from St Cyprian's works.

Approximately contemporary with Tertullian—perhaps rather earlier—was Clement of Alexandria, who quotes the Revelation[1] as St John's work, and refers historically to his exile in Patmos.

Of about the same age, probably, is the anonymous work on the Canon, known as the *Muratorian Fragment*, and supposed to be an African version of a Greek original written at Rome. In this "the Apocalypse of John" is recognised: so is an "Apocalypse of Peter," but more doubtfully: we are told that some do not like to hear the latter read in the Church. This proves that the former was so read, and read as canonical Scripture.

About this same period there appears another kind of evidence, shewing still more plainly the belief, not of individual divines alone, but of large provincial Churches—the versions of the New Testament made for ecclesiastical use in Churches where Greek was not generally spoken. The old Latin version was in use by Tertullian's time, and must almost certainly have included the Apocalypse. The versions, however, in the different Egyptian dialects do not seem to have contained it till a

---

[1] This is not noticed by Eusebius, though he mentions the fact of his quoting other "disputed" books. This makes his silence as to Papias less decisive against his having quoted the book.

later date. As to the Syriac, perhaps the oldest version of all, the evidence is more doubtful. The Peschitto, or vulgate Syrian version in use from the fourth century onwards, does not contain the book: but according to the view now taken by what seem to be the highest authorities, this is only a revision of the oldest version, that being one which has not been recovered, except (in part) for the Gospels. As the Apocalypse is quoted, and its authority recognised, by St Ephraim of Edessa, the great poet and divine of the Syrian Church, it cannot be thought an arbitrary opinion, that the Syriac canon did originally include the book: but neither can it be directly proved.

If we are now past the time when living tradition can be appealed to as decisive evidence, we have reached the time when scientific principles of criticism began to be applied to the traditional beliefs of Christendom. Justin, Irenaeus, Clement, Tertullian, were all well-educated men: the first and third ranked as "philosophers," in the sense in which that term was used in their age: Tertullian was a man of real original power of thought. Origen, the pupil and successor of Clement, was not only a learned student, but an able critic. He discusses ably and sensibly the question, admitted to be doubtful, of the authorship of the Epistle to the Hebrews: he notices the doubts, though without doing much to solve them, that existed as to that of the Second Epistle of St Peter: but as to the Apocalypse, he seems to know of no doubts at all, or none worth heeding.

A man of almost equal learning, of about the same date, was Hippolytus, bishop of Portus, near Rome, or perhaps a claimant of the Roman see. In his extant works he constantly and unhesitatingly ascribes the Revelation to the Apostle John: but from a catalogue of his whole works it seems that he thought it necessary to defend its authenticity.

The last witness who need be quoted at this stage of the enquiry is St Victorinus, a bishop and martyr in the Diocletian persecution. He wrote a Commentary on the Revelation, which is said to be extant: but the work bearing his name, if his in any sense, must have been considerably altered. Still there can be no doubt that he accepted the book as St John's. And though the extant commentary is not one of very high ability, there seems little doubt that the author was in possession of traditions about the book of great value, and probably of great antiquity.

After the Diocletian persecution there is a certain change in the view taken on the subject: the question is less, "Is the Revelation attested by ancient tradition to have come from the Apostle John?" and more, "Is the Revelation one of the books acknowledged as sacred by the living Church of our day?" As we have said, the two questions were not regarded as independent of one another: the genuine work of an Apostle must, it was confessed, be of authority in the Church: but it was rather the judgement of the Church that was expected to determine the critical question of authorship, than the critical judgement that was to decide the opinion of the Church. Hence it is not necessary for us to enumerate in detail those of the later Fathers who do or who do not recognise the book: it is enough to say that both the Eastern and Western Churches finally admitted its title to full canonical authority, though the former long hesitated before doing so. The Church of the *further* East, speaking Syriac, rejected the book: but this Church was separated from the Catholic in the course of the fifth and sixth centuries, by controversies with which this question had nothing to do.

II. The earliest people we hear of as denying the authenticity of the Revelation are an Asiatic sect, extreme opponents of Montanism, who thought it necessary to discredit the writings of St John, because their Montanist countrymen appealed to his authority in support of their own views. These heretics were nicknamed by their orthodox opponents *Alogi* or Unreasonable, on account of their denial of the *Logos*, the Word or Reason of God proclaimed by St John. The fact that they rejected *all* the Johannine writings is evidence rather for than against the strength of the tradition in favour of the genuineness of this: for it proves that tradition was consistent and homogeneous in favour of all alike. It is plain that neither the ancient hypothesis, that the Gospel and Epistles were genuine but the Apocalypse not, nor the modern one that the Apocalypse was genuine but the Gospel and Epistles not, had occurred to anyone in Asia in the second century. Their objections seem to have been altogether *à priori*, or at any rate based on internal evidence: they said they found the book unprofitable—very likely *they* did. A better argument was, that they alleged that no Church existed in Thyatira: but on this point the evidence of the Apocalypse itself is sufficient, whatever view be taken of the character of the book. Clearly these people do nothing to shake the credit of the book they attack.

A more respectable and sober opponent of the authenticity of the Apocalypse was Gaius, a learned presbyter of the Church of Rome in the early part of the third century—a contemporary, approximately, of Tertullian and Hippolytus. He wrote against the Montanists, and in a work called an "Inquiry," probably one concerned in this controversy, he speaks of "Cerinthus, who by revelations professedly written by a great Apostle passes off upon us false marvels, professedly shewn to him by angels; and says that after the Resurrection the kingdom of Christ will be earthly; and that the flesh will again be domiciled in Jerusalem, serving lusts and pleasures. And, being an enemy to the Scriptures of God, desiring to deceive, he says that the number is made up of 1000 years in a festive wedding" (*ap.* Eus. *H. E.* III. xxviii. 1). There is no reasonable doubt, that in this he alludes to the now canonical Revelation of St John—that he decidedly denies its genuineness and authority, ascribing it, not to St John but to St John's opponent, Cerinthus. Gaius was, so far as we know, at least as consistently orthodox as Hippolytus, so that the testimony of the latter does not appear to prove that the book was received, at least unhesitatingly, in the Church of Rome: though this *would* be proved, if it were certain, as it is probable, that the *Muratorian Fragment* proceeded from the Church of Rome, and gives the canon there recognised at the end of the second century. It certainly seems strange to our notions, that an orthodox Church should include opposite opinions on a question so important as that of the canonicity or heresy of a book of the New Testament: but the works of Hippolytus prove that there were, in the Roman Church of the third century, very bitter disputes, if not an actual schism: and that both parties were headed by bishops, of repute as divines in their own day, and recognised as saints and martyrs by the later Church.

III. St Dionysius of Alexandria (bishop A.D. 249—265), the most famous of the famous and holy men who proceeded from the school of Origen, had, it is plain, received the Apocalypse[1], without question, like his master, as one of the New Testament Scriptures recognised by the Church. But, in what seems to have been a later work[2], he had occasion to discuss the question critically. He recapitulates the arguments of those who rejected the book, with special reference, no doubt, to Gaius, and probably to the so-called Alogi. The argument sounds a little like theirs as quoted by St Epiphanius, "that the title is false: for, they say, it is not John's, nor yet is it a Revelation, being completely veiled by the thick curtain of ignorance."

But Dionysius himself treats the question in exactly the spirit, at once devout and critical, in which such questions ought to be treated: and the result is, that he sweeps away the bad arguments against St John's authorship, and states the good ones in a form that really has never been improved upon between his day and ours. Those who denied the canonicity and orthodoxy of the book had only two grounds to go upon—its obscurity, and its alleged description of the Kingdom of Christ as earthly. Now on the latter point St Dionysius thoroughly sympathised with the objectors: he had engaged in a controversy with Nepos, an Egyptian bishop who maintained millenarian views, and succeeded in convincing him and his followers that they were wrong. But Dionysius saw that it was neither reverent nor critical, to make the authority of the book stand or fall with a particular interpretation of a particular passage in it. To the charge of obscurity, he replies, "Even if I do not understand, I yet conceive some deeper sense to lie in the words. Not measuring and judging these things by private reasoning, but giving the chief weight to faith, I have supposed it too high to be comprehended by me: and do not reject these things which I have not seen, but admire them the more, because I

---

[1] *Ep. ad Hermamm. ap.* Eus. *H. E.* VII. x. 1.
[2] *On the Promises, ap.* Eus. *H. E.* VII. xxv.

have not." He then expresses his own opinion, and the grounds for it, as follows:

"That he was called John, and that this writing is [St] John's, I will not dispute: for I agree that it is the work of a holy and inspired man. Still, I would not readily admit that this John is the Apostle, the son of Zebedee, the brother of James, the author of the Gospel that bears the title according to John, and of the Catholic Epistle. I argue from the temper of the two, from the style of the language, and from what is called the purport of the book, that they are not the same. For the Evangelist never introduces his own name, nor proclaims himself, either in the Gospel or in the Epistle. St John nowhere [speaks of the Apostle by name?] either as being himself or as another: but the writer of the Revelation puts himself forward at the very beginning, 'The Revelation of Jesus Christ, which He gave to Him, to shew unto His Servants shortly. And He sent and signified it by His Angel to His Servant John, who bare witness of the Word of God and His testimony, whatsoever he saw.' Then he also writes an Epistle, 'John to the seven Churches which are in Asia, grace be to you and peace.' But the Evangelist has not written his name even at the beginning of the Catholic Epistle, but begins without preamble with the mystery of the divine revelation itself, 'That which was from the beginning, which we have heard, which we have seen with our eyes.' For on account of *this* revelation the Lord also called Peter blessed, saying, 'Blessed art thou, Simon bar-Jona: for flesh and blood hath not revealed it unto thee, but My heavenly Father.' But neither in the second and third Epistles current as John's, short as they are, is the name of John put forward, but 'the Elder' is written without name. But this writer has not even thought it enough, when he has named himself once for all, but takes it up again, 'I John, your brother, and partaker with you in the tribulation and kingdom and in the patience of Christ, was in the isle that is called Patmos, for the Word of God and the testimony of Jesus.' And again, near the end, he says this, 'Blessed is he that keepeth the words of the prophecy of this book, and I John who see and hear these things.' Now that it is a John who writes this, we ought to believe on his own word, but what John is uncertain. For he has not said, as in many places of the Gospel, that he is the Disciple beloved of Jesus, nor who leaned upon His breast, nor the brother of James, nor that he was eye and ear witness of the Lord: for he would have said some of these things which I have mentioned, if he wished to indicate himself clearly. But, instead of any of these, he calls himself our brother and partaker with us, and a witness (or martyr) of Jesus, and blessed as seeing and hearing the revelations. But I suppose there were many of the same name as John the Apostle, who for their love for him, admiration, and desire to imitate him and to be beloved like him of the Lord, were glad to assume the same name, as Paul and Peter are frequent names among the children of the faithful[1]. There is in fact another John in the Acts of the Apostles, who was surnamed Mark[2]: whom Barnabas and Paul took with them, of whom it says again, 'And they had also John to their minister.' But whether he is the writer, I would not say: for it is written that he did not come with them into Asia, but 'Paul and his company set sail from Paphos, and came to Perga in Pamphylia; and John departed from them and returned to Jerusalem.' But I think that there was some other of those who lived in Asia: for in fact they say that there are *two tombs at Ephesus, each called that of John*. And further, from their thoughts, language, and composition, this may reasonably be considered a different person from the others. For the Gospel and the Epistle harmonise with one another, and begin alike, the one 'In the beginning was the Word,' the other, 'That which was from the beginning.' The one says, 'And the Word became flesh, and dwelt among us, and we beheld His glory, glory as of the Only-begotten from the Father:' the other the same a little

---

[1] Of course this is an anachronism. John was a common Jewish name, and no doubt many Jewish Johns became Christians: but it had not had time to become a common Christian name, used for love of the Apostle, till long after the date of the Revelation.

[2] We may fairly gather from the way that this Mark is spoken of that St Dionysius did not identify him with the evangelist, the founder of his own Church. If he had, he could hardly have failed to notice the unlikeness of style between *that* Gospel and the Revelation.

varied, 'That which we have heard, that which we have seen with our eyes, that which we beheld, and our hands handled, concerning the Word of life: and the life was manifested.' For this is his prelude to his main contention, as he makes plain in what follows, against those who said that the Lord had not come in the flesh: wherefore he continues carefully, 'And we bear witness of that which we have seen, and declare unto you the life, the eternal [life], which was with the Father, and was manifested unto us: that which we have seen and heard declare we unto you.' He keeps close to himself, and does not withdraw from his announcement, and sets forth all by means of the same headings and names, of which we will briefly mention some. He who studies the books carefully will find in each frequently *life*, *light*, repulse of *darkness*, constantly *truth*, *grace*, *joy*, the *flesh and blood* of the Lord, the *judgement*, the *forgiveness of sins*, the *love of God* towards us, the commandment for us to *love one another*, the duty of *keeping all the commandments*, the condemnation of the *world*, the *Devil*, the *Antichrist*: the promise of the Holy Spirit, the adoption on the part of God, the constant demand of *faith* on our part, the Father and the Son everywhere: altogether, by every possible mark, we are allowed to see the same colouring in the Gospel and the Epistle. But compared with these the Revelation is utterly different and strange, neither touching nor approaching (one may almost say) any of these, nor having a syllable in common with them. Nor again has either the Epistle (I pass over the Gospel) any recollection or thought of the Revelation, nor the Revelation of the Epistle: whereas Paul in his Epistles has given some hint of his revelations, which he did not write separately. Further, one may also argue from the difference of language of the Gospel and Epistle compared with the Revelation. For they are written, not only without error in the Greek language, but with the greatest literary skill in the words, the reasonings, the arrangements of the exposition: far from there being any barbarous word, ungrammatical phrase, or in fact vulgarisms of any sort found there. For he had, as it seems, both forms of the Word, the Lord having granted him both, the word of knowledge and that of expression. But to this author

I will not deny that he had seen a revelation, and received knowledge and prophecy; but I can see that his dialect and language are not correct Greek, but that he uses barbaric constructions, sometimes ungrammatical. These it is not necessary now to recount: for I do not say this for ridicule—let no one suppose it—but only defining the unlikeness of the writings."

No ancient or modern critic has really added anything to this forcible argument against the unity of authorship of the Revelation and Gospel, with the exception of Eusebius. He calls attention to a passage of Papias, where he distinguishes, apparently, from the Apostle St John another "Disciple of the Lord," whom he calls "John the Elder" or "Presbyter"; thus giving direct evidence of what, in St Dionysius, is not much more than a conjecture—the existence at Ephesus, or at least in proconsular Asia, of *two* leaders of the Christian Church, both named John.

IV. No one in ancient times seems to have cared to question the inspiration, or reject the authority, of the Revelation, except those who, in the anti-millenarian controversy, thought it necessary to deny its orthodoxy. Thus the view that it is indeed a genuine work, belonging to the main stream of Christian thought, but that it can claim no higher inspiration than that of a subjective enthusiasm, does not present itself till modern times, and mostly on the part of rationalists: it involves matter of controversy which turns on *à priori* grounds, and cannot be discussed here: except so far as the question of interpretation involves the further question, "Have the Seer's predictions been fulfilled, or have Christians reason to expect that they will be?" By this test, no doubt, we are justified in judging the claims of what professes to be an inspired prophecy (Deut. xviii. 22): but we must ascertain *what* it is that is foretold, before we can judge whether it has "followed or come to pass," or is in the way to do so. For the present, it will be enough to say, that practically the whole Church has agreed to recognise the authority of the book, and that this ought to compel us to recognise it: though its authority does not, perhaps, stand so high as that of those books "of whose authority was never any doubt in the Church." Indeed, both in ancient and modern times, there has been a disposition to treat it with greater reserve, if not greater distrust, than the other canonical books. Everyone now past boyhood will remember, that in the English Church till 1872, while the rest of the New Testament was "read over orderly every year thrice, beside the Epistles and Gospels," out of the Apocalypse there were "only certain Proper Lessons appointed upon divers feasts." And something similar seems to have been the case in earlier times, from the fact that, while the theologians of Alexandria—even St Dionysius—acknowledged the canonical authority of the book, it was not translated till a comparatively late date into either of the vernacular dialects of Egypt. In the Greek-speaking Churches also it never came into general ecclesiastical use, and for this reason, probably, ancient copies of it are rare as compared with the other books of Scripture.

Conceding then the inspiration and canonicity of the book we approach without prejudice the question of its authorship. Its antiquity is undoubted, and the only person besides the Apostle suggested as its author was a personal "disciple of the Lord," so that we can readily conceive his writing by divine inspiration. We have only to judge, whether the internal evidence against its being by the author of the Gospel and Epistles is so strong, as to set aside the great body of external evidence, whereby all alike are ascribed to St John the Apostle.

V. The theory has been advanced in modern times, that the Revelation may be the work of the Apostle, but that if so the Gospel and Epistles cannot be—that they may at most be written by John the Presbyter, or some one else at Ephesus who inherited a genuine apostolic tradition. But to this the total absence of ancient support is an enormous objection. The question of the authorship of the Johannine writings was discussed, from the second century onwards, both from a theological and a critical point of view. Every theory was suggested but this: this could not fail to have been suggested, if there had been the smallest thread of tradition that could be alleged in its favour. No doubt the Revelation is rather more like than the Gospel to what we might have expected to be the work of the Galilean Apostle, the Son of Thunder: but the notion that, within 50 years of the Apostle's death—probably within 18—[1] the Gospel was accepted as his, when it was not his, becomes all the more incredible, if there was a genuine work of his current in the same Churches where the other was first circulated.

The internal evidence, moreover, for the apostolic authorship of the Gospel, though not obvious, is on the whole preponderating: on this question see the Prolegomena to the Gospel. If therefore the unity of authorship of the two be denied, it must be the Revelation that is non-apostolic.

We return therefore to the decisive question, Do St Dionysius' arguments prove diversity of authorship, in the face of the strong external evidence of unity? And on the whole, strong as they are, they seem hardly sufficient for this. It is a very extreme measure, to set aside contemporary evidence to the authorship of a book; especially of a book ascribed to an author who had been prominent and universally known among the community who received the book as his. No doubt there would be a real tendency to be over-hasty in assigning to a venerable name a work that claimed, and that deserved, high authority: a really inspired book, written by a namesake of an Apostle, might easily be ascribed to the Apostle *by future generations:* but hardly by the generation that had known the Apostle himself, and received from him his genuine writings.

Moreover, strong as is the internal evidence *against* the unity of authorship, it is not altogether so strong as it seems at first sight: while internal evidence *for* the unity is by no means wanting. The arguments of St Dionysius, and of other critics who have maintained his view, may be divided under two heads, the unlikeness of style and grammar, and the unlikeness of the theological terms and ideas, between the Revelation and the other Johannine writings.

Indeed, a third element of unlikeness is sometimes alleged, between the moral tone and temper of the two writers. But this is too delicate a consideration, too much a matter of subjective feeling, for much weight to be given to it: and as a matter of fact,

---

[1] The Epistle of St Polycarp to the Philippians dates, if entirely genuine, from A.D. 116. In this the First Epistle of St John is quoted, though without the author's name.

it is not put forward by those who have the best right to be heard. The character of a saint, at least of the greatest saints, is a complex and many-sided one: those who know most of the mind of the Spirit, and the saintly character which is His work, do not find much difficulty in forming a harmonious conception of the character of St John[1], which takes in, as one element, his authorship of the Revelation. And in fact, it is quite a mistake to think that the Apostle of love was incapable of severe condemnation. Not to mention the imperfectly disciplined temper shewn in St Luke ix. 54[2], in the Gospel itself, in the Epistles, and in the best authenticated traditions of his later life[3], we see that his zeal could be stern, even fierce, upon occasion. See in the Gospel i. 10, 11, ii. 24—5, iii. 18, 19, iv. 20, v. 14, 38—47, vi. 70, vii. 7, viii. 15, 21—24, 38—47, ix. 39—41, x. 26, xii. 37—43, 48: in the First Epistle ii. 15—19, 22, iii. 1 fin., 8, 13—15, iv. 3, 5, v. 16 fin.: in the Second, ver. 10, and in the Third vv. 9, 10, as evidence that the Evangelist sees nothing inconsistent with the "spirit he is of" in the stern condemnation of sin and unbelief or misbelief, either by the Saviour or by himself in His name. On the other hand, the tender charity of the Evangelist is not absent from the Apocalypse, though it may be admitted that the latter is, in its primary character, a vision of judgement: see i. 5 fin., 9, vii. 14—17, xxi. 3, 4, besides many other passages where the tenderness, if less unmixed, is perceptible.

The differences of theological conceptions characteristic of the Revelation and the other Johannine writings respectively are to a certain extent real, though not more than superficial: and it is important to remember, that a reverent Christian temper will lead us to ascribe more importance, not less, to superficial differences than a rationalist might. For if all the writers of the New Testament had the same Spirit in them, it follows of course

---

[1] See Keble's stanzas on page viii of this book, and the whole hymn containing it.

[2] It is a mistake to see a sign of the same temper *ib.* ver. 49. What that shews is, not that St John was more zealous than the other Apostles in silencing the unknown man, but that he was quicker in inferring that the Lord was not certain to approve of their silencing him.

[3] The story of his fleeing from Cerinthus in the bath, *ap.* S. Iren. III. iii. 4.

that the essentials of their doctrine must be the same: it can only be in superficial points—in their different manner of stating the same doctrine, or at most in the proportion in which special doctrines are insisted on—that their varying individuality can shew itself. If we thought that the doctrine of the Person of the Lord Jesus taught in St John's Gospel was not held by the other Apostles, or by the primitive Church generally, it might be an argument for the Apocalypse being the work of the Evangelist, that the same doctrine is taught there. But if the doctrine is true—if it formed part of the faith once for all delivered to the Saints—there is nothing incredible in the view that two Saints received it alike and taught it alike. We can only conclude that we have the teaching of the same Saint, if he teaches, not only the same doctrine, but in the same manner.

Now there is one great and important point, wherein the manner or method of stating this doctrine is the same in the Gospel and the Revelation. It is in these books only, that the name "The *Word*" is ascribed to the Lord Jesus. It is true, that the coincidence is not entire: in the Revelation (xix. 13) He is called "the Word of God," in the Epistle (i. 1) "the Word of life" (if there the term be used personally), and in the Gospel "the Word" absolutely: but there the context suggests that if the ellipsis be filled up, it can only be in the same manner as in the Revelation.

The case is similar as regards the description of the Son of God as a Lamb. Is. liii. 7 is quoted in Acts viii. 32, and He is *likened* to a lamb in 1 Pet. i. 19: but He is not *called* a Lamb except in St John i. 29, 36 and in the Apocalypse *passim*. But different Greek words are used for "Lamb" in the two books. That used in the Apocalypse occurs in the Gospel, xxi. 15, but is not there used of Christ.

Of the 18 or 19 characteristic Johannine phrases enumerated by Dionysius, we certainly meet with few in the Revelation in exactly the same form or with the same frequency: but, in some form, we meet with nearly all. (1) We never have the phrase "eternal life," but we constantly hear of "life" as an attribute of heavenly gifts—the Book of Life (cf. Phil. iv. 3), the Crown of Life (cf. James i. 12), the Tree of Life, and the Water of Life;

which last only differs in construction, not in sense, from St John's Gospel iv. 10—14, vii. 38. (2) The word "light" occurs rarely, and hardly ever in a directly spiritual sense: yet xxi. 11, 14 shew that the image was one that seemed to the seer natural and appropriate. (3) "Darkness" does not occur as a substantive, and the cognate verbs in viii. 12, ix. 2, xvi. 10 are images of punishment rather than of sin. (4) The substantive "Truth" does not occur, nor does the commoner of the Greek adjectives rendered "true." But the rarer word, meaning as a rule "real, genuine," is characteristic of the Johannine writings, and rare in the rest of the N. T. As an epithet of God or His Son, we meet it in the Gospel vii. 28, xvii. 3, and virtually i. 9, vi. 32, in the Ep. I. v. 20 (three times), and in the Revelation iii. 7, 14, vi. 10, xix. 11: nowhere else but 1 Thess. i. 9. And the use of the word in the Gospel xix. 35 is very like that in Rev. xix. 9, xxi. 5, xxii. 6. (5) *Grace* is not really a frequent word in St John. Except in the salutation at the head of the second Epistle, which is paralleled by Rev. i. 4, xxii. 21, we have it only in the Gospel i. 14—17. Hence it proves nothing that (except in the two places cited), it does not occur in the Revelation. (6) "Joy," and especially the phrase "joy *fulfilled*" is, on the contrary, a phrase characteristic of the Gospel and Epistles, and absent in the Revelation. Even the verb "rejoice" is rare; it occurs only twice (xi. 10, xix. 7), and only once of *holy* joy. Here then is a real diversity. (7) "The flesh and blood of the Lord" are mentioned in the Gospel i. 14, vi. 51 sqq., xix. 34, in the Epistles I. i. 7, iv. 2, v. 6—8, II. 7. For the most part, these relate to the doctrines of the Incarnation and—what is closely connected with this—of the Sacraments: the latter subject is not mentioned in the Revelation, and the word "flesh" is not used in connexion with the former. But in Ep. I. i. 7 we have a closer parallel in thought and imagery to Rev. vii. 14, xxii. 14 (true text) than anywhere else in the N. T.: see also i. 5 (whatever be the true reading) and v. 9. (8) The *word* "judgement" is as frequent in the Revelation as in the Gospel, more so than in the Epistle: and the *thought* of the Divine Judgement is, of course, all-pervading. It is a question of interpretation, not a self-evident point of style, whether the *nature* of the Divine Judgement is conceived in quite the same way in the different books. (9) The "forgiveness of sins" as a phrase does not occur in the Revelation nor in the Gospel or Epistles: in the Gospel however we have the cognate verbal phrase in xx. 23, and in the First Epistle in i. 9, ii. 12: and it is these, doubtless, that St Dionysius is thinking of. The *idea* of course is frequent throughout the N. T.—certainly not absent in the Revelation. (10) *The love of God*, as distinct from that of *Christ*, see i. 5, iii. 9 and (with a verbal variation found also in the Gospel), iii. 19 is only spoken of once, and that indirectly, in the Revelation (xx. 9). Here then is a real difference of manner and language—*not* of temper nor of theological thought, for God's electing love, as the first source of man's salvation, is as plainly set forth in Rev. xiii. 8 &c. as anywhere in Scripture. (11) The command to *love one another* is probably, though not certainly, on the same footing. The "love" of ii. 4, 19 *may* be mutual brotherly love, but probably is special love to Christ. If so, here is a very great difference indeed from St John's acknowledged writings—Christian love or charity being absolutely unnamed. (12) The phrase "keeping His Commandments," on the contrary, is as emphatic if not as frequent in the Revelation as in the Gospel and Epistle: see xii. 17, xiv. 12 (*not* xxii. 14; even if the received text were right, the phrase in it is varied). (13—15) The *world* is never used in the Revelation in an ethical sense, only in a physical (xiii. 8, xvii. 8: xi. 15 is not really an exception): and the *Devil* and *Antichrist* are usually designated, not by those names (see however xii. 9, xx. 2), but as "the Dragon" and "the Beast." As however the whole subject of the book is, God's judgement on the sinful world, on the Devil, and on Antichrist, this difference is no evidence at all against unity of authorship. Of course the two books differ in kind and method, and allowing for this, we find a unity not a diversity between their thoughts. (16) "The promise of the Spirit," spoken of in the Gospel cc. xiv.—xvi. &c. is not mentioned in similar terms in the Revelation: and "the seven Spirits of God" of Rev. i. 4, iii. 1, iv. 5, v. 6 are decidedly unlike the Gospel in language, whatever be the relation between the two theologically. "The Spirit" of the Epistles to the Churches (ii. 7, &c.) and of xiv. 13, xxii. 17 is indeed spoken of in a way like enough to that of the Gospel and Epistles: but the likeness is not greater than the common belief of the whole Church would necessitate. On the other hand, there is a likeness perhaps rather more individual between Ep. I. iv. 1—6, and Rev. xvi. 13, 14. (17) The *word* "adoption" is nowhere used in the Johannine writings, being, in the N. T. peculiar to St Paul. We have the *thought* in Rev. xxi. 7, but not only is it less prominent than in the Gospel and Epistle—it seems there to be spoken of as a present blessing, here as a future. Here then the discrepancy, though not very great, is real. (18) The word "Faith" occurs four times in the Revelation (ii. 13, 19, xiii. 10, xiv. 12), *once* in the first Epistle (v. 4), and *nowhere* in the Gospel. But what St Dionysius is thinking of is, the constant occurrence in the Gospels and Epistles of the various phrases "to believe God" or Christ, "to believe in Christ" or "in His Name." And it is certainly remarkable, that the word "believe" does not occur in the Revelation: but hardly more so, than that the word "faith" does not occur in the Gospel. The one can hardly be more than accidental, and so the other need not be. (19) The names of "the Father" and "the Son" are never coupled as correlative, or used absolutely, in the Revelation, as they are constantly in the Gospel and Epistles, and even in our Lord's saying reported in St Matt. xi. 27, St Luke x. 22. The nearest approach is xiv. 1 (true text). Christ is called "the Son of God" in ii. 18, and speaks of "My Father," as in the Gospels, in ii. 27, iii. 5, 21: but such expressions as these, and i. 6, belong to Christian theology, not Johannine phraseology.

On the whole then it appears that the difference of ideas is much less extensive than it seems. In the points numbered (3), (6), (10), (11), and perhaps (9), (16), (17) there is a real difference in the thoughts, but otherwise the matter resolves itself mainly into a difference of language—sometimes so merely a matter of style and grammar as that one book has an abstract word and the other the cognate concrete. Thus we pass to the other branch of the argument—the unlikeness in style and language of the Revelation to the other Johannine writings.

Now this unlikeness is undeniable, though it has been overstated, and some people, by refuting over-statements, have seemed to minimise it. It may perhaps be said that St Dionysius overstates it, not by exaggerating (as some modern critics have done) the peculiarities and harshnesses of the Revelation, but by over-estimating the literary power shewn in the Gospel and Epistles. It is quite true, that the author of these has a sufficient mastery of language for the adequate expression of his sublime and profound thoughts. Moreover, he writes in correct grammatical Greek, with less trace of Hebrew idiom than most of the N.T. writers: and he is rather fond of refining a point, sometimes of some theological importance, by the use of some delicate distinction of the Greek language, often quite untranslateable: e.g. the two nearly synonymous words rendered "ask" in ch. xvi., and those rendered "feed" and "love" in ch. xxi. And yet he does not write like a master of the Greek language. He does not write in the literary dialect of his time, echoing the language of the classical period, as St Luke does when he chooses: he does not, like the author of the Epistle to the Hebrews, write under the influence of the Alexandrine school of Hellenising Jewish literature: if his theology has something in common with Philo's, his language is unaffected by him. He says what he has to say in short, weighty, simple and rather unconnected sentences: his Greek is correct, because he never ventures on constructions complicated enough to risk a blunder.

The language of the Apocalypse, on the other hand, is fairly characterised by Dionysius. Indeed, the Greek is not *so* ungrammatical as it seems, nor are all its offences against the laws of grammar to be ascribed to ignorance or inability to write correctly: see i. 4 (true text) for a solecism obviously conscious and intentional. Moreover the language has laws of its own, e.g. as to the apposition of nouns, the connexion of participles with finite verbs, which, though they are not the laws recognised by classical or even by Hellenistic Greek, still are laws of language, and are observed with fair consistency. Still the fact remains that the Apocalypse is written in a language which, however well adapted to its subject and purpose, cannot be called good Greek, nor even good ecclesiastical Greek. It seems the work of a man who thinks in Hebrew, and turns the Hebrew sentences embodying his thoughts into Greek, not according to the traditional rules by which, since the composition of the Septuagint, a compromise had been made between the genius of the two languages, but quite independently, by rules of his own making.

Some of the grammatical peculiarities of the book will be pointed out in the Notes: it is impossible to discuss them fully here. With a few exceptions (see on xii. 7) they do not affect translation. But it must suffice here to say, that *primâ facie* the style of the Revelation is so utterly unlike that of St John's Gospel and Epistles, as to make it all but incredible that they are the work of the same author. We say *all but* incredible: for it is just conceivable that a man may change his style entirely, so that his writings of different periods shall seem like the writings of different men.

Is it then possible to assign the Apocalypse and the other Johannine writings to quite different periods in the Apostle's life? If so, it may be possible to reconcile the conflict between external and internal evidence. If we suppose (see the next chapter) that the Revelation was written by St John the Apostle between A.D. 68—70, and the Gospel and Epistles A.D. 80—100, we get a credible view of the history of the Apostle's mind, or at least of his style. A Jew of Palestine, habitually familiar with both the biblical Hebrew and the Aramaic vernacular, he was perhaps altogether ignorant of Greek till the age of 50 or 60. Then, being called on to take the pastoral charge of Greek-speaking Churches, he addressed them in their own language, which he had learnt as far as he could: but he refused to let his imperfect knowledge of the language hamper or even modify his expression of the message entrusted to him: he would say what he had to say *somehow*, even if he did not know how to say it in grammatical Greek. But, when he had lived from ten to thirty years in the midst of these Greek-speaking Churches, he learnt their language thoroughly, and became able to compose in it with vigour and correctness, if not with the mastery of a native. It is quite true that "the Greek of the Gospel and Epistle is not the Greek of the Apocalypse in a maturer state" (Alford), but it is conceivable that the man who had the one to unlearn might learn the other.

On the whole then the question of authorship must be made to depend on that of date. The internal evidence forbids us to believe that this and the other Johannine writings were composed by the same author *at the same time*—still more, perhaps, that the Apocalypse was composed after the Gospel. But if it appear that the Apocalypse is some years earlier than the other books, it becomes credible, though hardly *à priori* probable, that they may be by the same author: and we have such strong external evidence that they are so, as to justify a confident belief that they are.

CHAPTER II.

Date and Place of Composition.

The book itself tells us (i. 9) where the vision recorded in it was seen: it does not follow that the record was written in the same place. Such is, however, the probable conclusion. The English reader might indeed understand from the words "I *was* in the isle" that the writer was no longer there: and tradition, such as it is, seems to regard the book as written after the Seer's release. But the indications of the book itself are decidedly in favour of the composition in Patmos. The words just cited really mean, "I had *come to be* in the island," and do not in the least imply that he had left it: just as Daniel might equally have written "I *became* dumb" (x. 15) if, like Ezekiel and Zacharias, he had continued so for a long time, and had written in that state. And in i. 11, 19, xiv. 13, xix. 9, xxi. 5, and still more x. 4, it seems almost implied that the successive visions were written down as fast as they were seen; see however note on x. 4. But the command to write and send to the Seven Churches seems inconsistent with the Seer being, at the time of writing, resident at one of them, and free to visit the rest personally: and the style of the book, so far as any argument can be built on it, suggests that it was *written* in the same ecstatic state of mind in which the vision was unquestionably *seen*. Altogether, it seems likeliest that the book was written at Patmos, but the point is one of no great importance.

This cannot be said of the question of the date; which is much disputed, with strong arguments on both sides. We have already seen (p. xiii) that there is very strong evidence for ascribing it to the last three or four years of the Apostle's life, A.D. 95—98. "It was seen," says St Irenaeus, "...at the end of the reign of Domitian;" if it was not written till his return from exile, this was probably in the reign of Nerva. It is needless to quote later writers who say the same, for it is probable that most if not all of them derived their belief from this passage of Irenaeus. But it is certain, that his testimony was generally accepted by the Church at large, and that there is no trace of controversy as to the date of the work, independent of the controversy as to its authorship.

Nevertheless, there are statements in early Christian writers which seem to shew that the tradition on this point was not absolutely unanimous. Several of the earliest who refer to St John's exile avoid naming the emperor who condemned him, while the earliest of all who refer to the book do not, as it happens, mention the fact of the exile. Thus there is no evidence earlier than St Irenaeus either opposed to his or merely negative.

The evidence nearest in time to his is negative, but on the whole harmonises with the date under Domitian. St Clement of Alexandria, in his treatise "Who is the rich man that can be saved," tells the beautiful and often-repeated story (which, he is very careful to assure us, is historical not legendary) of St John reclaiming a young convert who had become a robber chief. He dates the beginning of the story "when, after the death of the *tyrant*, he had returned from the isle of Patmos to Ephesus." Now we know that Domitian sentenced many Christians to banishment, and that they were released after his death by his successor Nerva: moreover, Domitian's character, and that of his government, was far more likely to make a

Greek writer describe him as a "tyrant[1]" than that of any other early emperor. The only other emperor whose victims we can suppose to have been, as a matter of course, released on his death was Nero: he certainly did persecute the Christians, but we do not hear of banishment as ever inflicted by him, as it certainly was by Domitian.

Yet Clement's story that follows seems far more consistent with a date under (we may say) Vespasian than under Nerva or Trajan. At the later date, St John must have been at least ninety years old, and it is most improbable that his bodily vigour can have been unimpaired. In fact, a still better known legend (though not resting on equally early authority[2]) describes him as being, for some time before his death, entirely decrepit, though fully retaining his mental faculties. But St Clement (and here all tradition agrees with him) describes the Apostle after his exile as making Ephesus indeed his head-quarters, but travelling thence in all directions, "in some places to establish bishops, in some to arrange whole churches, and in some to ordain to the clergy one or more of those indicated by the Spirit." Some months, at least, are implied to have been thus spent: some years seem to be required for the instruction of the young man, his gradual fall into vice, and the time when he is recognised by the Church as "dead to God." But at the end of this time, we find that the local Church "when some occasion arose, again summoned John:" and not only does he readily make the journey when summoned, but, as soon as he hears of the fall of his disciple, he rides off on horseback to the mountains to seek for him. When the robbers have seized him and (presumably) taken his horse, their captain recognises him and, from shame, takes to flight: then no doubt it is thought remarkable that the Apostle "pursued him at full speed, forgetting his old age:" but this, which would be re-

---

[1] Under the later Empire the word "tyrant" came to be used as modern historians use "usurper." In this sense, neither Nero nor Domitian can be so called.

[2] The legend of "Little children, love one another" is told by no extant author before St Jerome.

markable in a man of 70, is all but incredible in a man of 97[1]. And finally, it is implied that the robber had to pass through a long course of penance before he was restored to the Church, through which the Apostle was able to guide and assist him.

Tertullian, in a work apparently orthodox and therefore early (*Praescr. Haer.* 36), says that at Rome "the Apostle John, after he had been plunged in burning oil without suffering anything, was banished to an island." He mentions this in close connexion with the martyrdoms of SS. Peter and Paul, which certainly took place under Nero: still it cannot be said that he implies that it was at the same time. But St Jerome (*adv. Jov.* i. 26) quotes Tertullian as saying that "being put by *Nero* into a jar of boiling oil, he came out cleaner and more vigorous than he went in." Now St Jerome was quite capable of lax quotation, of improving upon his authorities, and of confusing what he inferred from them with what they said. But on the other hand, we know that he used works of Tertullian now lost; and that, unless Nero was really mentioned by Tertullian (or someone else who repeated the same tradition), it would have been far easier to infer from the mention of St John's banishment that his intended martyrdom took place under Domitian than from the mention of the other Apostles that it took place under Nero. And the banishment, it is quite plain from the extant passage, followed immediately on the miraculous escape from death.

Origen, in his commentary on St Matthew xx. 22 sqq., speaks of "tradition" as teaching that "the Emperor of the Romans condemned John, being a witness" (or "martyr") "for the word of truth, to the isle of Patmos. John," he continues, "teaches us about his own martyrdom, *not telling who condemned him*, saying 'I John...was in the isle that is called Patmos for the word of God and the testimony of Jesus Christ' (Rev. i. 9). And he *seems* to have seen the Revelation in the island." Here it is implied that there was a tradition about St John's

---

[1] If we consider, not St John's appearance in modern pictures, but the nature of the work to which our Lord called him, a year before the Crucifixion, then, as the latter probably took place in A.D. 29, we can hardly date the Apostle's birth later than A.D. 5.

banishment, independent of the book itself: perhaps also, that this tradition stated the name of the Emperor who condemned the Saint. But, if Origen knew a tradition on this subject, he does not give it: and, in default of evidence to the contrary, it is presumable that the tradition was the usual or Irenaean one—that if it named anybody it named Domitian.

St Epiphanius twice (*Haer.* LI. 12, 33) in defiance of all other tradition and probability, ascribes St John's banishment to *Claudius*, dating his return also in the same reign. In the former place, he says that, "in his advanced old age, after 90 years of his life, after his return from Patmos which took place under Claudius Caesar," he wrote the Gospel. Now it is grammatically possible, but hardly natural, to take this sentence as meaning, that he wrote the Gospel when aged 90, *some* 40 *years* after his exile, which took place when he was hardly 50. Moreover, it is scarcely credible that the exile should have taken place in the reign of Claudius, when Christianity had not begun to attract the notice or hostility of the Roman government. It is true that Epiphanius does not, like Origen and, by implication, Clement and Tertullian, ascribe the banishment to the personal sentence of the Emperor: but who else had authority to pass such a sentence? certainly not Herod, the only *judicial* persecutor whom we know of in Claudius' days. Thus the mention of Claudius is almost certainly a mistake. We minimise that mistake as far as possible, if we suppose the exile to have been under Nero, who as Claudius' adopted son would bear the name of Claudius: but he would no more be spoken of as "Claudius Caesar" by a writer of the fourth century (or even by a contemporary) than by a modern historian: no more, we may say, than we could suppose that an act ascribed to Charles II. was really done by Charles I., who *might* have been called Charles II. on the plea that his father's name was Charles James.

Traces are found in later writers, of about the sixth century, of a tradition ascribing the Apostle's banishment to Nero: but they are the less trustworthy, as they associate with his banishment the composition, not of the Apocalypse but of the Gospel; the latter must be almost certainly of the age of Domitian.

These stories seem therefore to have their roots, not in any real tradition reaching back to the time when the facts were known, but to an unreal conventional treatment of sacred history, whereby it was attempted to supply the missing links between the age of the New Testament and that of the fully constituted Church.

It is otherwise with the evidence of St Victorinus, if we could be sure what his evidence was. *In the present state of his Commentary,* the Revelation is distinctly ascribed to the reign of Domitian. On the other hand, we are told very positively, that "he wrote the Gospel afterwards:" now if the Revelation was a work of the close of Domitian's reign, the Gospel could not be written *very long* afterwards. For no one supposes the Apostle to have lived later than the early years of Trajan, cir. A.D. 100; now it is scarcely credible that tradition—it is impossible that internal evidence—should have defined the exact order of two works so nearly contemporaneous as these would then be. Who imagines that a writer of the fourth century knew confidently whether St Paul wrote to the Galatians before or after the Corinthians? to the Philippians before or after the Ephesians and Colossians? On the other hand, if the two works belonged to quite different periods of the Apostle's life, there would be no more difficulty in remembering the distinction between them than in noting that between the Pastoral Epistles and those written before St Paul's imprisonment.

And further, the passage where the date under Domitian is most definitely affirmed is one which it is scarcely possible to suppose to be in its original form. In the Commentary on xvii. 10, the "seven kings" are identified as Galba, Otho, Vitellius, Vespasian, Titus ("five are fallen"): "one is," Domitian, "the other is not yet come, and when he cometh, he must continue a little space," i.e. Nerva, who only reigned two years. Now we ask, on what earthly principle the enumeration of the Emperors of Rome (if these be meant by the "kings") should begin with the ephemeral princes of disputed title who struggled with one another through the eighteen months after Nero's death? In popular apprehension, among the provincials at least, the first Roman Emperor was Julius Caesar: in strict constitutional law, the first who held the Empire as an established form of government was Augustus. The series of Emperors might legitimately begin with either of these, but with no one later. If the principle of interpretation here adopted be right—if the "seven kings" be individual Roman Emperors—it can hardly be doubted that they stand for the *first* seven, and that the Apocalypse was seen in the days of the sixth—though there is room for differences of calculation as to who the sixth is.

Further, the above interpretation of the series would, if consistently followed, lead to an utter and scandalous absurdity. Who is "the Beast that was and is not," who "is both himself the eighth, and is of the seven"? If the seventh king is the shortlived Nerva, the eighth must be the noble, upright, conscientious Trajan, the best ruler that the Empire ever had! It is almost blasphemous to suppose that St John—or even that a general Christian tradition, accepted by a holy Christian Bishop like Victorinus—can have taken such an unworthy view of Trajan's character and historical position. It is true, that Trajan gave a partial sanction to the persecution of the Christians in Bithynia: we may perhaps accept the tradition, that he was personally responsible for the condemnation of St Ignatius of Antioch. But though Trajan was a thorough Pagan, ignorant of the Gospel and contemptuous towards it, it is absurd, or worse than absurd, to suppose that he can be described as the great enemy of God and of righteousness.

Almost certainly, then, either Victorinus or the editor who has reduced his commentary to its present form is here distorting the traditional interpretation he means to give, in order to reconcile it with the common story, that the Revelation was seen under Domitian. Assume that the Apostle is writing under Nero or Nero's successor, and all becomes clear. The five fallen kings are the first five Emperors (whether beginning with Julius or Augustus): the character of the sixth is not defined, but he must have been more or less of a persecutor. The seventh will have a short but (apparently) not a merely ephemeral reign : the eighth will be an Antichristian revival of one of his predecessors.

Now it is possible to point out several schemes, according to which this prediction was more or less accurately fulfilled. Perhaps the most satisfactory is, to take the five fallen kings to be those from Augustus to Nero inclusive, and to suppose the three claimants of empire, Galba, Otho, and Vitellius, not to be counted as actual emperors. Then the sixth will be Vespasian, the seventh the shortlived Titus, and the eighth Domitian, a tyrant and a persecutor, who was recognised both by Christians and Pagans as a revival of Nero. It is probable that this was the interpretation really given, if not by St Victorinus, at all events by the authorities he used and ought to have followed.

It harmonises with this, that in ch. xi. Jerusalem and the Temple there are apparently spoken of as still existing. It is true, we cannot be sure how far we are to understand such passages literally, how far "the Holy City" and "the Temple of God" are to be understood spiritually of their evangelical antitypes. But on the whole it appears simplest to take the literal sense, which appears to be the traditional one. There is even a respectable amount of traditional evidence for referring to the fall of Jerusalem the vision of the seven seals in ch. vi.: and this interpretation is supported by the close resemblance between the imagery there, and that in our Lord's prophecy, St Matt. xxiv. &c.

Thus on the question of date, as of authorship, we seem to find external evidence in conflict with internal. On the former question, we found the possibility of reconciliation between the two to be conditional on our decision on this point: on the other hand, it is a consideration in deciding this, what view will best harmonise all the evidence on all the questions affecting the book. And on the whole, the most probable view seems to be, that the Revelation was written by the Apostle John, at some time between the death of Nero in June A.D. 68, and the capture of Jerusalem in August A.D. 70: the Gospel and Epistles being much later works of the same author. Thus we accept all the mass of well-attested evidence which, as we have seen, we have to the authorship of the book: while its peculiarities, and the difficulties in the way of referring it to the Evangelist, if not entirely explained or accounted for, cease to be insuperable objections. There is only one well-attested statement that we are obliged to reject—that of St Irenaeus about the date. And it is possible to account for this, without supposing it a mere blunder. If the story in Tertullian be true, it is likely enough to have happened, as St Jerome understood, under Nero. Savage punishments like those mentioned were inflicted by him on the Christians, and turned the popular hatred against them into pity; and it is credible that, when one of the victims was saved by a miracle or what looked like one, public opinion should have enforced a commutation of his sentence to simple exile. But, as exile was not a penalty often inflicted in Nero's persecution, but was in Domitian's, Irenaeus may have assumed that St John's exile took place at the same time as that of other confessors. Or it is possible, that the Apostle was condemned by Domitian, or at least in his name, in the beginning of A.D. 70, when he, after the victory of Vespasian's army, was the only member of the new imperial family at Rome, and enjoyed the titular office of city praetor. It would then be a comparatively slight error if St Irenaeus, knowing that St John was sent into exile by Domitian, assumed that he was sent at the same time as other 'witnesses', i.e. at the end of Domitian's own reign, instead of the beginning of his father's.

Most recent critics are disposed to admit both St John's authorship of the Revelation and its early date. In England, indeed, many, perhaps most, orthodox commentators still adhere to the Irenaean or traditional date. But it is utterly unfair to suppose that there is any necessary connexion between the interpretation mentioned above of ch. xvii. and the rationalistic views of some of its advocates: as we have seen, believers in the divine truth of the prophecy need be at no loss for seeing how, on this view, it received at least a partial and typical fulfilment. How far that fulfilment was adequate—in what sense this or other predictions of the book have yet been fulfilled, or to what extent they yet remain to be fulfilled—these are questions of interpretation. If the date and circumstances of the vision can be determined on critical grounds, they will throw some light on the interpretation, when we come to attempt it: but the critical question may be, and ought to be, treated without prejudice from the supposed necessities of exegesis.

CHAPTER III.

Principles of Interpretation.

EVERY student of the Apocalypse must be aware, that the interpretation of its visions has been a matter of controversy, almost ever since the age when it was written: and in view of this fact, it would clearly be presumptuous to propose any detailed scheme of interpretation with any approach to confidence. Still more obviously, it would be beyond the scope of an elementary sketch like the present Introduction, to enter into the controversy, or even to put forward the arguments by which the various schools have maintained their respective causes. And it would be beyond our limits to trace, in more than the barest outline, the history of opinion on the subject of the interpretation of the book: though that history may serve for a patient student, at once to suggest true principles and to warn him of the need of caution in applying them.

The presumptuous confidence with which, a generation or two ago, definite and detailed predictions of the future history of the world were grounded upon the visions of this book, and supposed to enjoy its authority, has now provoked a reaction. Many orthodox readers are content to leave at least the bulk of the book absolutely uninterpreted. The letters to the Seven Churches, it is obvious, are full of moral and spiritual instruction to the Church of all ages: the imagery of the first, fourth, and fifth chapters, perhaps of the twelfth, and certainly of the two last, is so transparent that no believer can fail to see the foundation of our salvation figured in the former, and its consummation in the latter. But the rest of the book is commonly left unread, or read only with a literary interest, as a phantasmagoria of sublime images: if people are too reverent to regard the book as a riddle without an answer, they treat it as one which they can never hope to guess, but must wait till the answer shall be told.

It is however scarcely credible that this can be the right spirit in which to regard any part of God's Word: it is quite certain, that it is not the spirit in which the author of the Apocalypse expected or intended his own work to be regarded. Plainly, he throughout considers that he is conveying valuable information to his readers: this appears from the very title of the book, and the explanation which follows it in the opening words: see also i. 3, xiii. 9, 10, xix. 9, 10, xx. 6, xxii. 6, 7. It is true, that we are told that certain things contained in the vision are intentionally concealed (x. 4), and that certain others can only be interpreted by a rare gift of discernment (xiii. 18): but the general purport of the prophecy is expected to be intelligible, and most of its details to be instructive, to the Church at large.

If then the visions contained in the book were expected and intended by the author to be intelligible, it is only reasonable to suppose that we shall find them so, if we will read them without prejudice, and from a point of view as near as possible to that of the readers who were addressed in the first instance. For, while it is likely that the book (assuming it to be a truly inspired prophecy) will be of greater value to the generation that sees its complete fulfilment than to any before, it is plain that it was expected to edify its first and immediate recipients: it can scarcely then be unintelligible or useless to the many generations that lie between.

I. This may then be taken as the first of the principles to direct us in the attempt to understand the book: its first readers must have had a clue to it. Such a clue may have been furnished in any of three ways—(1) by the Old Testament prophecies which the Seer repeats and makes his own, *if* we can ascertain the sense in which Jews or Christians of St John's day understood them; (2) by the oral teaching of St John and other Apostles, or by the earlier writings of the New Testament; (3) by the events of past or contemporary history.

(1) The Revelation of St John is full of reminiscences—of

what may almost be called imitations—of the prophecies of the Old Testament. In some cases it may sufficiently account for these, that the Seer uses an image or a phrase familiar to his own mind and his readers', though not using it exactly in its original sense. But there are other cases—more important if not more numerous—where it is plainly implied that the new prophecy has a meaning analogous to, if not identical with, that of the old: e.g. in ii. 27 the promise of Ps. ii. 9 is applied to the faithful and courageous Christian: but the last words of the verse shew that St John understood the original promise as made not to the Christian but to Christ. On the other hand, it is quite certain that the Beast described in xiii. 1, 2 is either identical with one, or is an embodiment of all, of the beasts described in Dan. vii. Again, the "time, times, and half a time" of Rev. xii. 14, and the apparently coincident 42 months or 1260 days (xi. 2, 3, xii. 6, xiii. 5) plainly stand in a close relation with the identical or similar periods in Dan. vii. 25, xii. 7, 11, 12: though here it may be said that the earlier prophecy is at least as obscure as the later. In fact, familiarity with Daniel's prophecy, and the generally received interpretation of it, must have made St John's readers readily understand his prophecy as directed against Rome, and against a person wielding the power of Rome (though the power in his hands was separable from Rome locally), who was to be such an oppressor to the new People of God as Antiochus Epiphanes had been to the old.

(2) And such an oppressor—or at least such a blasphemous enemy to God—had been foretold by the Apostles from very early times: more plainly, perhaps, in their oral teaching than in their writings. For the only place where he is clearly foretold in an apostolic writing earlier than the Revelation is 2 Thess. ii.: and there St Paul seems to use a certain reserve, and certainly refers to his oral teaching as serving to supplement what he writes. In this subject, therefore, it seems that the tradition of the early Church is entitled to more than usual authority, as to the interpretation of the designedly obscure predictions of the Apostle's written words. And here the earliest tradition agrees approximately with the doctrine of the Apoca-

lypse, while it is manifestly independent of it. The Beast in the Apocalypse is a support and ally of Rome, yet becomes in the end the enemy of Rome, and his most daring defiance of God is after her fall. The Man of Sin in 2 Thess. is only to be revealed in his full self-deifying lawlessness, when "that which withholdeth" (variously described as a person or as a power) is taken out of the way: that is, if tradition be trusted, when the Roman Emperor or Empire has been put down.

At the same time, the dominion of the Man of Sin is connected, not with Rome only but with Jerusalem. This power will be at least as much spiritual as temporal, and thus it affiliates itself as well to the divinely chosen Sanctuary as to the divinely appointed seat of Empire. But in the one case, even more than in the other, his enmity to the divine purpose is as distinctly marked as his desire to serve himself heir to it. "He sitteth in the Temple of God, setting himself forth as God," says St Paul. St John describes how the dead bodies of his victims shall lie "in the street of the great City...where also their Lord was crucified." And both Apostles tell us, how his power would be supported by the quasi-spiritual evidence of miracles—miracles as striking as those of our Lord Himself, or any of the Prophets before Him, and only distinguished from theirs by the absence of the spirit of charity and of holiness.

Looking on to the tradition of the post-apostolic ages, we find that, though the *details* of apocalyptic interpretation were as obscure, and opinions about them varied as much, as in modern times, yet as to the outline of future events revealed in this Book and elsewhere, there was an agreement complete except in one point (that of the Millennium). From the time of Tertullian and St Hippolytus—not to say of SS. Justin and Irenæus—we have a consistent expectation of the course of events that will precede the Last Judgement. Their views are not indeed derived from the Apocalypse exclusively, but they almost always give a meaning, and always give the same meaning, to its predictions. The Roman Empire was to be broken up into ten kingdoms, bearing (we must understand from Daniel) the same relation to it that the Hellenised kingdoms of the East bore to the Empire of Alexander. Among these kingdoms will arise a new Empire, reviving the old pretensions of Rome to world-wide instead of merely local dominion; but instead of resting on law, patriotism, and submission to the will of Providence, this new Empire will have no other basis than the self-will, the self-assertion, at least the self-deification, of its Ruler. He will come (if one may apply to the kingdom of evil the analogies of language used of the Kingdom of God) "in the spiritual power" of Epiphanes and of Nero: he may be called Nero in the sense in which our Lord is in prophecy called David, or His forerunner Elias. He will be a man free from coarse vices, such as hinder the consistent pursuit of any aim, but equally free from any restraint imposed by the fear of God, or by regard for human opinion. Claiming for himself the honour due to God and the supreme obedience due to His Law, he will persecute the Christian Church: his persecution being so relentless, so systematic and well-directed, that the Church would be exterminated did not God supernaturally interpose to "shorten the days." But, while persecuting Christianity, he will extend a more or less hearty patronage to Judaism, being possibly himself of Israelitish birth. Having in some sense revived the Roman Empire, he will yet shew himself an enemy to the City of Rome, which will be finally destroyed, either by his armies or by the direct act of God: and he will, perhaps on occasion of this destruction, choose Jerusalem for his seat of empire. To this end he will restore the Jews to their own land: he will perhaps be recognised by them as their Christ: he will restore their Temple, but will make it serve rather to his own glory than to that of the Lord God of Israel.

So far, his career has apparently been unchecked. Now God sends against him two Prophets—probably Moses and Elijah, or Enoch and Elijah—who, by their words and miracles, to some extent counteract his. But they will be put to death in his persecution, and then his power will appear finally established: but only for a few days. God will raise them from the dead, and call them up into Heaven: and by this miracle, together with the preaching that preceded their death, the Jews will be converted. Elijah will have fulfilled his destined work, of "turning the hearts of the fathers to the children," i.e. of God's old People to His new.

Still Antichrist's universal empire appears scarcely shaken by the secession of the one little nation of Israel: he will assemble the armies of the world for its reconquest, and it will seem far easier for him to reduce his second capital than his first. But when in the Land of Israel, he and his army will be met and destroyed, not in a carnal battle with the forces of Israel after the flesh, but by the power of God in the hand of His Son.

Here, according to what seems to be the oldest form of the tradition, and certainly that standing in closest relation to the Apocalypse, follows what is popularly called the Millennium. The whole reign of Antichrist lasted, apparently, but three years and a half: the divine triumph after his overthrow will last for a thousand years. This will begin, perhaps, with the appearance of the Lord Jesus on earth, certainly with the resurrection of the Martyrs, Prophets, and other chief Saints. Whether these remain on earth or no, the condition of the earth is made such that it shall not be an unworthy abode for them. Moral evil, if not annihilated, at least has its power broken. Jerusalem remains what Antichrist had made it—the spiritual and temporal metropolis of the world : but this world-wide power is now in the hands, not of God's enemy, but of God Himself: and the world under the rule of Jerusalem realises the most glorious prophetic descriptions of the Kingdom of God.

Yet this Kingdom of God is not the final and eternal one: indeed some in all ages have been disposed to doubt whether such an earthly Kingdom of God will be established at all. From the time of SS. Jerome and Augustine (the latter distinctly *changed* the older opinion for this), the general opinion of the Church has been that such a measure of liberty and predominance as has been hers since the conversion of Constantine is the only earthly Kingdom of God to be looked for. And if—feeling the inadequacy of this fulfilment to the language of St John and other Prophets—we incline to recur to the earlier view, we must confess that even so *Pauca tamen suberunt priscae vestigia fraudis.*

Not only does the natural order of the world go on—with deaths and (what shocked fourth century feeling most) marriages and births occurring; but there must be some root of moral evil remaining, to account for the end of this age of peace. The Devil will at last for a short time recover his power: while the central regions of the world remain faithful to God, the outlying ones are stirred up to revolt against Him, and press in to crush His Kingdom by the brute force of numbers. They are on the point of success—nearer to it, perhaps, than their predecessor Antichrist had been—when they are, like Antichrist, overpowered by the direct interposition of God. Then, all God's enemies being subdued, comes the end of all things— the General Resurrection of the Dead, the final Judgement, and the Eternal Kingdom of God.

(3) If we heartily believe that Daniel, St Paul, St John, and the other Prophets from whom the foregoing anticipations are derived, had received from the all-knowing God genuine revelations of the future, there is really no difficulty in accepting this as, in the main, the true interpretation of the Apocalypse. It is not of course a complete interpretation of all its details, but it gives a framework, in which every detail may find its place: and for the explanation of details we may be content to wait, till the time shall come when they are manifest to those whose faith sees the consistent fulfilment of the prophecy as a whole. Yet those who have faith to expect the entire fulfilment cannot help asking—indeed they are bound to ask—what special predictions are already fulfilled or fulfilling, what signs of the coming end are already visible: and so they are led to go over the same ground as unbelievers, who, not recognizing the Prophets as recipients of a supernatural revelation of the future, are obliged to ask how their predictions were suggested by the circumstances of the present.

And if the view be accepted that the Apocalypse was written within a year or two after the death of Nero, circumstances that might have suggested such forecasts are certainly not wanting. Nero himself realises the character of Antichrist in almost every feature. He was a cruel persecutor of Christianity: he was indifferent or even hostile to the national sentiments and national religion of Rome. Though the nearest approach he had to ruling principle was derived from the aesthetic culture of Greece, what religious feeling he had was oriental, perhaps even Jewish: his mistress and empress Poppaea seems to have been a Jewish proselyte. When his loss of the empire was imminent, he spoke of destroying Rome and transferring his throne to Jerusalem; and it was held that his motives for this plan were as much superstitious as political. But in truth Nero was too self-willed to "regard any god:" even the "Syrian goddess," to whom he had shewn some of the devotion which he denied to "the gods of his fathers," was discarded before his death: if he did not openly deify himself, like his predecessor Gaius, he shewed himself incapable of hearty worship for any other god but self.

One feature only is wanting to complete the resemblance of the two characters. Antichrist (if we accept the application to him of the latter part of Dan. xi.) "shall not regard the desire of women[1]," he shall be free from the sensual vices to which Nero was enslaved from boyhood to the end of his life. And, while with this one exception the *characters* of the two coincide so closely, their *careers* do not. Nero was a legitimate Roman Emperor, acknowledged as such by the Apostles themselves: it was in the early days of his reign, that the benefits of the Empire to mankind were most fully realised. And atheist, tyrant, and persecutor as Nero was, he certainly did not accomplish half of what the Revelation ascribes to Antichrist. He did not destroy Rome, nor reign and claim divine honours in Jerusalem: at most, it may be believed that he for a moment partially effected the first, and contemplated the second. Neither was he overthrown in the same way as Antichrist. While his generals were engaged in a successful war with the unbelieving Jews, he himself was overthrown by a revolt, or series of revolts, on the part of the army and the Senate—by a course

---

[1] In the natural sense of these words they are as little appropriate to Antiochus Epiphanes as to Nero. It is usual, though hardly natural, to understand them of that "Syrian goddess," whose temple Antiochus vainly attempted to profane. Even so, Nero's apostasy from her worship seems a suggestive parallel.

of events in which there was the same mixture of good and evil as in ordinary human action, and in which it is impossible to see any direct or miraculous intervention of God.

This admits, however, of a more or less satisfactory reply. The career of Antichrist is the career, not of Nero as known to us, as a personage of ancient history, nor as known to the Seer, as a personage of recent history, but of Nero as, the Seer thought, he was to be—of Nero risen from the dead, or restored after a period of seeming death. Although there appears to have been no room for reasonable doubt of the fact of Nero's suicide, there was a widely spread popular belief that he was alive, perhaps in the far east, and that his return from thence might be looked for. During his own generation, this belief gave occasion for pretenders to appear: we hear distinctly of two if not three, one as late as the reign of Domitian, who nearly succeeded in engaging the armies of Parthia in his cause. When it had become manifestly impossible that Nero could, in a merely natural way, be alive and in hiding, still the expectation of his reappearance by no means died out: only it assumed the form of a superstition. Both among heathens and Christians, the expectation continued down to the age of the Barbarian inroads: and among the Christians, it connected itself more or less closely with the expectation of the Antichrist foretold in the Apocalypse. Was this connexion recognised by the Seer of the Apocalypse himself?

We have already had occasion to notice an opinion according to which it was. If the Beast's seven heads, in xiii. 1, 2, xvii. 10, 11 are rightly understood of individual Emperors of Rome, there can hardly be a doubt that Nero is one of them, and that he is, in some sense, identified with the predicted Antichrist. In all probability, the head "smitten unto death" symbolises the death (not denied to have been real) of Nero: he is reckoned (together with Augustus, Tiberius, Gaius, and Claudius) among the five kings that are fallen. But his reappearance as Antichrist is anticipated: after the reign of the contemporary Emperor and the short one of his immediate successor, will appear "the Beast which was, and is not," who "both himself is the eighth, and is of the seven, and goeth into perdition." That is, the eighth Roman Emperor will be the revival of one of his predecessors (viz. the fifth), only in his revival he will be animated by the spirit of devilish, instead of merely human wickedness, as he will be possessed of devilish instead of merely human power.

Of course, it is certain that the Roman Empire was not terminated, or the visible kingdom of God established by a miraculous interposition cutting short the reign of the eighth Emperor of Rome. If the Seer of the Apocalypse commits himself to the assertion that this was destined to happen, it is certain that his prediction failed. This will present, of course, no difficulty either to unbelievers in the communication to the Prophets of supernatural knowledge of the future, or to those who deny the claims of the Apocalypse to the character of a true supernatural prophecy: on either of these principles it is easy to say, "This is what the Seer expected to happen, but it did not." Does it follow that, if we accept the divine authority of the Revelation made to St John, we must reject this interpretation of his visions, as one not borne out by the events? The analogy of other prophecies will suggest another course. The resemblances between the Nero of history and the Antichrist of prophecy are too close to be accidental: so are the resemblances, it may be added, between several other historical characters and Antichrist. On the other hand, Nero and each of these other Antichristian figures differs from the Antichrist of prophecy in some more or less essential features: and none of them has done the acts, or achieved the career, or met with the end, foretold for him. The inference seems to be, that in these "many antichrists" there have been *partial* and *typical* fulfilments of the prophecies of *the* Antichrist, in whom they will find their final and exact fulfilment: just as the various Messianic prophecies of the Old Testament have found or will find their final and exact fulfilment in Christ, while many of them were partially fulfilled—some of them even suggested—by events which the Prophets who foretold them lived to see.

In particular, there is absolutely no room for doubt that this explanation must be applied to the prophecies of the Old Testament which most closely resemble the Apocalypse—those in the seventh, eighth, and eleventh chapters of Daniel. The eighth chapter, and at least part of the eleventh, undeniably describe the reign, the persecution, and the overthrow of Antiochus Epiphanes: but, if these be regarded as having no further reference, the latter at least must be condemned as wanting that perfect truth which appears essential to a divinely inspired prophecy. If however we regard Antiochus as a type of Antichrist, it becomes credible—one may even say probable—that those parts of the prediction which have not been fulfilled by the one will be by the other. Thus understood, the three separate visions throw light upon one another. In c. vii. the reference is, apparently, to the final Enemy only—the imagery is almost[1] exactly that afterwards used by St John in the Apocalypse, and the meaning presumably the same. In c. viii., on the other hand, while the imagery is—not indeed identical, but—closely parallel with that of the preceding chapter, it seems plain that the Enemy described is Antiochus, and his history forms an adequate fulfilment of the prediction. Lastly, in c. xi. we have the historical antecedents of Antiochus described, in even more unmistakeable detail than in c. viii.: we hear of Antiochus himself, and of the conflict between him and Israel: then suddenly the historical Antiochus, with his ridiculous follies and miserable human vices, seems to vanish, and make way for a figure of demoniac grandeur, defying God on what, except to faith, seem equal terms. When *this* Enemy of God and His People has arisen, and developed his full power, the remedy is no longer to be looked for in the sword of the Maccabees: the champion Israel needs is the Archangel Michael, or indeed the Almighty Himself: the general Resurrection follows, and the general Judgement.

If the Book of Daniel be accepted as a really inspired prophecy, this series of visions admits of but one explanation. The oppression of Antiochus is foretold, in part for its own sake, as an important episode in the temporal and religious history of God's People: in part also as a type of a greater and still more important oppression. And it seems probable,

[1] Only it seems that Daniel's beast had one head, not seven (ver. 20).

that Nero is treated by the New Testament Seer exactly as Antiochus was by his predecessor—that the historical Nero is treated as the type of Antichrist, that the descriptions of the one pass insensibly into descriptions of the other. We may, consistently with our reverence for the prophecy, say, "So much of this prediction was realised in the Seer's age: the rest has not yet been fulfilled:" for we shall hold that the partial fulfilment was a foretaste and a type of a fulfilment which, when it comes, will be complete.

The partial fulfilment of the prophecy concerning the Empire has been already mentioned (p. xlix). We may say that Nero's real successor in the Empire was Vespasian—the 18 months between his accession and Nero's death being really a time of anarchy. The pretenders or claimants of empire who arose in almost every province may or may not be indicated by the "ten kings that have received no kingdom as yet," but it is arbitrary to select from among them, and recognise as *de facto* emperors, the three who were, for a few months, successively recognised at Rome. If we accept Nero then as the fifth of the "five fallen" emperors, Vespasian, the destroyer of Jerusalem, is the sixth, under whom, it is on this view probable, the vision was seen. His successor Titus was "not yet come, and when he came was to continue a little space"—*i.e.* not to have a merely ephemeral reign like those of Galba, Otho, and Vitellius, but yet a short one—about two years. And *his* successor—his brother Domitian—was to be a Nero: and so he was.

This is, however, an imperfect and inadequate fulfilment of the prophecies of Antichrist in this book. Domitian was, it is true, a revival of Nero in his cruelty; he was like Nero, a persecutor of the Church: he was also—like Nero and unlike the predicted Antichrist—foully unclean in life. But he differed from Nero in possessing talents and principles which, while to some extent they bring him nearer to the type of spiritual wickedness, may also be regarded as giving him the dignity of that power which "withholdeth" the manifestation of the Lawless One. Domitian was no blasphemous atheist, but was, as a Pagan, sincerely and even fanatically religious: and his gross personal vices did not prevent his having a zeal for virtue, which seems to have been sincere. And, for good or evil, he was a Roman—not like Antiochus, Nero, or Antichrist, a denationalised cosmopolitan. It may be doubtful to what extent the Empire suffered dishonour in Domitian's days: but at worst he must be acquitted of having wilfully betrayed its honour.

Thus it seems necessary to look for a completer fulfilment of the prophecy than any that has yet been seen, while yet it is possible to point to *a* fulfilment that, *to some extent*, corresponds with the prediction even in the minutest details. We may thus recognise an element of truth in the two rival schemes of interpretation commonly called the "preterist" and the "futurist" —that which sees in the Revelation only a prediction or forecast of events near the Seer's own time, and now past, and that which sees a prediction of events wholly or almost wholly future, and only to be fulfilled in the few last years of the world's existence. Just as the 72nd Psalm is recognised as setting forth the greatness of Solomon's, "in type, and in truth of Christ's Kingdom," so the Revelation may be regarded as a picture of the persecution of the Church, "in type" by such Emperors as Nero and Domitian, "in truth" by the Antichrist of the last days, and as a prophecy of Christ's victory over both enemies, the type and the antitype.

II. With the "Preterist" and "Futurist" schemes of interpretation is usually coordinated a third, called the "Continuous Historical." According to this scheme what is foretold in the Book is not only a series of events contemporary with the Seer, or at least within his natural range of anticipation, nor only the series of events which will immediately precede the Lord's final coming to Judgement, but the *whole* series of events, from the first to the last, beginning at the date (whenever we suppose that to be) of the vision, and ending with (or rather after) the end of the world, but embracing the whole course of history in between.

The strong point of this view is, that it enables us to give a meaning, not merely to every vision, every image, in the Apocalypse, but to the order and connexion in which the visions and images are arranged. It is quite certain, that that order is not arbitrary nor accidental, that the arrangement is (if we may apply the terms of human criticism) as elaborate, as artistic, and as symmetrical as any of the descriptions: and consequently it may fairly be held, that the arrangement forms an essential part of the Seer's teaching, and that no interpretation can be adequate which does not give a reason and a meaning for the arrangement. And the most obvious and natural view of the meaning is, that the arrangement is chronological—that every successive vision is a description, more or less figurative, of events successive to one another in the same order.

Yet no one has attempted to carry out this view quite consistently, and to interpret every vision as describing an event later than the vision before it. It is quite true that, as a rule, the visions are not only described in successive order, but are felt by the Seer to be successive—in the later ones he refers to the earlier (e.g. xiv. 1 (true text), xx. 2, xvii. 1, xxi. 9). But not only do some of the visions remain in view while later ones have risen which seem to take their place (see xi. 16, 19, xv. 5—8, xvi. 7, xix. 4): there are cases (e.g. xi. 7, xiii. 1—10, xvii. 3) where we seem to have unmistakeably the same figures or events described twice over, with only a difference in the point of view. Hence, some have gone so far as to analyse the whole book into a series of groups of visions, *each one* of which covers the whole range of human history, from the Seer's time (or even earlier) to the end of the world.

And certainly, it is difficult to understand vi. 12—17 of anything except the time immediately before the Last Judgement, or xiv. 14—20 of anything but the Last Judgement itself. Yet, when we find the latter passage immediately followed, not by the "beginning of the eternal rest[1]," but by a fresh series of plagues, which are, we are told, "the last, for in them is fulfilled the wrath of God," it is hard to avoid reconsidering the obvious and natural interpretation: and in *no other case* do we find anything resembling a description of the final Judgement, till it is described, quite unmistakeably in xx. 11—15: often as the Judgement has been prepared for and worked up to.

[1] See note on viii. 1.

In fact, the method and plan of the book seems to be, that we have again and again a series—most frequently a group of seven—of pictures that plainly symbolise the approach of the Judgement. Up to the penultimate stage, everything would lead us to think the Judgement was immediately to follow: but the penultimate stage itself is prolonged and expanded: and when at last it ends, and the series is complete, it is found to usher in, *not* the end of all things, but the beginning of a new series of events, still preparatory for the final Judgement.

Now whatever predictions of the Apocalypse have been or have not been fulfilled, there is no doubt that this feature of it has been realised conspicuously. In the first century—in the third—in the fifth—in the ninth—in the sixteenth—in the age of the French Revolution—perhaps in our own time the signs of the coming Judgement have multiplied. The faithful have seen them beginning to come to pass, and have looked up and lifted up their heads, as though their redemption were drawing nigh: while those who were *not* faithful, or at least whose faith was without love, have sought to hide from the face of Him that sitteth upon the Throne, and from the wrath of the Lamb. And yet, after a generation or two, the signs have passed away: the Judge has not come, the whole world has not been judged; rather, it has taken a new lease of life, and become a battlefield between new forms of good and evil, a court for new judgements of God between them. We cannot say indeed that those were wrong who expected the Judge to appear. They were bidden to expect Him—they were bidden to expect Him all the more, when they saw such signs as they did see: and so how could they do otherwise than they did? Indeed, dare we say that their expectation was disappointed? The world has not been judged, but the nation, the polity, the generation has been: the Kingdom of God's eternal rest has not been set up, but they that have believed do enter rest. The Vision of Judgement has been fulfilled in part and in type: the partial fulfilment serves to stay and support, without satisfying, faith's hunger for the final fulfilment.

Thus it seems possible to recognise an element of truth in both the "continuous" and what may be called the "resumptive" methods of interpretation, as we did in both the "preterist" and the "futurist" theories. We may believe, that the chief object of the book is, to teach the Church how to prepare for the Lord's coming to Judgement. With that object, we are told, not only in general terms what signs will mark His approach, but, in some detail, what events will immediately precede it. But in the providence of God, the signs of His approach, and events more or less resembling those immediately preceding it, have occurred repeatedly: and *this Book accordingly intimates*, that they will occur repeatedly. To Christians who had seen an almost perfect image of Antichrist in Nero, it was foretold that a new Nero, a perfect Antichrist, was to come: it was, not improbably, intimated that there would be in some sense a new Nero in the next generation, which was fulfilled in Domitian. Yet the "wars and rumours of wars" of the year 69—70 did not usher in the Second Advent: they passed off, and left the Empire in peace and prosperity. Jerusalem had fallen, and Rome had tottered: but the whole earth sat still and was quiet: and Rome, at least, had recovered from the shock. Again, in the conquests of the Teutonic barbarians, of the Arabs, of the Turks; or in the paganising apostasies of Julian, of the Renaissance, of the great Revolution, and of our own day, we may see likenesses, more or less close, of the things foretold in this Book: He Who inspired the Book doubtless intends that we should. Only, while the Book was written for the Church of all ages, it was written *specially* for the Church of the Apostles' own age, and for the Church of the last age of all: we need not therefore expect to find any intermediate age of affliction, or any intermediate enemy of the truth, indicated with such individualising detail as Nero and his persecution on the one hand, or Antichrist and his on the other.

Certainly, there is this objection to the various forms of the "continuous historical" theory, which have attempted to identify special visions in the Apocalypse with special events in mediaeval or modern history—that no just view of the history of any polity or system will support such a series of identifications. Indeed, there is this element of truth, or at least of plausibility, in such schemes, that the one national or local feature indicated by the Seer coincides with what men have learnt, more and more as time has gone on, to be the centre and heart of the continuous life of the world's history—The City on the Seven Mountains. The Revelation, it is plain, tells us what the history of Rome is in God's sight: and the history of Rome is the one thread that runs unbroken through the history of the world. But it is only by the most arbitrary treatment—passing without warning from the figurative to the literal, and from the literal to the figurative—that any appearance can be maintained of a resemblance between the history of Rome, or of the world gathered round Rome, and the successive visions of the Apocalypse: nor is it possible, in honesty or in charity, to ascribe to the Rome of past history a uniform character such as is ascribed to the Babylon of the Apocalypse. No doubt, there have been times,—(much later than those of Nero and Domitian,)—when a Roman Emperor or a Roman Pope has presented a figure which, to the eyes of faith and righteousness, looks terribly like that of Antichrist. Godless profligacy like that of Frederic II., cultivated, heathenish indifference to righteousness like that of the age of Leo X., was certainly felt—was, we cannot doubt, rightly felt—to be the antichristian power of their time, by the moral reformers of the Middle Ages and of the Renaissance: but it is unjust and unreasonable to hold the Empire in all ages, or the Papacy in all ages, responsible for the sins of the Empire or the Papacy in those ages. We who in our own age have seen the rival powers of the Empire and the Papacy represented by honourable Christian men like William I. and Leo XIII., ought to be able to do justice alike to Pagan Emperors like Trajan and Diocletian, to Christian Emperors like Henry III. and Barbarossa, and to Popes like Gregory I., Gregory VII., Innocent III., and Pius V. To treat either of these groups of men as the champions and representatives of Antichrist is hardly less than blasphemy against the work of God.

And in fact, the identification of the Papacy with Antichrist admits of direct refutation. " He is the Antichrist," says St John, (Ep. I. ii. 22) "who denieth the Father and the Son:" he defines " the spirit of Antichrist" as the " spirit which confesseth not that

Jesus Christ is come in the flesh" (Ep. I. iv. 3). Now, whatever the errors of the Papacy and of the Roman Church, it is certain that no Pope has ever denied the truth on the doctrines of the Trinity and Incarnation. The most questionable of Roman doctrines—in particular those relating to the person of the Blessed Virgin Mary—so far from contradicting the true doctrine of "Jesus Christ come in the flesh," presuppose it and are deduced (however unwarrantably) from it. It is likely enough that the Papacy has in many ages incurred "the Babylonian woe," not in respect of theological opinions, but in proportion as "the mitre and the crosier" were, in Bishop Coxe's words,

"Sullied with the tinsel of the Caesar's diadems:"

but, when the Caesars themselves were the bar against Antichrist, their successors or their apes can hardly be identified with him. One thing is plain about the Apocalypse—that it describes a clearly defined moral conflict between good and evil, between Christ and His enemies: not a controversy in which good men, and men who love Christ in sincerity, are to be found on different sides. It is an idle latitudinarianism which assumes that in such controversies truth is unimportant, or that compromise is the only guide to it: but it is something worse to waste on such controversies the zeal that should be reserved for the true war with the real Antichrist.

CHAPTER IV.

ANALYSIS.

i. 1—3. Title and description of the Book.

i. 4—iii. 22. Prologue and Dedication, shewing how St John received from Christ the command to write the vision, and send it to the Seven Churches.

    i. 4—20. The vision of the Son of Man.

    ii. 1—iii. 22. The Epistles to the Seven Churches.

v. 1—xxii. 7. The Vision or Revelation itself.

INTRODUCTION.

A. iv. 1—v. 14. Vision remaining visible through all the rest; shewing (ch. iv.) the Divine glory (see Ezek. i.; Is. vi.), and (ch. v.) the Lamb that was slain sharing it.

    (a) v. 1—14. The book of the seven seals and the Glory of the Lamb who is worthy to open it.

B. vi. 1—viii. 1. The opening of the seven seals, and the judgements attending thereon. Before the last seal, there appear

    (a) vii. 1—8. The sealing of the 144,000, and

    (b) 9—17. The assembly of the multitude of the justified.

C. viii. 2—xi. 19. The sounding of the seven trumpets, and the judgements attending thereon. Before the first trumpet appear

    (a) viii. 3—5. The Angel censing the prayers of the Saints. The last three trumpets are proclaimed (viii. 13) as Woes. Before the last of them appears

    (b) x. 1—11. A mighty Angel having a little Book, which the Seer is commanded to eat: and

    (c) xi. 1, 2. The measuring of the Temple.

    (d) xi. 3—14. The prophesying of the two Witnesses (Moses and Elijah?), their martyrdom and resurrection.

D. xii. 1—xiv. 13. The signs in Heaven and in Earth: the heads of the Kingdoms of God and Satan, or of Christ and Antichrist.

    (a) xii. 1—13. The Woman giving birth to the Man, persecuted by the Serpent (see Gen. iii. 15), and the War in Heaven.

    (b) xiii. 1—10. The Beast to whom the Serpent or Dragon (the Devil) gives his authority (see Dan. vii., xi. 36 sqq.; 2 Thess. ii. 3—10).

    (c) xiii. 11—18. The second Beast (the False Prophet) who secures the deification of the first Beast, and persecutes those who refuse him worship.

    (d) xiv. 1—5. The Lamb with the 144,000 of the redeemed.

    (e) xiv. 6—12. Three Angels proclaim God's Judgements, and (v. 13) a voice from Heaven His mercy.

E. xiv. 14—20. A symbolic vision of the Judgement of the earth (see Joel iii. 13).

F. xv. 1—xvi. 21. The outpouring of the seven vials, and the judgements attending thereon. Before the first vial there appears

    (a) xv. 2—4. The triumph-song of the victors in the war with the Beast.

Before the last vial,

    (b) xvi. 13—16. The spirits of devils gather the armies of Christ's enemies.

G. xvii. 1—xviii. 24. The fall of Babylon.

H. xix. 1—21. The campaign of the Word of God against the Beast.

    (a) 1—8. The triumph-song inspired by the fall of Babylon: the Lamb, the Victor and the Bridegroom (see Ps. xlv.).

    (b) 9—10. The revealing Angel proclaims himself not divine.

    (c) 11—21. The martial procession, and the victory.

I. xx. 1—6. The Millennial Peace.

K. xx. 7—10. The last campaign of the Devil.

L. xx. 11—15. The universal Judgement.

M. xxi. 1—xxii. 7. The glorious reign of God and His saints in the New Jerusalem.

    (8, 9. The revealing Angel again refuses divine honours.)

xxii. 10—21. Conclusion.

THE REVELATION

OF

S. JOHN THE DIVINE.

THE Revelation of Jesus Christ, which God gave unto him, 1
to shew unto his servants *things* which must shortly come

TITLE AND DESCRIPTION OF THE REVELATION. CHAP. I. 1—3.

1. *The Revelation*] Rightly so rendered in English idiom, though the definite article is not expressed in the Greek. The word, according to Jerome on Gal. i. 11, 12, is peculiar to the Scriptures, and is not used by Greek classical writers.

of Jesus Christ] i.e. which He makes; as is explained by the words which follow: "which God gave to Him,...and He sent and signified it, &c."

which God gave unto him] For as the Son is of the Father as regards His essential being, so He receives from the Father all that He has or knows. Compare in St John's Gospel vii. 16, xiv. 10, xvii. 7, 8; especially the last passage. Doubtless when the Son made this revelation, He had received from the Father the knowledge which in the time of His humiliation He had not (St Mark xiii. 32), or rather had abdicated (Phil. ii. 7).

his servants] Probably "God's" rather than "Jesus Christ's:" see xxii. 6.

things which must] The R.V. takes this as a further description of the "Revelation which God gave," and renders "*even* the things which must shortly come to pass," putting the A.V. in the margin.

must] as part of a Divine purpose, cf. Matt. xvii. 10, xxvi. 54; Luke xxiv. 26, &c.

shortly] So ver. 3 fin., xxii. 6, 7. Compare on the one hand Matt. xxiv. 29, 34, and on the other Hab. ii. 3; Luke xviii. 8; 2 Pet. iii. 8, 9. These last passages suggest, that the object of these words is to assure us of God's practical readiness to fulfil His promises, rather than to define any limit of time for their actual fulfilment. Slackness in fulfilling a promise is a moral fault (Prov. iii. 28), not to be ascribed to God: forbearance in executing a threat is not so. But we are not to press what St Peter says about the nothingness of time before God, so as to argue that these words mean nothing at all to human apprehensions: our Lord's words in St Matthew l. c. are so strong and definite as almost to necessitate the view that *a* fulfilment (if not necessarily the final and complete one) was really to come immediately.

to pass; and he sent and signified *it* by his angel unto his
2 servant John: who bare record of the word of God, and of
the testimony of Jesus Christ, and of all *things* that he saw.
3 Blessed *is* he that readeth, and they that hear the words of
this prophecy, and keep those *things* which are written therein: for the time *is* at hand.

he sent] "He" may be either "God" as in xxii. 6, or "Jesus Christ," as ibid. 16. It seems best to take it of the latter: the sense will be, "He, having received the Revelation from the Father, sent by His angel, and indicated it to His servant John." The angel is the same who is mentioned in xvii. 1, &c., xix. 9, xxi. 9, xxii. 6, 8, 16.

2. *who bare record*] i.e. who bears witness in the present work. The past tense is used, as constantly in Greek—e.g. in St John's own Epistle, I. ii. 14—of the act of a writer which *will* be past when his work comes to be read. The "witness" John is said to bear is that contained in this Book—not, as some have imagined, in his Gospel.

There is, however, some evidence to the identity of authorship of the two, in the resemblance between the attestations to the authority of this Book in these three verses, and to that of the Gospel in xxi. 24. The two may be presumed to proceed from the same persons, probably the elders of the Church of Ephesus.

the word of God] His word made known to man, especially as revealed to St John himself; not the *personal* Word of God of St John's Gospel i. 1 and Rev. xix. 13, as He is immediately mentioned under another name.

the testimony of Jesus Christ] See xxii. 16 for a similar description of the *special* Revelation of this book. Both 'the word' and 'the testimony' are repeated in *v*. 9 where they refer to the *general* Revelation of Christian truth for which the Seer was in exile.

3. *he that readeth, and they that hear*] Plainly the author of the Book, or of this endorsement of it, contemplates its being read publicly in the Church. The apostolic Epistles were thus read, first by the Churches to which they were addressed, then by others in the neighbourhood (Col. iv. 16): even the sub-apostolic Epistles of Clement and Polycarp, and the decidedly post-apostolic one of Soter, Bishop of Rome, were in like manner read in the churches that originally received them, or to which their authors belonged. In the course of the second century, both the Gospels and the apostolic Epistles came to be read in churches generally, as the Law and the Prophets had been read in the synagogues. In the time of Justin Martyr (Apol. I. 67), not to insist on 1 Tim. v. 18, 2 Pet. iii. 16, it is plain that the New Testament Scriptures were thus recognised as sharing the authority and sanctity of the Old.

and keep those things] Attend to them, *mind* them. He who reads and they who hear are only blessed if they do this; John xiii. 17; Matt. vii. 25 sq. The word is constantly used of 'keeping' the Law, the Commandments, &c., throughout the N. T.: but is commoner in *all* St John's writings than in any other.

JOHN to the seven churches which are in Asia: Grace *be* 4
unto you, and peace, from him which is, and which was,
and which is to come; and from the seven spirits which are

PROLOGUE, vv. 4—9.

4. *John*] The Apostle, the son of Zebedee, who (probably afterwards) wrote the Gospel: see Introduction.

seven churches] The number of course is symbolical or representative: there were other churches in Asia, e.g. at Colossae and Hierapolis (Col. iv. 13). But the Seven Churches represent "the Holy Church throughout all the world." It was very early observed, that St Paul also wrote to seven churches—the Thessalonians, Corinthians, Galatians, Romans, Philippians, Ephesians (?), and Colossians.

in Asia] The proconsular province of that name. In Acts xvi. 6 "Asia" seems to be used in a still narrower sense, being distinguished from the adjoining districts of Phrygia and Mysia, as well as from the provinces of Galatia and Bithynia; so that it would correspond approximately with the ancient kingdom of Lydia. But as Pergamum was in Mysia, and Laodicea in Phrygia, it seems that here the word is used to include the whole province.

Grace...and peace] So St Paul in all *his* Epistles to the Seven Churches, Rom. i. 7; 1 Cor. i. 3; 2 Cor. i. 2; Gal. i. 3; Eph. i. 2; Phil. i. 2; Col. i. 2; 1 Thess. i. 1; 2 Thess. i. 2; and so Philem. 3. In his later private letters the form varies—"Grace, *mercy*, and peace," 1 Tim. i. 2; 2 Tim. i. 2; Tit. i. 4—as in St John's second Epistle. St James (i. 1) uses the common secular salutation "greeting" (cf. Acts xv. 23): St Peter has "grace and peace" as here, but in his first Epistle does not say *from* Whom they are to come.

from him] The sacred Name is in the nominative, being treated as indeclinable: as though we should say in English "from He Who is," &c. For general remarks on the grammatical (or ungrammatical) peculiarities of this book, see Introduction, p. xxi. Here at least it is plain, that the anomaly is not due to ignorance, but to the writer's mode of thought being so vigorous that it must express itself in its own way, at whatever violence to the laws of language.

which is, and which was, and which is to come] A paraphrase of the "Ineffable name" revealed to Moses (Ex. iii. 14 sq.), which we, after Jewish usage, write "Jehovah" and pronounce "the LORD." Or, rather perhaps, a paraphrase of the explanation of the Name given to him l. c., "I am That I am"—which is rendered by the LXX. "I am He Which Is;" by the Targum of Palestine on Exod. "I am He who is and who will be." The same Targum on Deut. xxxii. 39 has "Behold now, I am He who Am and Was, and Will Be."

which was] is again ungrammatical in Greek: the only word that could be used grammatically, would mean "which was made" or "which began to be," and is therefore avoided. Compare the opposition of the "being" of God or Christ, and the "becoming" or "being made" of creatures, in St John's Gospel, i. 6, 8, 9, viii. 58.

is to come] Probably only used to express future time—not referring

I—2

5 before his throne; and from Jesus Christ, *who is* the faithful witness, *and* the first begotten of the dead, and the prince of the kings of the earth. Unto him that loved us, and washed

to the "*Coming*" of Christ; for thus far we have a threefold name for the Father—the Son is separately mentioned afterwards. Else, "He that is to come" is often used as a familiar and distinctive title of Christ: see Matt. xi. 3, xxi. 9; John vi. 14, xi. 27; Heb. x. 37; John Ep. II. 7: cf. Ep. I. ii. 18, where the same word is pointedly used of *Antichrist*. But with this more general sense we may compare "the wrath to come," 1 Thess. i. 10, "the world to come," Mark x. 30, and "things to come," John xvi. 13, xviii. 4.

seven Spirits] So iii. 1, iv. 5, v. 6. In the second of these passages it would be possible to understand the name of seven chief Angels (see viii. 2): but here it would scarcely seem possible that creatures should be, not merely coupled with the Creator as sources of blessing, but actually thrust into the midst of His being, between the two Divine Persons. "The seven Spirits" thus made coordinate with the Father and the Son can scarcely be other than the Holy Ghost, Who is known to us in His seven-fold operations and gifts, and Who *perhaps* has some seven-fold character in Himself; which we cannot and need not understand, but of which there seem to be intimations in the passages of this book referred to, and in Zech. iii. 9, iv. 10, by which these are certainly to be illustrated.

5. *who is*] These words are probably inserted in the A.V. and R.V. by way of marking the fact that "the faithful Witness" is in the nominative, not in apposition to the name "Jesus Christ." But whether this has the same object as the anacoluthon of the previous verse—a sort of reverence that forbids the divine Name to be "governed" by any other word—is more doubtful: the general usage of the book appears to ignore the classical rule of apposition.

the faithful witness] See 1 Tim. vi. 13: Jesus Christ was in His Death much more than a martyr, but He was also the perfect type and example of martyrdom. Observe His own words in John xviii. 37 —to which perhaps St Paul l. c. is referring. Here as in the next clause, see below, the *language* recalls Ps. lxxxix. 37, perhaps too Is. lv. 4.

first begotten of the dead] Explained by St Paul in Col. i. 18, where He is called "the First-born" (the word is the same) "*from* the dead." The sense of "first-born" or "first-begotten" is "first to enter life," without any fanciful image of death as the womb of earth. The thought in Rom. i. 4 is similar.

prince of the kings of the earth] A reminiscence (hardly to be called a quotation) of Ps. lxxxix. 27, "I will make Him My *First-born*, higher than *the kings of the earth*."

that loved] Read, **that loveth**. "It is His ever-abiding character, that He loveth His own, John xiii. 1" (Alford).

washed us] The balance of evidence is in favour of the reading "loosed us:" the preposition "*in*" might easily, in a Hebraistic book

us from our sins in his own blood, and hath made us kings 6
and priests unto God and his Father; to him *be* glory and
dominion for ever and ever. Amen.

Behold, he cometh with clouds; and every eye shall see 7
him, and they *also* which pierced him: and all kindreds of

like this, be used of an *instrument*, where we should say "by," or
"with." So we should probably render "redeemed us from our sins
by His own Blood"—the Blood of Christ being conceived as the price
of our redemption, as in 1 Pet. i. 18, 19—not, as in vii. 14, xxii. 14
(according to the preferable reading), and perhaps in St John's Ep.
I. i. 7, as the cleansing fountain foretold in Zech. xiii. 1. If therefore
we ask "*when* Christ thus freed us," the answer must be, at His
Passion, not at our conversion or baptism.

6. *and hath made*] Lit., **and He made**; the construction "that
loveth...and that freed..." is broken off, to be resumed by "to Him"
in the next clause.

kings and priests] Read, **a kingdom, priests**: a phrase synonymous
with the "royal priesthood" of 1 Pet. ii. 9. That is an exact quotation from the LXX. version of Exod. xix. 6 and a correct rendering of
the Hebrew; this is not.

God and his Father] A more natural translation is that of the R. V. **His
God and Father** as in Rom. xv. 6; 2 Cor. i. 3, xi. 31; Eph. i. 3; Col.
i. 3 (perhaps); 1 Pet. i. 3. Certainly there is nothing in this version
unworthy of our Lord's relation to His Father; cf. John xx. 17. But
some, while admitting the above to be the natural sense in the passages
quoted from SS. Peter and Paul, argue that here the A. V. is right;
because St John, especially in this book, usually repeats a possessive
pronoun with each of the substantives it belongs to, e.g. vi. 11, "*their*
fellow servants and *their* brethren;" so that he would have written
"*His* God and *His* Father," if that had been the sense intended.
Perhaps "My God" in iii. 12 may serve to decide which is the likelier
meaning in this Book.

7. This verse, as indeed may be said of the whole Book, is founded
chiefly on our Lord's own prophecy recorded in St Matt. xxiv., and
secondly on the Old Testament prophecies which He there refers to
and sums up.

with clouds] "With *the* clouds,"—"the clouds of heaven" of Dan.
vii. 13.

and they also which pierced him] Zech. xii. 10; in his Gospel, xix. 37,
St John translates that passage correctly, and here refers to the same
translation: that of the LXX. is wrong and almost meaningless. But
while the *words* here are taken from Zechariah, the *thought* is rather
that of Matt. xxvi. 64: "they which pierced Him" are thought of, not
as looking to Him by faith, and mourning for Him in penitence, but
as seeing Him Whom they had not believed in, and mourning in
despair.

all kindreds of the earth] Better, **all the tribes**—the reference is
still to Zech. l. c., through the medium of Matt. xxiv. 30. Thus we see

the earth shall wail because of him. Even so, Amen. I am Alpha and Omega, the beginning and the ending, saith the Lord, which is, and which was, and which is to come, the Almighty.

I John, who also am your brother, and companion in tribulation, and in the kingdom and patience of Jesus Christ, was in the isle that is called Patmos, for the word of God,

that the fact that the profitable and the unprofitable "mourning" (or "wailing"—the Greek word is the same in St Matthew as here) are foretold in the same terms, in solemnly suggestive contrast with each other, is due not to the Apostle but to his Master: it is He that tells us that all tribes of the earth *must* mourn, either now for the woe our sins caused Him, or then for the woe they will cause us.

because of him] Literally, "at him;" at sight of Him. R. V. "over Him," which can hardly be meant here.

Even so, Amen] Or, **Yea, Amen**—the two words, Greek and Hebrew, being similarly coupled in 2 Cor. i. 20. The second, like the first, is an emphatic word of *confirmation*—so used e.g. repeatedly by our Lord Himself, St Matt. v. 18, &c., where it is translated "verily." The popular tradition that "Amen" means "So be it" is only partially true: even in its liturgical use, we append it to creeds as well as prayers. It comes from the same Hebrew root as the words for "faith" and "truth;" the primary meaning being apparently "solidity." See on iii. 14.

8. *Alpha and Omega*] The first and last letters of the *Greek* alphabet used, as in Rabbinical proverbs the first and last letters of the *Hebrew* alphabet were, as symbols of "the beginning and the end." These latter words are not here a part of the genuine text; they come from xxii. 13.

Lord] Should be followed by "God;" the group of titles represents "the Lord, Jehovah the God of Hosts" of the O. T. The word we render "Almighty"—perhaps rather meaning "of all might"—is the usual representative in the LXX. of the word [Lord of] *Sabaoth*. So in the Athanasian Creed, "Almighty" is coupled with the divine *names* "God" and "Lord," not with the divine *attributes* "eternal, incomprehensible, uncreated."

9. *I John, who &c.*] Better and more simply, **I John your brother and partaker with you** (for the condescending choice of titles, cf. 1 Pet. v. 1) **in the tribulation and kingdom and patience in Jesus**. The collocation of the latter words is peculiar, and it is not very clear why "the kingdom" should be placed between "the tribulation" and "patience." Alford refers to Acts xiv. 22 for the association of the kingdom with the tribulation.

was] Had come there, found myself there. Here and in the next verse he avoids, perhaps intentionally, the use of the word for continuous and absolute "being:" see note on *v*. 4.

Patmos] One of the Sporades, the south-eastern group of the islands of the Aegean. According to the tradition, as given by Victorinus, he

and for the testimony of Jesus Christ. I was in the spirit 10
on the Lord's day, and heard behind me a great voice, as of
a trumpet, saying, I am Alpha and Omega, the first and the 11
last: and, What thou seest, write in a book, and send *it*
unto the seven churches which are in Asia; unto Ephesus,
and unto Smyrna, and unto Pergamos, and unto Thyatira,
and unto Sardis, and unto Philadelphia, and unto Laodicea.
And I turned to see the voice that spake with me. And 12

was condemned to work in the *mines*—which, if trustworthy, must mean marble quarries, as there are no mines, strictly speaking, in the island. Christians were sent to the mines (Roman Christians to those of Sardinia) at least as early as the reign of Commodus (Hipp. *Ref. Haer.* IX. 12), and this was much the commonest punishment during the Diocletian persecution in which Victorinus suffered himself. In St John's time it was commoner to put Christians to death; but the tradition is probably right; 'deportation,' confinement without hard labour on a lonely island was then and afterwards reserved for offenders of higher secular rank.

for the word, &c.] See note on *v.* 2. Comparing vi. 9 and xx. 4, it is hardly doubtful that these words support the traditional view, that he was banished there for being a Christian; that they do not mean, as else they might, that he had gone to the island to preach the Gospel, or (by special revelation or otherwise) had withdrawn there to await this vision.

Vision of the Son of Man, vv. 10—20.

10. *I was in the spirit*] Was caught into a state of spiritual rapture. So iv. 2 and (nearly) xvii. 3, xxi. 10; cf. 1 Kings xviii. 12; Ezek. iii. 12, 14, xxxvii. 1; also 2 Cor. xii. 2, 3.

the Lord's day] Undoubtedly here used (though for the first time) in the sense now traditional throughout Christendom. Many of the early Fathers, Ignatius, Justin Martyr, Clement of Alexandria, Tertullian, &c. use the word of the First Day of the week. A few commentators have proposed to translate, "I was, in spirit, on the day of the Lord," i.e. was carried away in spirit to the Great Day of the Lord's Coming; but the reference to iv. 2 refutes this.

as of a trumpet] As loud, and perhaps as clear.

11. *I am...the last: and*] Not genuine in this place: we therefore cannot say positively that the voice is His Who says in ver. 17 "I am the first and the last:" but the context makes it probable.

which are in Asia] Not genuine in this place.

unto Ephesus, &c.] The seven cities are enumerated in the order in which a traveller on circuit might visit them, going north from Ephesus to Smyrna and Pergamos, then inland to Thyatira, and southwards to Sardis, Philadelphia, and Laodicea.

Pergamos] *Pergamum* appears to be the correct form.

12. *to see the voice*] The meaning is obvious, and the inconsequence of language characteristic.

13 being turned, I saw seven golden candlesticks; and in the midst of the seven candlesticks one like unto the Son of man, clothed with a garment down to the foot, and girt about 14 the paps with a golden girdle. His head and *his* hairs *were* white like wool, *as* white as snow; and his eyes *were* as a 15 flame of fire; and his feet like unto fine brass, as if they

candlesticks] Or lamp-stands (Matt. v. 15). The ancients did not use candles like ours: the *candela* was rather a torch.

13. *one like unto the Son of man*] There is no article with either noun, while in the title of our Lord "the Son of Man" in the Gospels and in Acts vii. 56 it is expressed with both. The inference is, not that our Lord is not intended, but that the title is taken, not from His own use of it, but direct from the Greek of Dan. vii. 13—where also the art. is absent. Whether we should translate "a son of man" is a question rather of taste than of grammar: the words of themselves mean no more than "I saw a human figure," but their associations make it plain to anyone acquainted with the Book of Daniel, that it was a superhuman Being in human form; and to a Christian, of St John's days as of our own, Who that Being was.

a garment down to the foot] Certainly a garment of dignity (as Ecclus. xxvii. 8; Dan. x. 5; Ezek. ix. 2, 11): probably in particular of *priestly* dignity, as Ex. xxviii. 31 (where the next verse suggests comparison with John xix. 23). The same word as here is used in the so-called Epistle of Barnabas (c. 7) of the scarlet robe in which the Lord will appear to judgement: some suppose that the writer had in his mind this passage, and perhaps xix. 13.

girt about the paps] So xv. 6, of angels. We therefore can hardly press the distinction of this from Dan. x. 5 (and Ezek. ix. 2, LXX.), where the angels wear the girdles of gold or gems, as men would, on the loins.

14. *like wool, as white as snow*] Either these words are to be taken together, 'like wool white as snow' or we must punctuate "were white like white wool, like snow." Though the Person seen is the Son of Man of Dan. vii. 13, the description is more nearly that of the Ancient of Days, ibid. 9. We need not wonder that Their union was made more plain to the later Prophet.

15. *fine brass*] Decidedly the most probable sense, though the etymology of the word is obscure. It looks like a compound of the Greek words for "brass" (or more accurately bronze) and "incense"—the latter being borrowed from the Hebrew name, which comes from a root meaning "white." Perhaps the real meaning is "white brass," i.e. the Latin *orichalcum* (vid. Verg. Aen. XII. 87), which was like gold (Cic. Off. III. xxiii. 92)—i.e. perhaps was our "brass" as distinct from bronze. In Ezek. i. 4, 27, viii. 2 we have a word which probably (comparing ibid. i. 7, xl. 3, Dan. x. 6) means the same, but which the LXX. translate *electrum*—meaning perhaps by this not *amber*, but an alloy of gold with silver or other metal. Some think that sense suitable here, as symbolising the divine and human natures of our Lord.

burned in a furnace; and his voice as the sound of many waters. And he had in his right hand seven stars: and out of his mouth went a sharp twoedged sword: and his countenance *was* as the sun shineth in his strength. And when I saw him, I fell at his feet as dead. And he laid his right hand upon me, saying unto me, Fear not; I am the first and the last: I am he that liveth, and was dead; and behold, I am alive for evermore, Amen; and have the keys of

as if they burned] Read, **as if it burned** or rather with R. V. as **if it had been refined**—which seems to prove that "incense" cannot be the sense of the word just discussed, as incense would be burned in a censer not a furnace.

his voice as] Ezek. xliii. 2.

16. *he had*] Lit. **having**, and so the sword "going" out of His mouth. Throughout the book, participles are used coordinately with finite verbs, especially in descriptions: perhaps rather by a Hebraism than a mere carelessness of construction.

out of his mouth, &c.] The image is perhaps suggested by Is. xlix. 2; but the application made of it in ii. 16, xix. 15, 21 is more like in sense to Is. xi. 4; 2 Thess. ii. 8. It is relevant to compare Eph. vi. 17; Heb. iv. 12; but the use of similar images by different Apostles must not be allowed to lead us into a sort of Christian mythology, as though the imagery were as absolutely and unalterably fixed as the doctrine symbolized by it. In ch. xix. we see plainly that not the sword but the Owner of it is "the Word of God:" in ii. 23 we have the same sense as in Heb. l. c., but the image of the sword is *not* there used to illustrate it.

his countenance] The same word is used in John xi. 44 in the sense of "face," and so it is best to take it here, though it might mean "appearance" generally. In Ezek. i. 27, the LXX. use the word for "colour" not for "appearance."

17. *I fell at his feet as dead*] So Dan. viii. 17 sq., x. 8, 9, 15 (Ezek. i. 28, xliii. 3, xliv. 4 do not necessarily imply so much): cf. Ex. iii. 6, xx. 19, xxxiii. 20; Judg. vi. 22, xiii. 22; Is. vi. 5, and also Luke xxiv. 37; John xxi. 12. St John was in presence of both the sources of supernatural terror—of God's Presence made manifest, and of One come from the dead.

he laid his right hand, &c.] So Dan. x. 10, 16. As in Luke xxiv. 39, the Lord's *touch* serves to remind the Disciple of His still remaining perfect humanity. Sharing our nature, He is no longer the object of such blind terror as we should feel before an Angel or a disembodied spirit, or still more before God if revealed otherwise than in Christ.

the first and the last] i.e. the Eternal, as Is. xli. 4, xliv. 6, xlviii. 12.

18. *I am he*] Literally, **I am the First and the Last, and He that liveth; and I was dead and am alive.**

I am alive] The words "was" and "am" are emphatic—contrasting

19 hell and of death. Write *the things* which thou hast seen, and *the things* which are, and *the things* which shall be here-
20 after; the mystery of the seven stars which thou sawest in my right hand, and the seven golden candlesticks. The seven stars are the angels of the seven churches: and the seven candlesticks which thou sawest are the seven churches.

His temporal and temporary death with His eternal life: see on v. 4.
Amen] Should be omitted.
of hell and of death] Read, **of death and of hell**. "Hell" is Hades, the receptacle of the dead: usually personified in this book, as indeed is death, vi. 8, xx. 13, 14. But here they are rather conceived as places, prisons wherein the dead are confined, and from which Christ can deliver them. We read of "the gates of death" in Ps. ix. 13; Job xxxviii. 17, and "the gates of hell" in Is. xxxviii. 10; Matt. xvi. 18.

19. *Write*] Add **therefore**—The Lord reveals His exaltation in His Manhood as a reason why His servant is not to fear and is to write His words in faith and hope.
the things which are] Some take these words to mean "what they (viz. the things which thou hast seen) are," i.e. what they mean. But it is simpler to take the verse as meaning, that he is to write down the whole vision, whether of past, present, or future events. "The things which thou hast seen" are not, indeed, by any logical necessity visions of past events: but all that he had yet seen actually did symbolise the facts of Christ's Incarnation, Resurrection, and entrance into glory. It may be observed, that the Incarnation and Ascension are actually represented in a later scene of the vision, xii. 2, 5. "The things which are" will perhaps refer chiefly to the messages to the Seven Churches, "the things which shall be hereafter" beginning with ch. iv.

20. *the mystery*] The use of this word in the N. T. is not very far removed from its primary meaning in classical Greek. We may paraphrase it, "the hidden divine truth, now made known, but made known to God's favoured ones only:" see Eph. iii. 3—12 for the completest illustration of its meaning. Here the *sense* is, "I reveal to thee the secret and sacred meaning of..." The *construction* must be, "Write (among other things) the mystery of...:" for the context shews that the word "mystery" is an accusative not a nominative.
the seven golden candlesticks] In construction (but hardly in sense) these words are coordinate with "the mystery," not a genitive case dependent on it.
the angels of the seven churches] For the meaning of the word "Angels" here, see Excursus I.
the seven candlesticks] Plainly this image is suggested by the seven-branched candlestick of Ex. xxv. 31 sqq.—still more by the mystical vision of one resembling it, in Zech. iv. But here the image of seven *detached* candlesticks does not exactly correspond to the de-

Unto the angel of the church of Ephesus write; These 2
things saith he that holdeth the seven stars in his right hand,
who walketh in the midst of the seven golden candlesticks;
I know thy works, and thy labour, and thy patience, and 2
how thou canst not bear *them which are* evil: and thou hast
tried them which say *they* are apostles, and are not, and
hast found them liars: and hast borne, and hast patience, 3
and for my name's sake hast laboured, and hast not fainted.
Nevertheless I have *somewhat* against thee, because thou 4
hast left thy first love. Remember therefore from whence 5

scription of either, nor are we to assume that the significance of those is
exactly the same as of these.

The Church in Ephesus. Chap. II. 1—7.

These seven Epistles are marked by certain features common to
them all. (1) They are all dictated by the Lord Himself. (2) The
command to write to the Angel of the particular Church. (3) One of
the great titles of our Lord taken for the most part from the Vision in
chap. i. (4) An address to the Angel of the Church, always commencing
with 'I know,' describing the circumstances of the Church, exhorting to
repentance or to constancy, and ending with a prophetic announcement.
(5) A promise to "him that overcometh" generally accompanied with a
call to earnest attention, 'he that hath ears, &c.' (See Alford).

1. *the angel of the church of Ephesus*] Some think that this would
be St Timothy, and go so far as to find in St Paul's Epistles traits of his
character analogous to those here noted. But even if the "Angel"
here be a bishop, it is likelier that he would be one appointed by St
Timothy, if not by St John himself. 2 Tim. iv. 9, 21, compared with
Tit. iii. 12, seems to prove that permanent residence in one diocese was
not implied by the apostolical commission which St Paul, toward the
end of his life, gave to his disciples.

he that holdeth the seven stars] Ephesus being the chief city and, to
some extent, the mother Church of the district, the Lord addresses the
Church there in the character of Lord of *all* the Churches: as though
(to illustrate by the later organization of the Church) he addressed all
the Churches of the Province in the person of their Primate.

2. *canst not bear*] As too heavy a burden.

them which say they are apostles] Cf. 2 Cor. xi. 13 sqq. For the
question who these false Apostles at Ephesus were, see Excursus II.

hast found them liars] Rather, **didst find them false.** They had
profited by St Paul's warning, Acts xx. 28—30.

3. *and hast borne, &c.*] Read **and hast patience; and didst bear
for my Name's sake, and hast not been weary.**

4. *thy first love*] It is to be remembered that these words have not
in ecclesiastical (or indeed in any) Greek the same sentimental associations as in English; nevertheless it is not unlikely that conjugal love is
meant: cf. Jer. ii. 2. Some understand the word of love to the brethren,

thou art fallen, and repent, and do the first works; or else I *will* come unto thee quickly, and will remove thy candle-
6 stick out of his place, except thou repent. But this thou hast, that thou hatest the deeds of the Nicolaitans, which I
7 also hate. He that hath an ear, let him hear what the Spirit saith unto the churches; To him that overcometh will I give

because we have "the first works" in the next verse: but the argument is a bad one. Of course those good words (whether of "charity" in the narrower sense or not) proceeded from love to Christ.

 5. *repent*] Neither this word, nor the cognate subst. *repentance*, is used in St John's Gospel or Epistles.

do the first works] He does not say, "Love with the first love," though the works were only valuable as proceeding from love: for to love, though depending on the state of the will, is not a directly voluntary act. But He says "do the first works," for that is in thy power. Do again what love made thee do, that thou mayest learn to love again. The paradox is as true of spiritual graces as of natural virtues (Arist. Eth. Nic. II. iv. 1, 2) that the good habitual character is only gained by good acts, while really good acts are only possible as the product of the good character.

I will come] Literally, **I am coming**—the verb having, from its own nature, the sense of future time: cf. i. 4 and note.

remove thy candlestick out of his place] i.e. make thee cease to be a Church. It seems scarcely relevant to point to the destruction of the city by the Turks, and its present desolation, as a fulfilment of this threat. We may presume that the Church of Ephesus *did* repent, as it was famous and prosperous, and fertile in Saints, for centuries. It is likely enough that the Turkish conquest was God's judgement on the sins of the Eastern Empire and its Churches: but we cannot conclude that the Church of Ephesus was in the 14th century more corrupt than e.g. that of Smyrna, because it was more entirely exterminated.

 6. *But this thou hast*] This is one point in which thou art not wanting. Compare ii. 25, iii. 2, 11, where faithfulness is conceived as a treasure possessed and to be guarded.

thou hatest the deeds] Compatible with love to the persons: cf. St Jude 23.

Nicolaitans] See Excursus II.

 7. *He that hath an ear*] A repetition, with a merely verbal alteration, of one of our Lord's characteristic phrases in His teaching while on earth: St Matt. xi. 15, &c.

what the Spirit saith] Speaking through the Risen Church to John who was "in the Spirit."

To him that overcometh] A promise thus expressed, and an invitation to attention like that preceding it, are found at the end of each of these seven Epistles—the invitation standing first in the three first, and the promise in the four last. From this change in the order, it appears that attention is invited, not to the final promise only, but to the whole Epistle to each Church, as the Spirit's message.

to eat of the tree of life, which is in the midst of the paradise of God.

And unto the angel of the church in Smyrna write; These 8 *things* saith the first and the last, which was dead, and is alive; I know thy works, and tribulation, and poverty, (but 9 thou art rich) and *I know* the blasphemy of them which say

the tree of life] Cf. Gen. ii. 9, as well as Rev. xxii. 2, 14, 19. The Tree of Life appears, though not under that name, in Enoch xxiv., where we are told that there shall be no power to touch it until the period of the great judgement.

in the midst of the paradise] Read simply **in the Paradise**: the insertion is no doubt from Gen. ii. 9. "Paradise," a Persian word adopted in both Greek and Hebrew, means simply a park or pleasure-ground, and hence is used in the LXX. (*not* the Hebrew) of the garden of Eden: in 2 Cor. xii. 4; Luke xxiii. 43, we have it used of a region of the spiritual world, inhabited by the blessed dead. Whether the Paradise of God, where the Tree of Life is now, is identical either with the earthly Paradise where it grew of old, or with the New Jerusalem where it shall grow in the new earth under the new heaven, it would be rash to speculate.

of God] So "the garden of God" in Ezek. xxviii. 13, xxxi. 8, 9, and "the garden of the Lord" in Gen. xiii. 10; Is. li. 3. Some read "of *My* God," as in iii. 12, but on the whole the omission has more authority, and the exact O. T. phrase seems likelier.

THE CHURCH IN SMYRNA. 8—11.

8. *The angel*] Supposed by many of the ancient commentators to have been Polycarp.

which was dead] See on i. 18.

is alive] Lit., **lived**, i.e. came to life, revived. So xiii. 14, and Matt. ix. 18, John v. 25. The attributes of *death* and *life* are here especially ascribed to Christ, because the message He sends is a promise of life to them who die for His sake.

9. *thy works, and*] Should be omitted.

poverty] Perhaps the effect of the persecution, Jewish converts being, as in Heb. x. 34, deprived of their property when put out of the synagogue on their conversion. Or perhaps rather the cause of the persecution being more intense here—the Christians being people of no dignity or influence, it was safe to attack them.

but thou art rich] Contrast iii. 17, and compare James ii. 5.

blasphemy] Probably rather in the sense of calumny, coarse slanders against them, than blasphemy against their Lord: though of course both may have been combined, as when Christians were ridiculed as worshippers of the Crucified.

of them] We should read [coming] **from them**—i.e. the calumny not only uttered by them, but originating from them, and **very** likely received and repeated among the heathen.

they are Jews, and are not, but *are* the synagogue of Satan.
10 Fear none *of those things* which thou shalt suffer: behold,
the devil shall cast *some* of you into prison, that ye may be
tried; and ye shall have tribulation ten days: be thou faith-

which say they are Jews] No doubt the persons meant are real Jews by birth as well as by profession, but are denied to be worthy of the name. It is treated as still an honourable one, implying religious privileges, as by St Paul in Rom. ii. 17, 28—9, iii. 1. Contrast the way that "the Jews" are spoken of in St John's Gospel—always meaning the chief priests and scribes, the persistent enemies of the Gospel. Hence is drawn an argument, that this Book could not be written by the author of the Gospel, at any rate after he had written it: though if this Book were written before the fall of Jerusalem, and the Gospel long after, the change in his point of view will be intelligible.

and are not] Better, **and they are not**—the relative construction is not continued, at least if we suppose the sentence to be grammatical.

the synagogue of Satan] For an instance of the same severity from the same mouth, see John viii. 44. While they claimed to be, as the old Jewish Church was, "the congregation of the Lord." *Synagogue* is etymologically almost equivalent to *congregation*, and is, as St Augustine observes, a less noble word than that used for the Christian Church, *Ecclesia*, a summoned assembly: for while brutes may be "gathered together," reason (and we may add, freedom) is implied in being *summoned* together. But the distinction between the two words is not always maintained: Israel is called "the Church" in Acts vii. 38, and the assembly of *Christian* Jews is called a "synagogue" in St James ii. 2, and almost in Heb. x. 25.

10. *Fear none of*] Read simply **Fear not**.

those things which thou shalt suffer] Probably refer primarily to a persecution immediately impending; but they are no doubt meant to apply also to the subsequent persecutions of the Church there, especially to the famous one, under the Antonines, in which Polycarp the Bishop suffered martyrdom, in A.D. 155. It will depend on the date assigned to this Book, whether Polycarp can have been Bishop at the time of this message. It is to be noted that the Jews were specially active in urging his execution, though officially it was the act of the pagan magistrates.

that ye may be tried] Or, **tempted**: it is probably rather the Devil's object in raising the persecution than God's in permitting it that is meant. Cf. Luke xxii. 31.

ten days] Possibly a half proverbial expression for a short time, as we might say "a week or two." And no doubt the notion of a short and definite time is intended: but from the important significance in this book of definite numbers, and not least of definite measures of time, it is probable that something more is intended too—whether that the persecution would last ten *years*, or what, it would be rash to say.

be thou] Lit., **become**—not implying that he was not perfectly faithful now, but = "prove thyself," "quit thyself as."

ful unto death, and I will give thee a crown of life. He ¹¹
that hath an ear, let him hear what the Spirit saith unto the
churches; He that overcometh shall not be hurt of the
second death.

And to the angel of the church in Pergamos write; *These* ¹²
things saith he which hath the sharp sword with two edges;
I know thy works, and where thou dwellest, *even* where Satan's ¹³
seat *is*: and thou holdest fast my name, and hast not denied

a crown of life] i.e. eternal life as a crown; so St James i. 12. The phrase is like "the crown of glory" in 1 Pet. v. 4, and probably "the crown of righteousness," 2 Tim. iv. 8. As in the parallel promise, iii. 21, the throne is in the fullest sense a royal throne, the crown here is probably a *royal* crown (so Trench *Synonyms*), not a mere *garland of victory*. Throughout this Book the imagery is Jewish not Gentile, and all who are finally redeemed are Kings, v. 12. Both the thrones and the crowns of the elders, iv. 4, 10, might be ensigns of dignity less than royal, but not the crown of the Rider on the White Horse, vi. 3. Moreover the Crown of Thorns for which all the Evangelists use the same word as here was certainly a counterfeit of royalty. On the other hand in xix. 12 the King of Kings and Lord of Lords has on His head many *diadems*, the unmistakeable technical name for royal crowns, and there are diadems on the heads of the Dragon, xii. 3, and on the horns of the Beast, xiii. 1.

11. *the second death*] See xx. 6, 14, &c.

THE CHURCH IN PERGAMOS. 12—17.

12. *he which hath the sharp sword*] Mentioned because He threatens to use it, ver. 16.

13. *Satan's seat*] Better, **throne**—the word being the one so naturalised in English, and so translated in this book wherever used of the throne of God, iii. 21 &c. *Why* Satan's throne and dwelling-place is localised at Pergamum is uncertain; two explanations have been given: that it was a seat of the worship of Asclepius or Aesculapius, whose traditional image held a serpent, and who in some of his shrines (but apparently not at Pergamum) was actually worshipped under the form of a serpent: and since recent excavations it has been suggested that the phrase was intended to refer to the great altar of Zeus Soter, carved with the wars of gods and giants, which Attalus set up to commemorate his victory over the Gauls—the last great triumph of Hellenism over barbarism. No doubt, to a pious Jew or Christian the worship of the serpent might naturally and excusably seem more direct and avowed devil-worship than other idolatry, while the fame of the great altar might cause it to be treated as the chosen throne of the God of this world; but we may question whether an inspired Apostle, or rather the Lord Himself, would thus "look upon the outward appearance"—both the worship of Asclepius and the thank-offering of Attalus belonged to the better side of heathenism. Perhaps

my faith, even in *those* days wherein Antipas *was* my faithful martyr, who was slain among you, where Satan dwelleth. 14 But I have a few *things* against thee, because thou hast there them that hold the doctrine of Balaam, who taught Balac to cast a stumblingblock before the children of Israel, to eat 15 things sacrificed unto idols, and to commit fornication. So hast thou also them that hold the doctrine of the Nicolaitans, 16 which *thing* I hate. Repent; or else I *will* come unto thee

therefore the meaning is only, that Pergamum was in a special sense a home of the Satanic spirit of persecution (cf. *v.* 10).

even in those days wherein Antipas was] Read simply **in the days of Antipas, My martyr,** (or "witness") **My faithful one.** According to what seems the best text, the construction is not quite grammatically regular, but it is in accordance with the usage of this Book. A legend is given of the martyrdom under Domitian of Antipas Bishop of Pergamum: it can probably be traced up to the fifth or sixth century. But by that time the fashion had set in of the "invention" (half fraudulent, half imaginative) of relics and legends of martyrs: and it is more than doubtful whether anything authentic is known of Antipas except from this passage. Perhaps it is presumable that he was a Jew by birth: the name is a shortened form of Antipater. The latter, like Philip and other Macedonian names, had become common all over the Levant: but perhaps especially common among Jews, from its being borne by the father of Herod and (in this shortened form) by his son, the tetrarch of Galilee.

martyr] The word "witness" is already used in its technical ecclesiastical sense of one who bears witness to the Faith with his life: cf. vi. 9, xii. 11 ("testimony"). So xvii. 6; Acts xxii. 20.

14. *that hold the doctrine of Balaam, who taught*] As we should say "who adhere to the practice taught by Balaam, of eating...." It is called *doctrine*, because it is a thing that was *taught*—the words are cognate and correlative. For the fact of Israel being taught such practices, see Num. xxv. 1, 2: for Balaam's responsibility, ibid. xxxi. 16. That of Balac is not directly mentioned in the Pentateuch, but is naturally inferred, as we find Moab and Midian united throughout the story.

15. *thou also*] As well as Israel of old.

which thing I hate] Instead of these words read **in like manner.** This correction makes it certain that we are not to suppose two immoral sects prevailing at Pergamum, those who held the doctrine of Balaam and those who held that of the Nicolaitans: but one sect holding the doctrine taught by Balaam of old and the Nicolaitans now. The sense is, "thou hast with thee followers of Balaam: he taught God's people to fornicate and to communicate in idol-worship, and the Nicolaitans with thee teach the same." The passage gives no support to the theory that the Nicolaitans were so called from Balaam;—the etymology of whose name is doubtful, but according to a possible one

quickly, and will fight against them with the sword of my mouth. He that hath an ear, let him hear what the Spirit saith unto the churches; To him that overcometh will I give to eat of the hidden manna, and will give him a white stone, and in the stone a new name written, which no *man* knoweth saving he that receiveth *it*.

17

Nicolaus ("conqueror of the people") might be an approximate Greek equivalent to it. If not called after Nicolas the deacon, they no doubt were called after another Nicolas—as we hear from a tradition or conjecture, later than the one which traces them to him.

16. *Repent*] The Angel, i.e. the whole body of the Church represented by him, is bidden to repent: because not only are the Nicolaitans guilty of the sins their doctrine involved, but the whole Church (and more especially its Bishop, if we suppose him to be intended) is more or less guilty, for having extended to them the toleration which the Church of Ephesus was praised for refusing.

against them] Not "against thee:" the mass of the Church is faithful on the whole. But it is implied that if the whole Church does "repent", and do its duty, these erring members will be reclaimed: and that it will be a loss to the whole Church, if they are not reclaimed but have to be destroyed.

with the sword of my mouth] cf. i. 16 note.

17. *give to eat*] He shall receive the Bread of God (St John vi. 32 sqq.) instead of communicating at the table of devils (1 Cor. x. 21).

the hidden manna] The reference is to the pot of manna kept in the Tabernacle, in or before the Ark (Ex. xvi. 34; Heb. ix. 4), and therefore "hidden" in the unapproachable Sanctuary. The Jews appear to have cherished an opinion that the Ark of the Covenant, and other sacred objects which were wanting in the Second Temple, had not perished with the First, but were concealed before its destruction (see e.g. 2 Macc. i. 19 sqq., ii. 4 sqq.), and were preserved somewhere in earth or heaven, to be revealed in the days of the Messiah. But we are not to understand that this Book sanctions the first part of this belief, when xxi. 22 contradicts the second: passages like xi. 19 do not imply that the earthly Temple or its contents have been removed to Heaven, but that, whether the earthly Temple stands or falls, there remains in Heaven the archetype from which it was copied, according to the revelations made to Moses and (through David) to Solomon. See Ex. xxv. 40, xxvi. 30; 1 Chron. xxviii. 12; Heb. viii. 5, ix. 23 sq.

a white stone, and in the stone a new name written] Whatever be the precise meaning of this figure, the white stone and the new name are closely connected. This excludes the notion that the white stone is given as a token of acquittal because judges who voted to acquit the prisoner dropped a white stone, sometimes called the pebble of victory, into the urn, though the stone is white because that was the colour of innocence, of joy, of victory. The white stone is a gift

18 And unto the angel of the church in Thyatira write; *These things* saith the Son of God, who hath his eyes like unto a

in itself, not merely a vehicle of the new name, which it would be if the new name were the new name of Christ Himself, iii. 12 (which may be identical with His hidden Name, xix. 12), though this too is written upon those who overcome, as the Father's Name is written on the hundred and forty and four thousand. The stone and the name are the separate possession of each to whom they are given. Most likely both are a token entitling the bearer to some further benefit. It is no objection to this that we do not find the technical Greek word for such tokens, for the 'token' might be described without being named. The Greeks had feasts to which every feaster brought a token as a pledge that he would pay his share of the cost. Such a token might also prove his right to join the company. If so, it may be meant that when they who are worthy are called to the Marriage Supper each is called by the new name which he only knows, as each hears and enters, the white stone with the new name is his passport at the door. This would require us to believe that the hidden manna is given to strengthen the elect on the way (1 Kings xix. 8; Joh. iv. 32). Possibly again the token gives the right to enter through the gates into the city (xxii. 14)— for the angels at the gates may suffer none to pass who cannot name themselves by the new name and shew the white stone. It appears from Aristophanes (Av. 1199—1224) that foreigners (at least in time of war) had no right to be at large in a strange city without some token from its authorities. The parallel though suggestive is too remote in place and time to be convincing. The contemporary parallels of tickets for stated doles or occasional largesses are not exact. These which might be thrown to be scrambled for were marked with the amount of the gifts they represented, not with the owner's name. If the word used of a 'stone' could mean a gem as St Victorinus supposes, the key to the passage might lie in Wetstein's quotation from Joma 8 about the rain of pearls and precious stones which fell with the manna. The first readers of the Apocalypse had not to reflect with Bengel that they would know the meaning of the white stone and the new name if and when they overcame. Its symbolical language was plain at the time to those who had ears to hear. Perhaps the new and hidden name is a pledge that no enemy can have power upon him who receives it, for exorcists were supposed to have power over spirits good and evil by knowing their names, and this was only an instance of a widespread feeling which it is said led Cæsar to put a man to death for divulging the sacred secret name of Rome, which was Valentia. It is possible that some kindred mystery may attach to the names, Il. I. 403, xx. 74, which differ in the language of gods and men.

The Church in Thyatira. 18—29.

18. *the Son of God*] So designated, perhaps, because it is the power which He received from His Father which is the subject of the concluding promise, *v.* 27.

flame of fire, and his feet *are* like fine brass; I know thy 19
works, and charity, and service, and faith, and thy patience,
and thy works; and the last *to be* more than the first. Not- 20
withstanding I have a few *things* against thee, because thou
sufferest *that* woman Jezebel, which calleth herself a pro-
phetess, to teach and to seduce my servants to commit fornication, and to eat things sacrificed unto idols. And I gave 21

his eyes] Which search reins and heart, *v.* 23.

his feet] Of strength to break the nations to shivers like a potter's vessel.

19. *and thy works; and the last to be more*] Read, **and thy last works to be more**—in contrast with Ephesus, *v.* 4.

20. *a few things*] Should be omitted: it has come in from *v.* 14, while the real construction is as in *v.* 4, "I have [somewhat] against thee, because...," or better, "I have [this] against thee, that...."

that woman Jezebel] There is some authority for the reading "thy wife Jezebel," and even if the possessive pronoun be not rightly inserted in the Greek text, it is a question whether the article ought not to be understood as equivalent to one. If the sense "thy wife Jezebel" be right, the allusion must be to 1 Kings xxi. 25: there is some one (or something) at Thyatira who is, to the Angel of the Church, such a temptress as Jezebel was to Ahab. No doubt, if we suppose the Angel to be the Bishop, it is probable that his actual wife is intended; but even then the name Jezebel must have this meaning.

As a plain matter of verbal exegesis, "thy wife Jezebel" seems, in this context, the more natural translation. But it has its own diffi-culties. What analogy is there between a faithful servant of Christ, culpably tolerant of a bad wife, but not sharing her faults himself, and Ahab, who "did sell himself to work wickedness," and "did very abominably in following idols?" It may be added, that except in Jehu's taunt (2 Kings ix. 22), which need not be meant literally, there is no evidence whatever of Jezebel's unchastity: her behaviour towards her husband, as well as her influence over him, makes it probable that she was a good wife, in her own way.

On the whole, the best editors decline to adopt the reading which would make the sense "thy wife" certain: and this being so, it seems better to translate as the A.V. Who "Jezebel" was—whether a real woman, or a personification of a sect,—is almost equally doubtful on any view: but it seems simplest to suppose a real person.

to teach and to seduce] Literally, according to the right reading, **and she teacheth and seduceth.**

my servants] The possessive pronoun is emphatic—she leads those who belong to Me to act as do those in slavery to devils.

to commit fornication] No doubt to be taken literally, not (as so often in the O.T.) as a metaphor for idolatry: since this is mentioned coordinately.

21. Read, **And I gave her time that she should repent, and she will not [does not choose to] repent of her fornication.**

her space to repent of her fornication; and she repented
22 not. Behold, I *will* cast her into a bed, and them that
commit adultery with her into great tribulation, except they
23 repent of their deeds. And I will kill her children with
death; and all the churches shall know that I am he which
searcheth the reins and hearts: and I will give unto every
24 one of you according to your works. But unto you I say,
and unto the rest in Thyatira, as many as have not this
doctrine, and which have not known the depths of Satan, as

22. *I will cast*] lit. 'I am casting' i.e. am about to cast. Cf. 'I ascend', Joh. xx. 17.

a bed] Perhaps of sickness, as "death" in the next *v.* is perhaps to be taken of pestilence: cf. vi. 8.

with her] Possibly the sense is "I will cast them together with her into...," but the sense "the partners of her adulteries" is at least equally natural. It seems probably intended, that she and they are to be separated in punishment: Francesca's "Questi che mai da me non fia diviso" is rather a poetical sentiment than a moral one. But if Jezebel be understood to mean a sect rather than an individual woman, it will be possible to distinguish her "adulteries" as metaphorical from the literal "fornication" which she encouraged: if so, her paramours are the false teachers, her children their disciples.

23. *all the churches shall know*] cf. All flesh shall know, Is. xlv. 26; All flesh shall see, Is. xl. 5; Ezek. xx. 48. 'All the Churches' though less extensive than 'all flesh' (cf. John xvii. 2, xiv. 22) must still be taken as widely as possible, it means not merely all the seven Churches of Asia but 'all the churches in the world,' hardly as Alford adds 'to the end of time.' We know nothing (and have no reason to think St Irenæus knew more) of either the repentance or the punishment of the children of Jezebel.

that I am he which searcheth, &c.] Compare Psalms vii. 9, [10], xxvi. 2; Jer. xi. 20, xvii. 10, xx. 12; also 1 Chr. xxviii. 9, xxix. 17. But the closest parallel to this phrase is Rom. viii. 27, which suggests that this epithet was almost proverbial in the Apostolic age, whether applied to the Father as there or to the Son as here. It is hardly doubtful that the phrase is derived from David and Jeremiah ll. cc., but the verb used both here and in Rom. is different from any used by the LXX.

24. *unto you*] The form of address to the Angel of the Church is dropped, and the Church addressed directly. *And* should be omitted: the sense is "to the rest of you in Thyatira," or more literally, "to you, namely to the rest."

have not known the depths of Satan, as they speak] The heretics condemned in the preceding verses were doubtless a sect of those who called themselves Gnostics, probably at this time, certainly in the next generation. They contrasted their *knowledge* of "the depths" or "deep things of God" (cf. 1 Cor. ii. 10), with the *faith* of the orthodox in the plain simple doctrines that were openly preached to the world: the Lord

they speak; I will put upon you none other burden. But 25
that which ye have *already* hold fast till I come. And he 26
that overcometh, and keepeth my works unto the end, to
him will I give power over the nations: and he shall rule 27
them with a rod of iron; as the vessels of a potter *shall
they be broken to shivers*: even as I received of my Father.

answers, that the depths of knowledge that they attained were depths, not of God, but of Satan. It is uncertain how far the quotation of their own language marked by 'as they speak' extends, it is hardly possible that they themselves actually gloried in a knowledge of the depths of Satan (yet cf. 2 Cor. ii. 11); but it is to be remembered that the Gnostic systems of the second century, and probably those of the first also, included a strange mythology of half-personified abstractions; and it may be that the Lord rather identifies one of these with Satan than substitutes the name of Satan for that of God. It appears from Irenaeus that the Gnostics of his time talked of "the deep things of Depth" as well as "the deep things of God." It is curious that the phrase "the depths of knowledge" is quoted from the great Ephesian philosopher Heraclitus: possibly it was owing to his influence, that such notions found a congenial home in Asia Minor.

I will put] Right in sense, as "I will cast" in ver. 22, though here the true text has a present tense, as there.

none other burden] viz., than abstinence from fornication and things offered to idols, Acts xv. 28 sq. The A.V. rightly avoids exaggerating the verbal resemblance between the two passages, but a reference here to that phrase, adopted solemnly by the whole Church, is not impossible. Yet it is a question whether we may not understand the sentence as if the construction were "I will put on you no other burden *than to* hold fast that which ye have till I come."

25. *that which ye have*] Comparing ver. 6, we shall probably understand this "what thou hast to thy credit," thy present faithfulness: so that the sense will rather be like Phil. iii. 16 than Jude 3. Cf. iii. 11.

26. *And he that overcometh, &c.*] Literally, **And he that overcometh, and he that keepeth**, &c.

my works] "Such works as I do" is rather the sense than "such as I approve." Cf. John xiv. 12, "The works that I do shall he do also."

27. *shall rule them*] Lit., **shall be their shepherd**. So the LXX. read the word in Ps. ii. 9 which, according to the pronunciation now adopted in the received Hebrew text, will mean "bruise" or "break them." St John, we have seen, does not follow the LXX. blindly in their deviations from the Hebrew text (see on i. 6, 7): so from this passage and xii. 5, xix. 15 we see that he accepted "rule" as the right reading. Apart from this, shepherd is used in the Old Testament of human and superhuman rulers often enough to suggest its use here. The same metaphor is found in Classical Greek.

shall they be broken] Read, **are broken**: he is to rule the nations with as absolute a mastery as is expressed in crushing a potsherd.

even as I] Rather, **as I also**. Of course the meaning is, that Ps. ii.

²⁸₂₉ And I will give him the morning star. He that hath an ear, let him hear what the Spirit saith unto the churches.

3 And unto the angel of the church in Sardis write; These *things* saith he that hath the seven spirits of God, and the seven stars; I know thy works, that thou hast a name that 2 thou livest, and art dead. Be watchful, and strengthen the *things* which remain, that are ready to die: for I have not 3 found thy works perfect before God. Remember therefore

9 is assumed to be the promise of the Father to the Son; as is plain from the eighth verse.

28. *the morning star*] The only direct illustration of this image is xxii. 16, where Christ Himself is called the Morning Star: and the meaning here can hardly be "I will give myself to him." Some compare 2 Pet. i. 19, others, perhaps better, Dan. xii. 3: taking the sense to be, "I will give him the brightest star of all, that he may be clothed (cf. xii. 1) with its glory."

29. *He that hath* &c.] For the position of these words, see on ver. 7.

The Church in Sardis. Chap. III. 1—6.

1. *that hath the seven Spirits of God*] See the last note on i. 4. Though "the Seven Spirits" were mentioned there, we have not yet heard of them as specially belonging to Christ: but this we find in v. 6.

are the seven stars] Cf. ii. 1. We find the "Spirits" and the "stars," i.e. Angels, mentioned coordinately, a further argument against identifying the Spirits with Angels, even angels other than these. These attributes of Christ are mentioned, because He speaks as Judge of the Churches: cf. 1 Cor. ii. 15 for the conception of *judgement* as the Spirit's work.

2. *Be watchful*] Literally, **Become watching**: "awake and watch."

the things which remain] The elements of goodness, or means of goodness, which thou hast not yet lost. Cf. ii. 6, and the first note there.

that are ready] Read, **which were ready**, i.e., would *have* died, but for the strengthening them. We may perhaps say, that it seems to be taken for granted that the warning, sharp as it is, will be effectual.

perfect] Lit. **fulfilled**; as we say "up to the mark."

before God] Read **before my God**. The Church *had* a name of being alive among men: its works therefore may have come up to *their* standard.

3. *Remember*] Cf. ii. 5: but here it is the sound doctrine of the founders of the Church that is the standard to be regained: it does not appear that the former practice of the Church itself furnished such a standard.

how thou hast received and heard, and hold fast, and repent. If therefore thou shalt not watch, I will come on thee as a thief, and thou shalt not know what hour I will come upon thee. Thou hast a few names even in Sardis, which have 4 not defiled their garments; and they shall walk with me in white: for they are worthy. He that overcometh, the same 5 shall be clothed in white raiment; and I will not blot out

hold fast] Or **keep**: the word is the same as in i. 3, where see note. Here the sense is more like 1 Cor. xi. 2 ; 1 Tim. vi. 20, where however the Greek verb used is different: 1 Tim. vi. 14, where it is the same as here, bridges the interval between the two.
I will come...as a thief] So xvi. 15; Matt. xxiv. 43; Luke xii. 39; 1 Thess. v. 2, 4; 2 Pet. iii. 10. In all these places the image is used of the *Last* or universal Judgement, but here plainly of a particular judgement upon this one Church. The use of the same image in both the larger and narrower senses seems to sanction the system of interpretation commonly applied to St Matt. xxiv., and here attempted to be applied to this book also.
4. *Thou hast*] Read, **But thou hast**, and omit **even**.
a few names] Some understand, from the similar use of the word "names" in Acts i. 15, that at this time it was usual for every Church to keep a register of all its members. 1 Tim. v. 9 seems certainly to imply such a register of office-bearers at least. It is possible indeed that the "names" are spoken of as entered in the heavenly Book of Life (cf. the next verse): but the use of that image would be far more forcible, if the readers of the Revelation were familiar with an approximate counterpart to that Book on earth.
have not defiled their garments] Which were cleansed (vii. 14) by the Blood of Christ, but may be defiled again by deadly sin. See St John's 1 Ep. i. 6, 7; where we are told both of the absolute sufficiency, and of the conditional efficacy of that Blood for cleansing. It seems to be fanciful to inquire minutely what the "garments" are, whether their bodies or their baptismal robes: there may be an allusion to Zech. iii. 3 sqq.
in white] So vi. 11, vii. 9. It is idle to ask whether these are the *same* garments which they kept undefiled during their probation: but no doubt it is meant that their keeping these undefiled proves them "worthy" of those.
5. *the same shall be clothed*] Read, **shall thus be clothed**. Perhaps the sense is not so much "thus, as I have promised to the holy remnant in Sardis," but "thus as I am now." The colour of Christ's priestly robe (i. 13) was not stated (and see Pseudo-Barnabas, there quoted) but we are probably to understand that it was white, cf. Dan. vii. 9.
I will not blot out his name] See Ex. xxxii. 32 sq. (which it seems hard to tone down into meaning no more than 1 Kings xix. 4: compare rather Rom. ix. 3), Ps. lxix. 29 (28) (which can more easily be taken in the milder sense), and Dan. xii. 1. The image seems to be, that every-

his name out of the book of life, but I will confess his name
6 before my Father, and before his angels. He that hath an ear, let him hear what the Spirit saith unto the churches.
7 And to the angel of the church in Philadelphia write; These *things* saith he *that is* holy, he *that is* true, he that hath the key of David, he that openeth, and no *man* shutteth;
8 and shutteth, and no *man* openeth; I know thy works: behold, I have set before thee an open door, and no *man* can

one on professing himself Christ's soldier and servant has his name entered in the Book of Life, as on an army list or census-roll of the kingdom. It remains there during the time of his probation or warfare, even if, while he has thus "a name that he liveth," he is dead in sin: but if he die the second death it will be blotted out—if he overcome, it will remain for ever. See xx. 12, 15.

I will confess] A repetition of Matt. x. 32.

THE CHURCH IN PHILADELPHIA. 7—13.

7. *he that is holy, he that is true*] The same epithets are combined in vi. 10, where *apparently* they belong rather to the Father than the Son. In Mark i. 24, John vi. 69 (according to the true reading), Christ is called "the Holy One of God," and God's "Holy Servant" (according to the probable rendering) in Acts iv. 27, 30: also "the faithful and true" in this book, inf. *v.* 14 and xix. 11. "The Holy One" is used absolutely as a name of God in Job vi. 10; Is. xl. 25; Hab. iii. 3, and perhaps Hos. xi. 9, besides the phrase so frequent in Isaiah, and used by several other prophets, "the Holy One *of Israel:*" and we have "the true God," as opposed to idols, in 2 Chr. xv. 3; Ps. xxxi. 5, (6); Jer. x. 10; 1 Thess. i. 9; 1 John v. 20, and, without such opposition being specially marked, in Is. lxv. 16; John xvii. 3. Here the sense seems to be "He Who *is* the Holy One of God," as opposed to those in v. 9, who say that they are of the Holy people and are not.

he that hath the key of David] From Is. xxii. 22. There the meaning is, that Eliakim shall be made ruler of the house of David, i.e. chief minister of the kingdom (2 Kings xviii. 18 &c.), and that his will shall be final in all business of the kingdom. Here then in like manner Christ is described as Chief Minister in the Kingdom of God. But the promise in the next verse suggests that the image is not used in this general sense only: Christ says that He has the power of admitting to, or excluding from His Church, the power which He delegates (St Matt. xvi. 19) to the rulers in His Church, but which none, not even they, can really exercise in opposition to His will.

8. *an open door*] Through which thou mayest enter into the Kingdom, into the house of David.

and no man can shut it] Probably the false Jews mentioned in the next verse denied the title of the Christians in Philadelphia to the privileges of brotherhood—whence we may suppose that they were

shut it: for thou hast a little strength, and hast kept my word, and hast not denied my name. Behold, I *will* make ⁹ *them* of the synagogue of Satan, which say they are Jews, and are not, but do lie; behold, I will make them to come and worship before thy feet, and to know that I have loved thee. Because thou hast kept the word of my patience, I ¹⁰ also will keep thee from the hour of temptation, which shall come upon all the world, to try them that dwell upon the earth. Behold, I come quickly: hold *that* fast which thou ¹¹ hast, that no *man* take thy crown. Him that overcometh ¹² will I make a pillar in the temple of my God, and he shall

mostly Gentiles. Christ answers, that He would grant what they refused.

for thou hast] Rather, **that thou hast**, depending on "I know thy works," the intermediate words being parenthetical.

thou hast a little strength] Better, **thou hast little strength and [yet] hast kept** &c. The point is that his strength is not great, not that he has a little left in spite of the strain upon it.

9. *I will make them of* &c.] Literally, **I give of the** &c. The use of "give" in this verse is frequent in Hebrew: here the sentence is unfinished, and is resumed by "I will make thee come" &c. below.

the synagogue of Satan] See on ii. 9.

I will make them to come &c.] An application of Is. lx. 14.

that I have loved thee] The pronoun "I" is emphatic—which supports the view already suggested, that the title of this Church to Christian privileges was contested by the Jews, and that this message of the Lord is intended to decide a controversy.

10. *Because......I also*] It would be possible, but hardly in accordance with the usage of this book, to connect this with what goes before, "that I have loved thee, because thou hast kept......, and I will keep thee from... ."

11. *hold that fast which thou hast*] See on ii. 6, 25.

that no man take thy crown] i.e. rob thee of it: the image of a race or other contest for a prize does not seem in harmony with the context, nor with the style of this book.

12. *Him that overcometh*] Lit. **He that overcometh, I will make him**, as in ii. 26.

a pillar] Used of chief men in the Church in Gal. ii. 9, and perhaps 1 Tim. iii. 15. All Christians are living-stones in the Temple (Eph. ii. 20 sqq., 1 Pet. ii. 5), all necessary to its completeness, but some of course filling in it a more important position than others: and such important position is indicated by the image of the "pillars" ll.cc. But here the promise is not for Apostles or their successors only, but for all the faithful: the point is not "he shall be one of the great and beautiful stones on which the others rest," but "he shall be so placed that he cannot be removed while the whole fabric stands."

go no more out: and I will write upon him the name of my God, and the name of the city of my God, *which is* new Jerusalem, which cometh down out of heaven from my God:
13 and *I will write upon him* my new name. He that hath an ear, let him hear what the Spirit saith unto the churches.
14 And unto the angel of the church of the Laodiceans write; These *things* saith the Amen, the faithful and true witness,
15 the beginning of the creation of God; I know thy works,

I will write upon him] We repeatedly have in this book the image of the divine Name written on the foreheads of God's servants: see vii. 3, xiv. 1, xxii. 4. Hence the inscribing the name is here equally appropriate to the figure and the thing signified: probably the metaphor of the pillar is not dropped, but writing the name on the pillar means the same as writing it on the man.

the name of my God, and the name of the city] Cf. Is. xliv. 5; Jer. xxiii. 6, xxxiii. 16; Ezek. xlviii. 35, for the junction of these two names. The *three* names joined here are in a manner those of the Trinity, the Church being representative of the Spirit. It is probable that passages like this did much to suggest the use of the sign of the Cross on the forehead, both at Baptism and on other occasions that seemed to call for a profession of faith: and the image of the "new name" (cf. ii. 17) harmonises well with the much later usage of conferring a name in Baptism.

which cometh down] xxi. 2, 10.

my new name] See on ii. 17, and xix. 12 there referred to.

The Church in Laodicea. 14—22.

14. *the Amen*] See the last note on i. 7. Here the name is used, (i) because this is the last of the seven Epistles, that it may confirm the whole: (ii) as synonymous with the title "Faithful and True" that follows: for which see the latter group of references on *v.* 7. Is. lxv. 16 is specially noticeable, where "the God of *truth*" is in the Hebrew "the God of Amen": in the other O.T. passages a different but cognate form is used.

the faithful and true witness] See i. 5.

the beginning of the creation of God] Exactly equivalent to Col. i. 15, as explained by the words that follow: in both places the words are such as might grammatically be used of the first of creatures, but the context there, and the whole tone of the Book here, proves that the writer does not regard Him as a creature at all. But St John is not here, as in the first verses of his Gospel, describing our Lord's Nature theologically: it might be enough to say that here and in Prov. viii. 22 (where the words "the Lord possessed" or "created Me" lend themselves more easily than these to an Arian sense), the Word coming forth to create is conceived as part of His earthly mission, which culminates in the Incarnation, so that in a sense even creation is done by Him as a Creature.

that thou art neither cold nor hot: I would thou wert cold
or hot. So *then* because thou art lukewarm, and neither
cold nor hot, I will spue thee out of my mouth. Because
thou sayest, I am rich, and increased with goods, and have
need of nothing; and knowest not that thou art wretched,
and miserable, and poor, and blind, and naked: I counsel

15. *neither cold nor hot*] Neither untouched by spiritual life, dead
and cold, as an unregenerate heathen would be, nor "fervent (lit. **boiling**
—a cognate word to that here used) in spirit" (Rom. xii. 11). We
might naturally speak (perhaps the Lord does, Matt. xxiv. 12) of those
as "cold" who were such as the Laodiceans were, and of course here
something more is meant: but that further meaning can hardly be being
"actively opposed" to the Gospel, but only being utterly unaffected by it.

I would thou wert cold or hot] For the sentiment that it would be
better even to be "cold," cf. 2 Pet. ii. 21; though there the apostasy
described is no doubt more deadly than here. But according to the
Greek proverb (Ar. Eth. VII. ii. 10) of a man who sins against his
conscience, "When water chokes, what are you to wash it down with?"
You can instruct and convince a man who has either low or perverse
views of duty, but what can you do to one whom sound views do not
make to act rightly? And similarly an unbeliever can be converted
and regenerated, but what can be done for him in whom faith does not
work by love?

16. *because thou art lukewarm*] The image is of course taken from
the tendency of lukewarm water to excite vomiting. It is *intended* to
be an offensive one, interfering with the self-satisfied refinement to
which it is addressed.

I will] Rather, **I shall soon**, or, **I am likely to...**: the word used
does not necessarily imply that the intention is final, and *v.* 19 shews
that it is not.

17. *I am rich, and increased with goods*] The words in the original
are cognate, as it were, "I am rich, and have gotten riches." If there
be any distinction of sense between them, the second expresses pride in
the riches being his own acquisition, in addition to self-complacency in
the enjoyment.

For the sense, cf. Hos. xii. 8, where apparently the self-complacency
in material prosperity lends itself to and combines with religious self-
satisfaction. Hence it is not necessary to interpret these words either
of material wealth, or of fancied spiritual wealth, to the exclusion of the
other. St James ii. 1—6 shews that in the first century, as in the
nineteenth, the "respectable" classes found it easiest to be religious, to
their own satisfaction.

that thou art wretched] Inadequate: read **that thou art the wretched
and miserable one**, &c.: the one person truly to be called so, above all
others—at least, above all the other six Churches.

18. *I counsel thee*] "There is deep irony in this word. One *who has
need of nothing*, yet needs counsel on the vital points of self-preservation."

thee to buy of me gold tried in the fire, that thou mayest be rich; and white raiment, that thou mayest be clothed, and *that* the shame of thy nakedness do not appear; and 19 anoint thine eyes *with* eyesalve, that thou mayest see. As many as I love, I rebuke and chasten: be zealous therefore, 20 and repent. Behold, I stand at the door, and knock: if any

to buy] Cf. Is. lv. 1: the counsel to a poor beggar to *buy* is of course meaningless, unless he can buy "without money and without price," or, as the Hebrew of that passage more literally means, "for (what is) not money and for (what is) not a price." Thus the word is not a mere synonym for "receive:" the sense is, "Thou hast nothing to give, but thou must give all that thou hast" (Matt. xiii. 44, 46). The nothingness of human merit is a reason against exalting self, but not a reason for sparing self: the Lord does not bid us say, "We are unprofitable servants: we cannot and need not do what it is our duty to do." (Luke xvii. 10.)

gold tried in the fire] Right in sense, though "fresh burnt from the fire" would be perhaps more literal: cf. i. 15, where the same participle is used as here. The meaning of the "gold" is defined in the next words: it stands for spiritual "riches" of any sort.

white raiment] As in *vv.* 4, 5.

that the shame &c.] Cf. xvi. 15.

and anoint thine eyes with eyesalve] Read **and eyesalve to anoint thine eyes.** *Collyrium* was the common dressing for weak eyes, and could be applied by a barber (see Horace's Satires, *passim*), but perhaps hardly by the patient himself.

19. *As many as I love, I rebuke*] The pronoun "I" stands emphatically at the beginning of the sentence—as it were, "My way with those I love (the word is a strong one, expressing affection, not simply charity), is to shew them their faults," not to "prophesy smooth things," and encourage the self-complacent temper that was destroying the Laodiceans. In every other case, the Lord has noted both the good and the evil in the Church, and generally the good first: here He does nothing but find fault, but He adds in effect, "Do not suppose from this that I do not love you." The word "rebuke" is more often rendered "reprove:" see e.g. John xvi. 8; Eph. v. 11, 13: its meaning here is exactly what we express by "working conviction of sin." •

be zealous therefore, and repent] Shake off thy languid "lukewarm" temper: then thou wilt be able to start on a new life of righteousness.

20. *I stand at the door, and knock*] The Lord expresses His affection, from which He has intimated that the Laodiceans are not excluded, by this figure of intense and condescending tenderness. It is intended to remind the readers of Cant. v. 2: but the figure of the *lover's* midnight visit is too delicate to bear being represented, as here, with a mixture of the thing signified with the image, especially since the visit is not to the Church, personified as a single female, but to any individual, and of either sex; so it is toned down into a visit from a familiar friend.

man hear my voice, and open the door, I will come in to him, and will sup with him, and he with me. To him that 21 overcometh will I grant to sit with me in my throne, *even* as I also overcame, and am set down with my Father in his throne. He that hath an ear, let him hear what the Spirit 22 saith unto the churches.

After this I looked, and behold, a door *was* opened in 4

hear My voice] It is implied that anyone is sure to hear His knock, and be roused to ask who is there: but only those who love Him will know His voice (as Rhoda did St Peter's, Acts xii. 14) when He says "It is I."

will sup] The blessing promised is a *secret* one to the *individual*. There can thus hardly be a reference to the Holy Eucharist, which is shared publicly by the whole Church.

with him, and he with Me] The sense is, "I will take all he has to give Me, as though I had need of it, and benefited by it (cf. Matt. xxv. 37—40): but at the same time, it will really be I that give the feast, and he that receives it." There can hardly be a better illustration than a quaint and touching legend, given in a little book called *Patranas, or Spanish Stories*, with the title "Where one can dine, two can dine."

21. *To him that overcometh*] The construction is as in ii. 26, iii. 12, "He that overcometh, I will give him." For the sense, compare the former of these passages; but the promise of sharing Christ's inheritance (Rom. viii. 17) is even more fully expressed here.

as I also overcame] See St John's Gospel, xvi. 33.

with my Father in his throne] See v. 6, vii. 17. In the Jewish Cabbala (of which the oldest parts are ascribed to a date little later than St John, and perhaps embody still older traditions, though it received its present form quite late in the middle ages) we hear of Metatron, apparently a Greek word Hebraised for "Next to the Throne," or perhaps "in the midst of the Throne," a sort of mediator between God and the world, who is identified with the four Living Creatures of Ezekiel's vision. The Cabbala as it now exists has more affinity with Gnostic mythology than with scriptural or Catholic Christianity: but it is deserving of notice, as the outcome of tendencies in Jewish thought that might have developed, or found their satisfaction, in the Gospel. St John's Lamb "in the midst of the Throne" is perhaps just as far comparable with the Cabbalistic Metatron, as his doctrine of the personal "Word of God" is with Philo's. It is hardly wise to ask whether "My Throne" and "His Throne" are quite identical: for the doctrine that the faithful stand to Christ in the same relation as He to the Father, see St John's Gospel, c. xvii. 21—3, and 1 Cor. iii. 23, xi. 3.

HEAVEN OPENED. CHAP. IV. 1—9.

1. *I looked*] Better, **I beheld, and lo!** as v. 6, 11 &c.; Dan. vii. 6,

heaven: and the first voice which I heard *was* as *it were* of a trumpet talking with me; which said, Come up hither, 2 and I will shew thee *things* which must be hereafter. And immediately I was in the spirit: and behold, a throne was 3 set in heaven, and one sat on the throne. And he that sat was to look upon like a jasper and a sardine stone:

11 &c. The purport of the word is rather that he *continued* looking at what he had seen before, than that he looked in another direction. There *is* a transition: henceforth he goes to another point of view, and sees no more the Son of Man in the midst of the seven candlesticks: but the transition is not indicated in this word.

[*was*] *opened*] The participle is used without any verb: he saw the door standing open, he did not see the fact of its opening.

[*was*] *as it were*] Here the insertion of the verb is even more misleading. The true construction and sense is, "Behold a door set open in Heaven, and [behold] the first voice which I had heard, as of a trumpet [i. 10] saying...."

which said] The participle does not agree with the substantive "voice," and perhaps we ought to render "one saying."

hereafter] Lit., **after these things**, as in i. 19: i.e. after the state of things described in the Epistles to the Seven Churches. See note l.c.

2. *I was in the spirit*] As i. 10 q.v. It is implied that he was caught up through the open door into Heaven, and saw what was going on above.

was set] i.e. was there already—not that he saw it put in its place. There is a description of the Throne of God in the apocryphal Book of Enoch, xiv. 17—23, very like this: probably St John had read it (cf. Jude 15), and his language shews quotations of it, as well as of the canonical passages in Ezek. i. and Dan. vii.

and one sat on the throne] God the Father, not the Trinity: the presence of the other Persons being otherwise indicated, *v.* 5, and v. 6. It is intimated, though with an intentional vagueness, that the Divine Presence was symbolised by a human Form, as in Is. vi. 1, 5; Ezek. i. 26 sq.; Dan. vii. 9: contrast Deut. iv. 12, but compare Exod. xxiv. 10, 11, xxxiii. 23. Apparently God revealed Himself by such symbols to men whom He had educated to such a point that they should not imagine them to be *more* than symbols. Therefore perhaps to attempt to include representations of the Father in the range of Christian art is rather of dangerous boldness than *ipso facto* illegitimate: see on this question Ruskin's *Modern Painters*, Part. III. Sec. ii. Chap. V. § 7.

3. *a jasper and a sardine stone*] Our jasper, a stone the colour of which varies between red, green and yellow, does not seem very appropriate to the image here, nor to answer to the description in xxi. 11, as it is not sparkling nor transparent. But it seems proved that the jasper of the ancients (the word is substantially the same in Hebrew, in Greek and Latin, and in modern languages) was the translucent

vv. 4, 5.] REVELATION, IV. 31

and *there was* a rainbow round about the throne, in sight like unto an emerald. And round about the throne were 4 four and twenty seats: and upon the seats I saw four and twenty elders sitting, clothed in white raiment; and they had on their heads crowns of gold. And out of the throne 5 proceeded lightnings and thunderings and voices: and *there*

stone now known as Chalcedony—especially the green variety. The sardius (so we should read) is certainly the choicest kind of red carnelian, translucent and fiery in colour, but not exactly sparkling.

round about the throne] i.e. forming an arch over it.

in sight] The word is the same as "to look upon" just before, though the construction is somewhat varied.

like unto an emerald] Here there is no doubt what stone is meant: we have only the question whether the rainbow was *all* green, or only produced the same effect on the eye as an emerald—brilliant yet not dazzling. The ancients felt very strongly the relief given to the eye by looking at it. The rainbow in any case no doubt represents God's revelation by a covenant of grace, Gen. ix. 13 sqq.

4. *four and twenty seats*] Better, **thrones**; it is the same word that is used of *the* throne. Cf. Dan. vii. 9.

four and twenty elders] There are two views as to the significance of these, both leading to substantially the same result: (i) that they are the twelve Patriarchs, the heads of the Tribes of Israel, together with the twelve Apostles, the heads of the new People of God: (ii) that they answer to the heads of the 24 courses of the Priests, 1 Chr. xxiv. The *title* of those assessors to the divine Throne is already found in Is. xxiv. 23: and the conception of the twelve Apostles answering to the twelve Tribes appears in Matt. xix. 28; Luke xxii. 30, as well as in this Book, xxi. 12, 14. The resemblance between this passage and those in the O. T. and Gospels is not complete —in the account of the Judgement, xx. 11, the Elders are not mentioned: still on the whole they support the former interpretation. But perhaps the second is not inconsistent with it, for the Elders have certainly a priestly character. They are not *called* Priests in v. 10 according to the true text, and their white robes, though suitable, are not peculiar to priests: but they *act* as priests in v. 8: and we may add, their title is the ordinary Scriptural one for the Christian priesthood. Either way of explaining their *number* points to the same explanation of their *office*: they are the glorified embodiment and representatives of the people of God. It seems not necessary to read "*the* 24 elders," which would imply that their meaning, and perhaps their number, was known: if it be right, the chief reference is probably to Is. xxiv. 23.

crowns of gold] The word used does not necessarily imply royal crowns—we have a different one e.g. in xix. 12: but probably we are to understand that the elders are kings as well as priests. Cf. Zech. vi. 11—13.

were seven lamps of fire burning before the throne, which
6 are the seven spirits of God. And before the throne *there
was* a sea of glass like unto crystal: and in the midst of the
throne, and round about the throne, *were* four beasts full of
7 eyes before and behind. And the first beast *was* like a lion,
and the second beast like a calf, and the third beast had a
face as a man, and the fourth beast *was* like a flying eagle.

5. *seven*] Typified by the seven lamps of the candlestick in the Tabernacle, and represented by the "seven golden candlesticks" of the Church on earth: see on i. 20. The significance of the seven-branched candlestick in relation especially to the *Spirit* is suggested in Zech. iv.
seven Spirits] See the last note on i. 4.
6. *a sea of glass*] As there was a brazen "sea" in front of Solomon's Temple, 1 Kings vii. 23 &c. We find from xi. 19, xv. 5, &c. that St John was now in front of the heavenly Temple—whether the Throne was inside it seems doubtful: xvi. 17 looks as if it were, xi. 19 as if it were not. That Temple had a real sea in front of it—sea-like in extent, no doubt, but a *glassy* sea, calm and transparent, and apparently solid, xv. 2: its earthly representative (see Ecclus. l. 3, and note on ii. 17 above) was hardly more than a tank, though richly ornamented.
like unto crystal] Ancient glass being not so clear as ours, a further term of comparison seemed necessary. The word *may* mean "ice," but xxi. 11 confirms the A.V.
in the midst of the throne, and round about the throne] It is not quite clear how they are placed—whether with their bodies partly *under* the Throne, or only so far "in the midst" of it, that each of the four was in (or opposite to) the middle of one of its four sides. In Ezek. i. 22 we see that the Cherubim *support* the Throne of God, which points to the first view.
four beasts] Should be rendered **living creatures**, as Ezek. i. 5 &c.: the word for the "beasts" of ch. xiii. &c. is quite different: and that used here, like the Hebrew one in Ezekiel, is cognate with the word for "life."
7. The description of these living creatures does not exactly agree with any of the O.T. parallels: in Ezek. i., which is the nearest, the four Cherubim, as they are called, have human figures, calves' feet, and *each* has four faces, of the same four animals as these: also they have each four wings, while these have six, like the Seraphim of Is. vi. 2. Probably the meaning is, that these four represent the Cherubim *and* Seraphim who "continually do cry 'Holy, Holy, Holy, Lord God of Sabaoth'." We have no reason to suppose that the Angels, or these super-angelic beings, have proper bodies or invariable forms: they appear in such forms as may please God, or may be appropriate to the purpose for which He bids them appear. For further discussion as to their meaning, see Excursus I.
8. *And the four beasts* &c.] Render, **And the four living creatures,**

And the four beasts had each of them six wings about *him*; 8 and *they were* full of eyes within: and they rest not day and night, saying, Holy, holy, holy, Lord God Almighty, which was, and is, and is to come. And when *those* beasts give 9 glory and honour and thanks to him that sat on the throne, who liveth for ever and ever, the four and twenty elders fall 10 down before him that sat on the throne, and worship him that liveth for ever and ever, and cast their crowns before the throne, saying, Thou art worthy, O Lord, to receive 11 glory and honour and power: for thou hast created all *things*, and for thy pleasure they are and were created.

having each of them six wings, are full of eyes round about and within: " i. e. the statement of *v.* 6, that they are "full of eyes before and behind," is extended to tell us that they are covered with eyes, not only on the parts ordinarily visible, but when they spread their wings (and the Eagle at least was in the attitude of flight) it is seen that the inside of the wings, and the parts beneath it, are full of eyes too.

they rest not] Lit. **have no rest.** The order of words in the original makes it doubtful whether "day and night" should be connected with these words or with "saying:" but xiv. 11 (where the same words occur in a very different sense) proves that the A.V. is right. There is *some* resemblance between this place and Enoch xxxix. 11, where Is. vi. 3 is referred to, much as here: it is hardly likely that St John had the passage from Enoch in his mind.

Holy, holy, holy] Is vi. 3. It will be observed that "Almighty" represents the Hebrew [God] "of Hosts:" see on i. 8.

which was, &c.] i. 4.

9, 10. *And when those beasts,* &c.] Read **And when the living creatures shall give glory and honour and thanks to Him that sitteth upon the Throne, to Him that liveth for ever and ever, the four and twenty elders shall fall down before Him that sitteth..., and shall worship Him..., and shall cast....**" The meaning of the futures is doubtful: some take it as "implying eternal repetition of the act." Or the meaning may be (if one may say so reverently) a sort of stage direction: "during the future course of the vision, these (who never leave the scene) are to be understood to be thus employed." But it is always a question in this Book whether the use of tenses be not accommodated to the rules of Hebrew rather than Greek grammar: the sense may after all be merely frequentative.

cast their crowns] Alford compares Tac. *Ann.* XV. xxix. 3, 6, where Tiridates lays down his crown before the image of Nero, as a token of homage for his kingdom.

11. *Thou art worthy,* &c.] Here we have the praise of God the Creator by His Creatures as such: in the next ch. we have the praise of the Redeemer.

for thy pleasure] Better, **because of Thy will.**

they are] Read **they were**: not exactly "they came into being,"

And I saw in the right hand of him that sat on the throne a book written within and on the backside, sealed with seven

but "they had their being,"—as the simple verb substantive is very well translated in Acts xvii. 28.

THE BOOK WITH SEVEN SEALS. CHAP. V. vv. 1—8.

1. *in the right hand*] Lit. **on the right hand**—lying on the open palm.

a book] i. e. a roll : the ordinary meaning for the equivalent words in all ancient literature, though books arranged in leaves like ours were not unknown.

written within and on the backside] So Ezek. ii. 10. It was a recognised but quite exceptional way of getting an unusual amount of matter into a single volume : such rolls were called *opisthographi*. See Juv. i. 6, where he complains of an interminable poem, "written till the margin at the top of the book is full, and on the back, and not finished yet." If we are to ask, how St John saw that it was thus written, it may be said that he saw that there was writing on the part outside, between the seals, and took for granted that this implied that the side folded inwards was full of writing too. But perhaps this is too minute : St John saw the book now, and learnt (either now or afterwards) how it was written.

sealed] See Is. xxix. 11 ; Dan. xii. 4.

The traditional view, so far as there is one, of this sealed book is, that it represents the Old Testament, or more generally the prophecies of Scripture, which are only made intelligible by their fulfilment in Christ. But Christ's fulfilment of prophecy was, in St John's time, to a great extent past : and he was told (iv. 1) that what he was now to see was concerned with the future. Many post-Reformation commentators, both Romanist and Protestant, have supposed the Book to be the Apocalypse itself : some supposing, by a further refinement, that the seven seals were so arranged that, when each was opened, a few lines of the Book could be unrolled, viz. those describing what was seen after its opening : while the opening of the last would enable the whole roll to be spread out. But of this there is not the smallest evidence in the Apocalypse itself : nor do we ever find the Prophets of Scripture representing, as Mahomet did, that their writings are copies of an original archetype in Heaven. Most modern commentators therefore generalise, and suppose that it is the Book of God's counsels. Some insist on the fact that though the seals are all broken, "no portion of the roll is actually unfolded, nor is anything read out of the book :" they suppose it to stand for the *complete* counsel of God, which will not become intelligible till it has *all* been fulfilled, not therefore before the end of time. But this Book tells us what is to happen until all *has* been fulfilled, until time *has* ended : and why then do we not hear of the opening of the Book, even if it be not for us yet to know what is written therein? And to this we may answer, we *are* told, xx. 12,

seals. And I saw a strong angel proclaiming with a loud 2 voice, Who is worthy to open the book, and to loose the seals thereof? And no *man* in heaven, nor in earth, neither 3 under the earth, was able to open the book, neither to look thereon. And I wept much, because no *man* was found 4 worthy to open and to read the book, neither to look thereon. And one of the elders saith unto me, Weep not: behold, the 5 Lion of the tribe of Juda, the root of David, hath prevailed to open the book, and to loose the seven seals thereof. And 6 I beheld, and lo, in the midst of the throne and of the four

of the opening of a very important Book, the Book of Life; and that Book belongs to the Lamb that was slain, xiii. 8, xxi. 27. Is not then this Book the same as that? so that the opening of it will be "the manifestation of the sons of God" (Rom. viii. 19).

3. *no man*] Better, **no one**—the term includes others as well as men.
under the earth] i.e. in the world of the dead. In view of *v.* 13, we can hardly make it mean "in the sea," on the analogy of Ex. xx. 4 fin.
neither to look thereon] Which would have enabled him to read some fragments of its contents, viz. as much as was written on the outer fold of the back of the roll.

4. *And I*] The pronoun is emphatic: "no one could open it: I for my part wept for the impossibility." *Why* he wept will be variously explained, according to the view taken of the meaning of the Book. If it be the Book of Life, the reason is obvious: if it be the future purposes of God, the impossibility of opening it threatened to disappoint the promise of iv. 1.

5. *one of the elders*] It is idle to speculate which; even if it be assumed certain that the twenty-four are the Patriarchs and Apostles, they represent their federal office, not their individual character. We can hardly suppose that St John saw *himself* seated among them.
the Lion of the tribe of Juda] Gen. xlix. 9.
the root of David] xxii. 16; Is. xi. 1, 10, where however we have the Root of *Jesse*. Some distinguish the two phrases, that Christ is said to grow from the obscure Jesse in reference to the time of His humiliation, from the kingly David in reference to His exaltation.
hath prevailed to open] Lit. **hath conquered**: Christ's victory (see iii. 21 and ref.) has this consequence, that He can open. There is a well-supported reading, "the Lion hath conquered, Who openeth"... but this is grammatically easier, and less effective—both presumptions in favour of the text.
to loose] Should be omitted as a gloss: we hear of "opening the seals" all through the next chapter.

6. *and lo*] Should be omitted: the construction is, "And I saw in the midst of...a Lamb standing."
in the midst of the throne] See on iv. 6. In this passage, the sense might be merely "in the centre of the (semicircular?) space surrounded by...," but vii. 17 disproves this. If it be not rash to attempt to work

beasts, and in the midst of the elders, stood a Lamb as *it had been* slain, having seven horns and seven eyes, which are the seven spirits of God sent forth into all the earth. 7 And he came and took the book out of the right hand of 8 him that sat upon the throne. And when he had taken the book, the four beasts and four *and* twenty elders fell down before the Lamb, having every one *of them* harps, and golden

out the details of the picture, I would conjecture that the four living creatures were under the four corners of the Throne, with their heads and wings projecting beyond it: and the Lamb stood in the midst of the front of it, appearing as proceeding from between the feet of Him Who sat thereon.

stood] Expressed by a participle, and with the true reading (see above) should be so translated, "I saw...a Lamb standing."

Lamb] See Is. liii. 7; John i. 29, 36. Too much importance has been given to the fact that St John uses a different Greek word here from that in his Gospel, and in the LXX. of Isaiah. It is doubtful whether the LXX. is used in the O. T. references in this Book; and the form here used is a diminutive and a neuter. It is awkward to use a neuter noun of a Person, but in this Book St John boldly uses masculines in reference to the Lamb (as in his Gospel he once or twice does in reference to the Spirit): while in the Gospel he is less regardless of grammatical rules, and therefore prefers the masc. form.

as it had been slain] The true construction calls attention to the paradox, a Lamb appearing with its throat cut, yet not lying dead or dying, but standing. It serves to typify "Him that liveth and was dead, and is alive for evermore" (i. 18). The risen Christ bore, and doubtless bears, the wounds of His Passion unaltered—unhealed, though apparently not bleeding, John xx. 25, 27.

seven horns and seven eyes] The Spirit is to Him both strength and wisdom. The horn is throughout the Bible the symbol of conquering might and glory: see e.g. 1 Kings xxii. 11; Zech. i. 18 sqq., while 1 Sam. ii. 1, &c. shew that divine glory as well as earthly may be so expressed. For the seven eyes, see Zech. iii. 9, iv. 10. It is hardly fanciful to observe on the combination of *horns* and *eyes*, that a bull shuts his eyes when he charges. Sagacity in discerning truth in all its aspects, and power and promptitude in resolve and execution, are excellences scarcely ever combined in the great men of the world, the one usually varies inversely as the other; but "Christ the Power of God and the Wisdom of God" (1 Cor. i. 24) unites both.

seven spirits] i. 4, iv. 5.

sent forth, &c.] Taken, of course, from Zech. iv. 10 already referred to. The seven lamps of iv. 5 represent the Spirit as eternally proceeding from and belonging to the Father: these represent Him as sent by the Son and belonging to the Son.

8. *having every one of them*] Perhaps refers to the elders only; though it is not more difficult to *picture* the living creatures holding harps than the Lamb taking the Book and breaking the seals; nor is it more unfit

vials full of odours, which are the prayers of saints. And they sung a new song, saying, Thou art worthy to take the book, and to open the seals thereof: for thou wast slain, and hast redeemed us to God by thy blood out of every kindred, and tongue, and people, and nation; and hast made us unto our God kings and priests: and we shall reign on the earth.

that Cherubim and Seraphim should present the prayers of Saints than that a single Angel should bless them, as in viii. 3 sq.

golden vials] i.e. broad open bowls; more like saucers than any vessel in modern use.

which are the prayers] If the strict grammar of this sentence is to be pressed, it is the "vials" not the "odours" which are identified with the "prayers." See viii. 3 and note there. Cf. Ps. cxli. 2.

THE NEW SONG, vv. 9—13.

9. *And they sung*] Should be **they sing**. It may be only an historic present, but perhaps, though to the Seer the song of adoration appeared to begin now, and to stop in time to let other voices be heard, he means to intimate that in fact their adoration is continued to eternity. See on iv. 9, 10.

and hast redeemed] The word rendered "redeemed" means simply "bought," as it is rendered in 1 Cor. vi. 20, &c.: it does not express that the effect of the purchase was to restore those bought either to their rightful owner, or to liberty, though of course both are true, but all that this text expresses, is, that Christ has bought us, and that we now belong to His Father.

us] Should be omitted. The elders probably *represent* the whole multitude of the redeemed, but they are not here said to *belong* to their number, and the living creatures certainly do not. The true reading is, "Thou wast slain, and hast purchased to God by Thy Blood out of every tribe, and tongue, and people, and nations, and hast made them unto our God a kingdom and priests, and they [shall] reign upon the earth."

to God] Notice that the phrase is the exact reverse of some lax modern language on the Atonement, which speaks as if the Son redeemed men *from* the Father. To say that Christ redeemed men from God's *wrath* may be justified (e.g. by Gal. iii. 13); but even that mode of expression is not exactly Scriptural. The metaphor of a ransom, which is frequent in Scripture, must not be pressed.

out of every kindred] The first of many indications in this Book of the catholicity of the Church: of course, a conclusive refutation of the theories (see on ii. 2) which ascribe to this Book a controversial anti-Pauline purpose, and a spirit of Jewish exclusiveness. There is really hardly anything in St Paul as strong as this or vii. 9.

10. *unto our God kings and priests*] See on the last verse for the true reading: on i. 6 for the origin of the phrase.

we shall reign] Authorities are nearly evenly divided between the readings "they reign" and "they shall reign." Perhaps the present is

11   And I beheld, and I heard the voice of many angels round about the throne and the beasts and the elders: and the number of them was ten thousand times ten thousand, 12 and thousands of thousands; saying with a loud voice, Worthy is the Lamb that was slain to receive power, and riches, and wisdom, and strength, and honour, and glory, 13 and blessing.   And every creature which is in heaven, and on the earth, and under the earth, and such as are in the

to be preferred, as the more difficult in sense; the future could be easily understood of the millennial reign (xx. 4), whatever that means. If we accept the present, it can hardly be used *for* a future, every one must feel that ii. 22, &c. are not really parallel: rather, we may say that the faithful on earth are, even in their exile, kings *de jure*, as David was "when he was in the wilderness of Judah" (Ps. lxiii. ult. cf. title).

11.   *I beheld*]   See on iv. 1.   The sense is, of course, that he saw the Angels whose voice he heard.

round about]   We cannot tell if they formed a complete circle round the Throne, or a semicircle between it and the Seer, or a semicircle on the side away from him. But though we cannot answer these questions, it is worth while to ask them: for it is plain that St John did see a definite picture.

ten thousand times ten thousand]   Lit. **myriads of myriads**, the Greek (and Hebrew) language having a single word for the number 10,000: so that the effect is as if we should say "millions of millions and thousands of thousands" (in Gen. xxiv. 60 words equivalent to these are translated "thousands of millions.") In Dan. vii. 10 the order is the reverse, "thousand thousands...and ten thousand times ten thousand," with the obvious motive of a climax: here the effect is, "there were hundreds of millions massed together, and if you counted those in the mass, the numbers you would leave over would be millions still." The passage in Daniel is also imitated in Enoch xiv. 24, xl. 1.

12.   *power*, &c.]   Lit. **the power.**   Notice that the praises ascribed are either sevenfold, as here; fourfold, as in the next verse; or threefold, as in iv. 11, xix. 1 (true text).

13.   *every creature*]   Cf. Phil. ii. 10.

under the earth]   See on v. 3.   It seems harsh to understand the words of an *unwilling* cooperation of the devils in glorifying God and His Son, besides that Jude 6 seems hardly to prove that *all* fallen spirits are yet confined "under the earth:" Matt. viii. 29 compared with Luke viii. 31 suggests the contrary. It is more possible to suppose the dead, even the holy dead, to be described as "under the earth." In Enoch lxii. we have a hymn, somewhat resembling those of this Book, actually sung by the souls of the lost—apparently in the intervals of their suffering. The souls of the Martyrs appear from this Book to be in Heaven, vi. 9 sqq.: but we cannot be sure that this is

sea, and all that are in them, heard I saying, Blessing, and honour, and glory, and power, *be* unto him that sitteth upon the throne, and unto the Lamb for ever and ever. And the 14 four beasts said, Amen. And the four *and* twenty elders fell down and worshipped him that liveth for ever and ever.

And I saw when the Lamb opened one of the seals, and 6 I heard, as *it were* the noise of thunder, one of the four beasts saying, Come and see. And I saw, and behold a 2

true of all the faithful, and it is not certain that a disembodied soul can be said, except figuratively, to be in any place at all: so that the place where their bodies lie is perhaps the only place where the dead can properly be said to be.

such as are in the sea] Read simply **on the sea**: including those in ships, and marine animals: see Ps. civ. 26.

Blessing, and honour] Lit. **the blessing, and the honour**, &c.—the art. being repeated with each noun, not, as in the preceding verse, standing once for all. The repetition of the article has perhaps none but a rhetorical or euphonic purpose. Whatever "power and riches...," whatever "blessing and honour..." the world contains, all belongs of right to Him. Watts' "Blessings *more than we can give*" is a perfectly legitimate developement of the sense.

14. *And the four and twenty...for ever and ever*] We should read simply, "and the elders fell down and worshipped"—in silence. The brevity of the phrase, imitating their silent adoration, is really grander than the completer sentence of the A.V.

The Opening of the Seven Seals.

The First Seal. Chap. VI. vv. 1, 2.

1. *one of the four*] Presumably the Lion, as the other voices are described as those of the second, third, and fourth. But the voice (so the word "noise" should be rendered: cf. x. 3, 4) like thunder does not refer to the lion's roaring: no doubt the other three voices were as loud.

Come and see] The two last words are almost certainly spurious here and in *vv.* 3, 5, 7: the cry is only "Come!" in all four cases. Who then is to come? Some say the received reading, originally no doubt a gloss, is a correct gloss—the Seer is to draw near. But the word is quite different from the "Come hither" of xvii. 1, xxi. 9: also there is no sign that he does draw near or has need to do so, and if he has done so once, why is he bidden to do it thrice again? Others take it to be a summons to the Horseman who in fact does come: and this at least is in harmony with the context, and makes good sense, and applies equally to the opening of the first four seals where the same expression occurs. Others, comparing xxii. 17, 20, take it as addressed to the

white horse: and he that sat on him had a bow; and a crown was given unto him: and he went forth conquering, and to conquer.

Lord Jesus. His creatures pray Him to come—and behold, instead of His coming immediately, there come these terrible precursors of His, so increasingly unlike Him. But in an address to the Lord, surely His Name must have been added. It would have been not merely 'Come,' but 'Come, Lord Jesus.'

2. *behold a white horse*] The image of these four horses is certainly suggested by the vision of four chariots (with perhaps four horses in each, and so related to this exactly as Ezekiel's vision of the living creatures to that in ch. iv.) in Zech. vi. 1—8: cf. ibid. i. 8. But that passage throws little light on this: it is in fact the obscurer of the two. Here, the colours of the four horses plainly symbolise *triumph, slaughter, mourning,* and *death*; we are told expressly who the fourth Rider is: and hardly anyone doubts that the second and third represent War and Scarcity respectively. But about the first there is controversy. His white horse and golden crown resemble His Who appears in xix. 11, Whose Name is called the Word of God: and hence many think that this Rider is Christ, or at least the representative of Christ's Kingdom. But is it possible that when He has come, the plagues that follow should come after him? or why should the living creatures continue to cry to Him to come, if He be come already? It would be more credible, that the first Rider is a *false* Christ, just as Matt. xxiv. 5 precedes *vv.* 6, 7. But on the whole it seems more reasonable to suppose that all four riders symbolise the woes before Christ's coming foretold in the two latter verses: and that the first is the spirit of Conquest:—the description is like that in ch. xix., because there Christ is described as a Conqueror, and here we have a Conqueror who is nothing more. Then what is the difference between the first and the second Rider? Conquest is necessarily painful—it may be unjust and cruel, but it may be beneficent even to the conquered: at least it is not necessarily demoralising to the conquerors, as war is, when it sinks from conquest into mere mutual slaughter. This Rider has a bow, that a sword: the first is prepared to fight, and slay if necessary, but he will do so without passion or cruelty—just as it is commonly observed, that fire-arms have tended to make war less brutal, by removing the soldiers from the excitement of a personal struggle.

was given unto him] Apparently he comes into view armed with the bow, but his crown (either that of an honoured soldier or of a king, see on iv. 4) is given to him afterwards perhaps as his title to the dominion he is to conquer. But the phrase "was given" is from Dan. vii. 4, 6, 14: which proves that it is not necessary to suppose that the Seer actually saw some one crown him.

he went forth] Apparently out of the field of vision—perhaps out of Heaven to carry his conquests over the earth.

conquering, and to conquer] He makes war successfully, but his purpose is the securing the victory, not the excitement of the battle and carnage.

And when he had opened the second seal, I heard the 3 second beast say, Come and see. And there went out 4 another horse *that was* red: and *power* was given to him that sat thereon to take peace from the earth, and that they should kill one another: and there was given unto him a great sword.

And when he had opened the third seal, I heard the third 5 beast say, Come and see. And I beheld, and lo a black horse; and he that sat on him had a pair of balances in his hand. And I heard a voice in the midst of the four beasts 6

THE SECOND SEAL, vv. 3, 4.

4. *to take peace*] The word "peace" has the article, which according to Greek usage may mean merely "peace in general, peace in the abstract," but may also very well stand for "*the* peace" which the conquests of the previous Rider have left as their fruit.

that they should kill one another] Some understand this of *civil* war exclusively: and such wars have indeed most of the character of war as indicated under this seal. But its full meaning perhaps includes all wars, so far as they are aimless bloodshedding, not painful steps towards human progress. Here we can agree almost entirely with the "continuous historical" interpreters, who see the fulfilment of these four seals in the reigns of the "five good emperors," when Trajan carried imperial conquest to its utmost height: in the civil wars and mutinies during and after the age of the Severi, in the famines that followed: and in the general distress that made the Barbarian conquest possible. Only we need not regard their meaning as exhausted in the fifth century (much less in the third). We may see e.g. the contrast of the two first seals in the Crusades compared with the religious wars of the Reformation: in the conquests of the French Republic and Empire, compared with the Red and the White Terror, and the mutual crimes of the Holy Alliance and the Carbonari: even in our own country, in a comparison of the reigns of Edward III. and Henry V. with those of their respective successors, or of Elizabeth's with Charles I.'s: while again the civil war of the latter was noble and fruitful compared with the Dutch war of his son.

THE THIRD SEAL, vv. 5, 6.

5. *a pair of balances*] The primary meaning of the word is a *yoke:* but no doubt the A.V. is right, as what follows proves that scarcity rather than oppression is to be symbolised. The sense is, that mankind shall be placed on limited rations of bread, like the people of a besieged city; as in Levit. xxvi. 26; Ezek. iv. 16.

6. *I heard a voice*] One of the many voices heard throughout this book without anyone being defined as the speaker.

say, A measure of wheat for a penny, and three measures of barley for a penny; and *see* thou hurt not the oil and the wine.

7, 8 And when he had opened the fourth seal, I heard the voice of the fourth beast say, Come and see. And I looked, and behold a pale horse: and his name that sat on him *was*

A measure of wheat] The object of the voice is rather to *define* the extent of the scarcity than, as some say, to mitigate it. A quart (or somewhat less) of corn is to be bought for a silver penny (about $8\frac{1}{2}d$.); the former was the estimated ration for an able-bodied man's daily fare, the latter the daily pay of a soldier, apparently a liberal daily pay (see Matt. xx. 2) for a labourer. So there is not such a famine that the poor must starve, and the rich "give their pleasant things for meat to relieve the soul:" the working man can, if he pleases, earn the ordinary necessaries of life for himself: he may even procure a bare comfortless subsistence (for barley, an ordinary article of human food down to the time of the kings of Israel, was now considered as fodder for cattle) for a family, if not too numerous. Meanwhile, nothing is said about the fish and vegetables, which the plain-living man of the Mediterranean ate with his bread, as the plain-living Englishman eats bacon or cheese: but the comparatively superfluous luxuries of wine and oil are carefully protected. In short, we have a picture of "bad times," when no one need be absolutely without bare necessaries, and those who can afford it need not go without luxuries. All that we know of the age of the decline of the Roman Empire points to this prophecy having been eminently fulfilled then; but we need not go so far for fulfilments of it any more than of the two former: indeed this is much nearer to us than the grand army and the barricades, or Waterloo and Peterloo.

THE FOURTH SEAL, vv. 7, 8.

7. *I heard the voice of*] The slight variation of phrase serves to mark the fourth rider off, as partly distinct in character from the rest. They have brought an increasing series of scourges to the earth: his work is utter and unmitigated woe, combining the worst features of theirs.

8. *a pale horse*] Or **livid**, lit. **green**, as in viii. 7, but used constantly of the paleness of the human face when terror-struck, or dead or dying. It is not certain whether it here expresses a possible colour for a real horse: it seems not very appropriate for the "grisled" of Zech. vi. 3. Perhaps it might apply to the colour of the bare skin of a *mangy* horse.

and his name &c.] Lit. **and he that sat upon him, his name was Death.**

that sat on him] Alford remarks on the fact that the phrase for "upon him" is different from that used of the previous riders, and may be rendered "on the top of him," perhaps taking it to suggest that the

Death, and Hell followed with him. And power was given unto them over the fourth *part* of the earth, to kill with sword, and with hunger, and with death, and with the beasts of the earth.

And when he had opened the fifth seal, I saw under the 9 spectre (or skeleton, or demon ?) did not ride astride and manage his horse, but simply sat clumsily on his back.

and Hell] Hades, personified as a demon, as in xx. 13, 14. He follows Death, to devour those slain by him.

the fourth part of the earth] No good explanation of this proportion has been given : the best is, that the four riders divide the earth between them, and that the three afflict or decimate their subjects, while the last exterminates his.

with sword, and with hunger, and with death, and with the beasts of the earth] God's "four sore judgements," Ezek. xiv. 21. For "pestilence" there the LXX have "death," which fixes the sense of the word in this clause: but the personified Death, the rider, is not to be so limited; *he* is the sovereign over all four modes of death. The preposition "with the beasts of the earth" is different from those before: it might be rendered "by" instead of "with."

The first four Seals are distinguished from the rest (*a*) by Personification; (*b*) by the part which the four living creatures bear in the representation.

THE FIFTH SEAL, vv. 8—11.

9. This series of seven visions, like the other groups of seven throughout the book, is divided into two parts. We have seen (ii. 7, 29) that the messages to the seven Churches were divided into a group of *three* and one of *four:* here the first *four* seals are marked off from the last *three*, and similarly with the four trumpets of chap. viii. from the three that follow in chaps. ix.—xi.: perhaps also, though less clearly, with the vials of chap. xvi.

under the altar] Here first mentioned; it is a part of the arrangements of the heavenly Temple: see on iv. 6. Are we to understand that its position was that of the *golden* altar within the Holy Place (Ex. xxx. 1 sqq.) or of the *brazen* altar in the open court before the Temple (Ex. xxvii. 1 sqq.)? i.e. is it an altar of incense or of burnt offering? In viii. 3 sqq. we find incense offered at a heavenly golden Altar, and it is not distinguished from this: yet it may be thought that the image here is more suitable to the altar of sacrifice. For at the foot of it the blood of the victims was poured out (Ex. xxix. 12), and the blood, we are told repeatedly, is the life: then is it not meant that the lives or souls (the words are interchangeable, as Matt. xvi. 25 sqq.) of the martyrs are poured out at the foot of the heavenly altar, when they sacrificed their lives to God? Probably it *is* meant: but we are not to assume without evidence that the altar here is different from that in chap. viii. Admitting that the Israelite tabernacle and Temple were copies of a really subsisting heavenly archetype, it is not certain

altar the souls of them that were slain for the word of God, 10 and for the testimony which they held: and they cried with a loud voice, saying, How long, O Lord, holy and

that they were exact copies in all respects: they might have to be modified to suit material conditions. Just as it was impossible to have a real sea (see on iv. 6) in front of the earthly temple, so it may have been necessary to have on earth an inner and an outer Sanctuary, an altar before each, whereon to present the symbols of those things which in heaven are offered on one.

the souls] There is undoubtedly a distinction throughout the N.T. between the words for "soul," the mere principle of natural life and "spirit," the immortal and heavenly part of man: see especially 1 Cor. xv. 44 sqq. Yet it is probably an overstatement of this distinction to say that these are mere lost lives, crying to God for vengeance like Abel's blood (Gen. iv. 10), but different from the immortal souls, which have all their wants satisfied, and desire the salvation, not the punishment, of their murderers. They are the "lives" of the slain: their being under the altar is well illustrated by the ceremonial outpouring of the blood, and their cry for vengeance by that of the blood of Abel, but what follows in the next verse is surely addressed to the inmost souls of the saints, not to impersonal abstract "lives."

of them that were slain] As the four former verbs correspond to Matt. xxiv. 6—8, so this to ibid. 9. In Enoch xl. 5, a voice (that of "him who presides over every suffering and every wound of the sons of men, the holy Raphael," ib. 9) is heard "blessing the elect One, and the elect who are crucified on account of the Lord of spirits." There is a passage more like this in sense in the same book, xlvii. 2, "In that day shall the holy ones assemble who dwell above the heavens, and with united voice petition, supplicate, praise, laud, and bless the name of the Lord of spirits, on account of the blood of the righteous which has been shed, that the prayer of the righteous may not be intermitted before the Lord of spirits; that for them He would execute judgement, and that His patience may not endure for ever."

for the word of God, and for the testimony] Cf. i. 9, xx, 4.

the testimony which they held] For the construction cf. xii. 17 fin. The verb rendered "held" here and "have" there being the same. Some argue from the name of *Jesus* not being used here, as in the three places referred to, for describing their testimony, that there are Old Testament martyrs, like those in Heb. xi. *ad fin*. But surely *their* blood was very amply avenged, and very speedily: of the three great persecutors, Jezebel and Antiochus perished miserably, and Manasseh suffered equal misery, though he repented in time to receive some alleviation of it. We have, however, a Jewish parallel to the thought of this passage in Enoch xxii. 5 sqq., where Enoch hears in heaven the accusing cry of the soul (not, as in Genesis, the blood) of Abel.

10. *How long*] Cf. Ps. xciv. 3.

O Lord] Not the ordinary word of reverence applied to God, but one meaning (as we say) "lord and master." It is used of God in

true, dost thou not judge and avenge our blood on them that dwell on the earth? And white robes were given 11 unto every one of them; and it was said unto them,

Luke ii. 29, Acts iv. 24; and of Christ in Jude 4 (according to the right reading and probable translation), 2 Pet. ii. 1. Perhaps, as the usual word "Lord" in the N.T. and other Hellenistic writings stands for the Name Jehovah, so this is used where the *sense* "Lord" is really meant, i.e. it answers to the name *Adonai*, which the Jews pronounced instead of the Unutterable Name, and which Symeon and the Apostolic Church no doubt used in their thanksgivings. Their use of the word, especially in the latter instance, shews that it is no argument for these Martyrs being only Jews—as though it proved a servile rather than filial spirit, as some have imagined: at most, it only proves Jewish habits of expression, and it needs no proof that such prevail throughout this Book.

dost thou not...avenge] It has been argued again from this, that the temper of the Martyrs' souls is less than Christian. But however right it may be to contrast 2 Chr. xxiv. 22 with Acts vii. 60, no one can surely imagine that the spirit of this passage is a selfish desire for personal vengeance. As we meet with the germ of the thought in Ps. xciv. 3, so we have a developement of it, substantially identical with this, from the mouth of Christ Himself, Luke xviii. 2—8. Faith looks on evil with a hatred like God's own—shares God's will that it shall not triumph, and trusts in God that it will not: but without sharing the depth of God's counsels, Who knows best how and when to overthrow it. Therefore the Church on earth (the probable meaning of the Widow) and the Saints in heaven, cry alike to God to execute His own purpose, and bring the reign of evil to an end—and He does not yet, but He surely will.

11. *And white robes were given*] We should read, **and there was given them to each one a white robe**, bringing out still more fully than the old text, that the white robe is an individual, not a common blessing. It serves to mark them both as *innocent* and as *conquerors:* what it *is* is better felt than said. We see that the "souls" appeared in some visible form, like enough to bodies to wear garments: one of the considerations against regarding them as abstractions, not personal beings. There can hardly be any doubt that this verse (cf. iii. 4, 5) represents a portion of the reward given by God to His Saints, and if so, evidently such a portion of their reward as they receive in the interval before the Resurrection. But whether all the elect are in the same position as the Martyrs, or whether we have here described a special privilege granted to them only, is more doubtful: the prevalent belief of Christendom has been, that Martyrs and the like more excellent Saints have, in this intermediate state, a privilege above all the other justified ones.

and it was said unto them] From the nature of the case, their cry and the answer to it had to be heard by St John successively. But doubtless in fact they are contemporaneous: the Saints at once share

that they should rest yet for a little season, until their
fellowservants also and their brethren, that should be killed
as they *were*, should be fulfilled.

God's desire for the triumph of righteousness over sin, and rest in God's
assurance that it is for good reason that that triumph is delayed.
  that they should rest] i.e. not be impatient and disquieted. Something
more is meant than to be at peace, freed from the troubles of their earthly
life (as xiv. 13): but the word does not in the least imply that they are
to be unconscious, or as it were asleep.
  yet for a little season] Yet to Stephen and his companions it is not
less than 1840 years: and though the Old Testament Martyrs be not
exclusively meant, they are no doubt included. But notice that it is
contemplated that there will be an interval between the Martyrs of the
Primitive Church and those of the last days.
  their fellowservants also and their brethren] It would be possible to
construe the words "*both* their fellowservants and their brethren," as
though two classes were spoken of. In xix. 10, xxii. 9, where we get
the same words coupled, though in another construction, it may be
thought that St John is called a brother of Martyrs and Prophets in a
special sense. It would therefore be possible to distinguish the two
classes, "their fellowservants (viz. all their true fellow-believers), and
their brethren which should be killed as they were." But it is much
simpler to translate as the A.V., making both nouns antecedents to the
clause that follows.
  that should be killed as they were] The word "as" is slightly emphasised,
"*even* as they." The Martyrs of the last days are to be like those of the
first, Martyrs in the strictest sense—Christians slain because they hold
the Christian faith, and will not renounce it. Such Martyrs there have
been, no doubt, in the interval between the great ages of persecution
under the Roman emperors and under Antichrist, e.g. in the Mohammedan
conquests, in the age of the conversion of central Europe, in Japan in
the seventeenth century, and in Madagascar, China, New Zealand, and
Zululand in our own time. It is likely enough also that martyrs to
charity—men like St Telemachus and St Philip of Moscow, Abp. Affré
and Bp. Patteson—have their portion with the perfect martyrs to faith:
in some cases, as in the last, it is hard to draw a line between the two:
any way, those who suffer for righteousness' sake suffer for Christ, as
St Anselm said when Lanfranc wished to deny the honours of a martyr
to St Alphege. But to suffer for conscience' sake, however noble, is
not necessarily quite the same thing: and it is hardly right to claim the
name of martyr for the victims—certainly not for the victims on one side
only—in the fratricidal contests of Christians. "The Lord knoweth
them that are His;" He knows whether Becket or Huss, More or
Latimer, Charles I. or Margaret Wilson, had most of the Martyr's
spirit: we had better not anticipate His judgement whether any or all of
them are worthy of the Martyr's white robe.
  should be fulfilled] Probably we should read, **should have fulfilled**—
i.e. their course, as Acts xiii. 25, or their work.

And I beheld when he had opened the sixth seal, and lo, ¹² there was a great earthquake; and the sun became black as sackcloth of hair, and the moon became as blood; and the ¹³ stars of heaven fell unto the earth, *even* as a fig tree casteth her untimely figs, when she is shaken of a mighty wind. And the heaven departed as a scrole when it is rolled to- ¹⁴ gether; and every mountain and island were moved out of their places. And the kings of the earth, and the great ¹⁵ men, and the rich *men*, and the chief captains, and the

THE SIXTH SEAL, vv. 12—17.

12. *a great earthquake*] Earthquakes follow wars, famines, and pestilences in Matt. xxiv. 7, as the *earlier* signs of the approach of Christ's Coming. But here it is coupled with the darkening of the sun and fall of the stars which, ibid. 29, precede His Coming *immediately:* whence Alford says, that here it is more than the earth that quakes—that it is a fulfilment of Hag. ii. 6, cf. Heb. xii. 26 sqq.

black as sackcloth] The image is used in Is. l. 3.

the moon became] Read, **the moon wholly became**, or, **the whole** [i.e. full] **moon became.**

as blood] From Joel ii. 31, "the sun shall be turned into darkness, and the moon into blood." The image, no doubt, is suggested by the phenomena of natural total eclipses, when the sun disappears entirely, but the moon, though ceasing to be luminous, does not in general become invisible, but assumes a dull reddish colour. We are told of "signs in the Heaven" before the fall of Jerusalem which, if natural, must be assigned to this last cause, and in any case may be regarded as partial fulfilments of these prophecies, and types of their final fulfilment. See Jos. *B. J.* VI. v. 3; Tac. *Hist.* V. xiii. 1.

13. *and the stars of heaven*] So still in Matt. xxiv. 29.

as a fig tree] It is curious that a "parable of the fig-tree" follows in Matt. xxiv. 32, immediately after the "fall of the stars." But this image is taken, not from our Lord's prophecy l.c., but from Is. xxxiv. 4 (the Hebrew, not LXX.). The "untimely fig" is the fig which, having formed too late to ripen in the autumn, hangs through the winter, but almost always drops off before the sap begins to rise in spring, so as not to come to maturity. See Comm. on Matt. xxi. 19 and parallels.

14. *And the heaven departed*] i.e. parted asunder. The verb *depart* was so used (only in a transitive sense) in the Marriage Service until the last revision of the Prayer-Book, "till death us depart," i.e. "till death part us." Here we still have a reference to Is. xxxiv. 4. The word for "scroll" is the same as that rendered "book" in c. v. &c.

every mountain and island, &c.] Cf. xvi. 20. There the convulsion is greater than here: and even there it does not imply quite so much as xx. 11—a fact to be remembered in the interpretation of this passage.

15. *chief captains*] Should be transposed with "rich men." The word means lit. "captains of thousands," and was in St John's time the

mighty *men*, and every bondman, and every free *man*, hid themselves in the dens and in the rocks of the mountains; 16 and said to the mountains and rocks, Fall on us, and hide us from the face of him that sitteth on the throne, 17 and from the wrath of the Lamb: for the great day of his wrath is come; and who shall be able to stand?

recognised equivalent (as e.g. Acts xxi. 31, &c.) for the *tribunus* of the Roman army. Probably St John is thinking of Is. iii. 2, 3.
in the dens, &c.] Is. ii. 19, 21.
16. *and said*] should be **and they say**.
to the mountains, &c.] Hos. x. 8: adopted by our Lord, Luke xxiii. 30. In that passage, it is entirely natural to understand Him to refer to the destruction of Jerusalem *only:* and therefore it does not seem necessary to understand this vision as implying that the *Last* Judgement is immediately to come. *A* judgement of the Lord has now been prepared for, by all the signs that He foretold of it: His Disciples, no doubt, will "look up and lift up their heads," while the world which does not "love His appearing" is terrified. And we see in the next chapter that the faith of those is not unrewarded: but the dread of these is not immediately realised. In fact, the last "Day of the Lord" will come "when they shall say, 'Peace and safety'" (1 Thess. v. 3)—not therefore, apparently, preceded by terrors like those among the ungodly, but rather by an unbelief (not so uncommon now) that has outlived such alarms, and asks, "Where is the promise of His Coming? for since the fathers fell asleep, all things continue as they were from the beginning of the creation."
from the face of him that sitteth, &c.] In spite of John v. 22, it seems plain that the Father as well as the Son will be specially present and specially revealed in the judgement. See Matt. xvi. 27 and parallels: which are to be taken into account in the interpretation of Tit. ii. 13, and of ch. xx. 11 in the book.
from the wrath of the Lamb] It is scarcely necessary to point out the paradoxical character of the words, and its deep significance.
17. *for the great day of his wrath is come*] So the world has thought in every great social convulsion, since they have learnt so far to believe the Gospel, as to confess that such a day is coming. The thought has led men to repentance or to despair, as they were worthy of one or other: but, since the world has so often thought wrongly that the Day has come, it does not follow that, when this Book tells us that the world thinks it has come, we must suppose the world to be right.
who shall be able to stand?] Cf. Mal. iii. 2.

CHAPTER VII.

The two Visions in this Chapter, 1—8, 9—17, each introduced by the same phrase "After this" extend the opening of the Sixth Seal very considerably beyond that of the others; but are really episodical.

And after these *things* I saw four angels standing on the 7
four corners of the earth, holding the four winds of the earth,
that the wind should not blow on the earth, nor on the sea,
nor on any tree. And I saw another angel ascending from 2
the east, having the seal of the living God: and he cried

THE VISION OF THE FOUR ANGELS OF THE FOUR WINDS.
CHAP. VII. vv. 1—3.

1. *four angels*] Presumably the Angels of the four winds, as we have other elemental Angels in xiv. 18, xvi. 5. Cf. Ps. civ. 4, of which the probable sense is, "Who maketh His Angels winds," i.e. sends them into the air to cause the wind to blow, so that the wind is the manifestation of their presence.

on the four corners of the earth] Probably the four cardinal points, the extreme north, south, east, and west of it. It is hardly likely that the "four winds of the earth" should be conceived as NE., SW., SE., and NW.: in the climate of the Levant, there would not be as much physical truth in such a classification as in our own, and the usage of nomenclature, in Greek and still more in Hebrew, proves that the four winds are N., E., S., W. We therefore cannot argue from the "four corners" that St John conceives the earth is a rectangle—for it would be most unnatural to conceive it as set *corner-wise:* in Jer. xlix. 36, the four winds blow from the four *ends* of the earth. But it appears that the machinery, so to speak, throughout the vision does imply that the earth is conceived as a plane. St John is in Heaven, and is able to look down (or even to go down) to the earth, which he sees spread beneath him like a map, from Euphrates to Rome and very likely further. We have somewhat similar language in Enoch xviii. 3, "I also beheld the four winds which bear up the earth and the firmament of heaven." But St John does not, like Pseudo-Enoch, put forward his imagery as absolute physical truth.

that the wind should not blow] Every one will remember Keble's beautiful illustration of this image, by the natural phenomenon of the "All Saints' Summer." But the next *v.* shews, that it is by the Angels' action that the winds blow, as well as that they are restrained from blowing: we are not to conceive the winds (as in *Od.* x., *Aen.* 1.) as wild expansive forces, that will blow if not mechanically confined.

2. *ascending*] Probably the Heaven from which St John looks down on the earth formed a vault over it, or at least rested on walls surrounding the earth; cf. Enoch xviii. 8, "I saw, from the end of the earth, the firmament of the heaven which rests upon it." This Angel, then, mounted up the eastern side of this vault or circling wall (probably flying up, just outside it), till he was high enough to see, and to be heard by all the four Angels, even the one on the extreme western side of the earth.

having the seal] Perhaps this marks this Angel as one specially favoured and trusted: see Gen xli. 42; Esth. iii. 10, viii. 2. But there seems no good reason for the notion, popular in modern times, that this

with a loud voice to the four angels, to whom it was given
3 to hurt the earth and the sea, saying, Hurt not the earth,
neither the sea, nor the trees, till we have sealed the servants
4 of our God in their foreheads. And I heard the number of
them which were sealed: *and there were* sealed an hundred
and forty *and* four thousand of all the tribes of the children
of Israel.

angel, or any other, is to be taken as representative of Christ. He appears, when He does appear, either in His own person, or under a symbol that is obviously symbolic: it would be out of harmony with the scope of this Book, and indeed with New Testament theology generally, to obscure the distinction between Him and created Angels. The words "our God" in the next *v.* marks this Angel as a fellow-servant both of the other four, and of the elect on earth. It is far better to illustrate this vision by Matt. xxiv. 31, as we have seen the earlier images of that chapter reproduced under the former seals. This Angel's office, however, is the marking, not the gathering of the elect: he represents and effectuates God's love in its individual, not in its comprehensive aspect.

to hurt the earth, &c.] viz., by letting the winds forth, to blow and produce storms.

3. *till we have sealed*] The object of the sealing is twofold. (1) to mark them as God's own, beyond the risk of loss; we may almost certainly infer, from this chapter compared with xiv. 1, that the inscription of the seal is the Name of God and of the Lamb; and (2) to mark them as to be saved from the judgements that the other angels are to execute upon the world. Hence we are to compare this sealing, on the one hand with the mark (a less careful and indelible one than here—a cross marked with ink, not a name stamped with a seal) set on the protesting remnant in Ezek. ix. 4, 6 (R. V.): on the other hand, with 2 Tim. ii. 19; Eph. i. 13, iv. 30. It is scarcely likely indeed that St John refers consciously to these passages in St Paul, but it is likely that the image of the seal was the common property of the Apostolic Church, perhaps that the name was already applied, as in later times, to the rite which we call confirmation.

THE SEALING OF THE 144,000, vv. 4—8.

4. *an hundred* and *forty* and *four thousand*] As there are twelve tribes, so in each tribe there are to be twelve thousands: possibly with a reminiscence of the primitive political and military organisation, when a "thousand" was a recognised subdivision of a tribe. See Judges vi. 15; Mic. v. 2. Any way, we are probably to understand that each portion of Israel is a miniature likeness of the whole.

of all the tribes of the children of Israel] It is one of the most controverted of the minor questions of interpretation of this Book, whether Israel is here to be understood in the literal or the spiritual sense. This vision of a certain number of Israelites, and the next of an innumerable multitude of all nations, are certainly correlative to each other: and the

Of the tribe of Juda *were* sealed twelve thousand. 5
Of the tribe of Reuben *were* sealed twelve thousand.
Of the tribe of Gad *were* sealed twelve thousand.
Of the tribe of Aser *were* sealed twelve thousand. 6
Of the tribe of Nephthalim *were* sealed twelve thousand.
Of the tribe of Manasses *were* sealed twelve thousand.
Of the tribe of Simeon *were* sealed twelve thousand. 7
Of the tribe of Levi *were* sealed twelve thousand.
Of the tribe of Isachar *were* sealed twelve thousand.

most obvious way of understanding them is, that among God's elect there will be many faithful Israelites, and yet few comparatively to the number of faithful Gentiles. Others however understand these 144,000, and the innumerable multitude of *v.* 9, to represent the same persons regarded in two different aspects. To God they are all His own people, all duly numbered and organised and marshalled as His army, and everyone known to Him by name: on the other hand, from a human point of view they belong to all nations, and are too many to be counted. Lastly, in xiv. 1 we hear of a company of 144,000 whom (not from their number only) it is natural to identify with these: and it appears that these represent, not the whole multitude of the elect, but a group specially faithful and specially favoured, even among them. It seems worth asking, whether the true solution be not a combination of the first and last, whether we are to understand that Christ's nearest and dearest ones still come from God's old people, who are still "beloved for the fathers' sake," though they attain such nearness to Him, not by virtue of their descent, but by graces of the same kind as sanctify Gentile saints also.

5—8. *Were sealed* is not genuine except in the first and last clauses: and even then it is strictly a participle, not a verb: read "**of the tribe of Judah, 12,000 sealed, of the tribe of Reuben, 12,000, of the tribe of Gad, 12,000, &c.... of the tribe of Benjamin 12,000 sealed.**" It is a question whether there is any principle in the order of the names. Judah is no doubt named first, as the tribe of David and of the Son of David: then Reuben as the eldest son of Israel, while Joseph and Benjamin, the two youngest, come last. Gad and Asher, Simeon and Levi, Issachar and Zebulun are also mentioned in pairs, according to their parentage and the order of their births: but the pairs themselves are not grouped either in order of age or of the dignity of the mother. It is curious, and has never been really satisfactorily accounted for, that while we have *Joseph* given under that name, instead of *Ephraim*, we have Manasseh mentioned coordinately as one of the twelve tribes: room being made for him, not as in many O.T. enumerations, by the omission of Levi, who had no part nor inheritance with his brethren, but by the omission of Dan. Num. xiii. 11 is some sort of analogy for the name of Joseph being appropriated to one of the two tribes descended from him: for the omission of Dan, the nearest analogy is the omission of Simeon in the blessing of Moses, Deut. xxxiii. The traditional view is, that Dan

8 Of the tribe of Zabulon *were* sealed twelve thousand.
Of the tribe of Joseph *were* sealed twelve thousand.
Of the tribe of Benjamin *were* sealed twelve thousand.
9 After this I beheld, and lo, a great multitude, which no *man* could number, of all nations, and kindreds, and people, and tongues, stood before the throne, and before the Lamb, 10 clothed with white robes, and palms in their hands; and cried with a loud voice, saying, Salvation to our God which 11 sitteth upon the throne, and unto the Lamb. And all the angels stood round about the throne, and *about* the elders

is omitted because Antichrist will come of that tribe: but the grounds for that opinion are very slight; it rests mainly on this omission itself, for no one would naturally understand Gen. xlix. 17 as implying that Dan would be an evil power. Others have suggested that Dan is omitted because they early fell into idolatry (Judg. xviii.); but all Israel fell into worse idolatry, sooner or later: others again imagine that this tribe had been long extinct, because it is omitted in the enumeration of the tribes in the early chapters of Chronicles: but Zebulun is also omitted there, though both tribes were powerful in David's time, 1 Chr. xii. 33, 35. The case is not quite parallel where, in xxi. 12, 14, we have only room for the names of twelve tribes and twelve apostles: it will follow from Ezek. xlviii. 31—34, that Dan *is* there included, and that Joseph only counts as one: and though either the name of St Paul or St Matthias (probably the former) must be omitted to keep the number of the apostles down to twelve, yet the omission is not pointed or express. We have no occasion to ask there *why* St Paul is omitted, while here we cannot help asking why Dan is: probably there is a reason, but we had better confess we do not know it. It is worth noticing that in *v.* 7 there is some authority for the reading *Isaschar*—the name is always so spelt in the O.T., though traditionally pronounced as in the A.V.

THE PRAISE OF THE GREAT MULTITUDE OF THE REDEEMED, vv. 9—17.

9. *of all nations, and kindreds,* &c.] Lit. **out of every nation, and tribes, and peoples, and tongues.**
white robes] Cf. iii. 5, vi. 11.
palms] Opinions differ as to the meaning of this image, whether we are to compare the Pagan use of the palm-branch as a symbol of victory, given e.g. to winners at the public games, or the Israelite custom of bearing branches of palm, as of other sacred trees, at the Feast of Tabernacles: see Lev. xxiii. 40, and cf. St John xii. 13. Although Jewish rather than Gentile imagery is to be expected in this book, the former view seems on the whole more reasonable, as it gives a more obvious and a more appropriate meaning to the symbol.
10. *Salvation to our God*] The word "salvation" has the article, according to Hebrew usage, as, e.g. Ps. iii. 8 [Heb. 9], where the article

and the four beasts, and fell before the throne on their faces, and worshipped God, saying, Amen: Blessing, and glory, and wisdom, and thanksgiving, and honour, and power, and might, *be* unto our God for ever and ever. Amen. And one of the elders answered, saying unto me, What are these which are arrayed in white robes? and whence came they? And I said unto him, Sir, thou knowest. And he said to me, These are they which came out of great tribulation, and have washed their robes, and have made them white in the blood of the Lamb. Therefore are they before the throne of God, and serve him day and night in his temple: and he that sitteth on the throne shall dwell among them. They

may denote either "the promised salvation" or the salvation in all its fulness including *victory*. We must remember that "salvation" is in the Bible a positive conception—not only being saved *from* some evil, but being placed in a state of positive blessedness: and these words will thus be a confession that such blessedness not only is of God, but belongs by right to God.

12. *Blessing, and glory* &c.] The seven words of praise have each the article: see on ch. v. 13.

13. *one of the elders*] See on v. 5. We have similarly "one (no matter which) of the seven Angels" in xvii. 1, xxi. 9.

14. *Sir*] Read, **My lord**: cf. Dan. x. 16, 17; Zech. iv. 5, 13. In the latter place we have, as here, the heavenly interlocutor apparently assuming that the Seer ought to understand the vision without explanation.

thou knowest] Cf. Ezek. xxxvii. 3.

which came] More accurately, **which come**.

great tribulation] Should be, **the great tribulation**: the article is strongly emphasised. It probably means, "*the* great tribulation foretold by the Lord," St Matt. xxiv. 21: cf. Dan. xii. 1. For a similar use of the art. cf. ch. i. 7, "*the* clouds."

made them white in the blood] A paradox something like that of vi. 16 fin. For the image, cf. perhaps i. 5 (but see note there); certainly xxii. 14 (true text), and probably St John Ep. I. i. 7. Heb. ix. 14, which is sometimes quoted, is less closely parallel: there the image seems to be taken from ritual rather than physical cleansing.

15. *before the throne*] Perhaps in a more favoured position than is given to *all*, even among Saints: as we have similar language about the most favoured Angels, Matt. xviii. 10; Luke i. 19.

serve Him] Cf. xxii. 3. The sense would be clearer if the word were rendered "worship:" it does not mean that they have active work to do for Him, but that they do what is the appropriate service of His Temple.

shall dwell among them] Rather, as R. V., **shall spread his tabernacle over them**: in xxi. 3 the verb is the same, but there the preposition

shall hunger no more, neither thirst any more; neither shall the sun light on them, nor any heat. 17 For the Lamb which is in the midst of the throne shall feed them, and shall lead them unto living fountains of waters: and God shall wipe away all tears from their eyes.

8 And when he had opened the seventh seal, there was silence in heaven about the space of half an hour.

"with" is right. The word is used in the N. T., and in Hellenistic writers generally, to express the dwelling of the Divine Presence in any of its manifestations: see esp. St John's Gospel, i. 14. The Greek word for "tabernacle," *scēnē*, was the more readily used in this sense because of its assonance with the late Hebrew word *Shĕchínăh* for "the cloud of glory shadowing the Mercy-seat." Here perhaps the thought is rather of that manifestation of God's Presence than of the fuller and later Presence in the Incarnation.

16, 17. Taken from Is. xlix. 10. We have again the solemn paradox, that the Lamb is Shepherd (of course we are reminded of St John x., but we ought to remember Ps. xxiii. as well, and its many O. T. imitations, including Is. l.c., in all of which the Shepherd is the Lord God of Israel), and the men are His flock—cf. Ezek. xxxiv. 31, xxxvi. 37, 38.

that is in the midst of the throne] See on v. 6.

living fountains of waters] Lit., **fountains of waters of life**, cf. xxii. 1: but the A.V. is right, in keeping the order of the words rather than the construction.

God shall wipe &c.] From Is. xxv. 8.

The Seventh Seal. Chap. VIII. v. 1.

1. *there was silence*] All the promised signs of Christ's Coming have been fulfilled—everything has, apparently, been made ready for it: and we expect Him to come, and the world to come to an end: but the series of signs concludes—not with a catastrophe but—in silence. The same is the case, though less markedly, after the seventh trumpet in ch. xi. 15; and in fact, similar cases occur throughout the book. We have the choice between three explanations of this phenomenon. (I.) The preceding series of visions does describe the events leading up to Christ's Coming: when they are ended, He does come, but His Coming itself is not described. Here, it is passed over in silence, or only symbolised by the opening of the seventh seal: the half-hour's silence is, as St Victorinus grandly says, "*initium quietis aeternae*." (II.) The previous series of visions describes events preparatory, indeed, to Christ's Coming, but not leading directly up to it: the events symbolised by these visions *have* been fulfilled, but those of the rest of the Book must be fulfilled also, before He really comes. (III.) These visions represent, *on a smaller scale*, the preparations for Christ's final Coming and Judgement: but they do not wait for their fulfilment

and the four beasts, and fell before the throne on their faces, and worshipped God, saying, Amen: Blessing, and glory, and wisdom, and thanksgiving, and honour, and power, and might, *be* unto our God for ever and ever. Amen. And one of the elders answered, saying unto me, What are these which are arrayed in white robes? and whence came they? And I said unto him, Sir, thou knowest. And he said to me, These are they which came out of great tribulation, and have washed their robes, and have made them white in the blood of the Lamb. Therefore are they before the throne of God, and serve him day and night in his temple: and he that sitteth on the throne shall dwell among them. They

may denote either "the promised salvation" or the salvation in all its fulness including *victory*. We must remember that "salvation" is in the Bible a positive conception—not only being saved *from* some evil, but being placed in a state of positive blessedness: and these words will thus be a confession that such blessedness not only is of God, but belongs by right to God.

12. *Blessing, and glory* &c.] The seven words of praise have each the article: see on ch. v. 13.

13. *one of the elders*] See on v. 5. We have similarly "one (no matter which) of the seven Angels" in xvii. 1, xxi. 9.

14. *Sir*] Read, **My lord**: cf. Dan. x. 16, 17; Zech. iv. 5, 13. In the latter place we have, as here, the heavenly interlocutor apparently assuming that the Seer ought to understand the vision without explanation.

thou knowest] Cf. Ezek. xxxvii. 3.

which came] More accurately, **which come**.

great tribulation] Should be, **the great tribulation**: the article is strongly emphasised. It probably means, "*the* great tribulation foretold by the Lord," St Matt. xxiv. 21: cf. Dan. xii. 1. For a similar use of the art. cf. ch. i. 7, "*the* clouds."

made them white in the blood] A paradox something like that of vi. 16 fin. For the image, cf. perhaps i. 5 (but see note there); certainly xxii. 14 (true text), and probably St John Ep. 1. i. 7. Heb. ix. 14, which is sometimes quoted, is less closely parallel: there the image seems to be taken from ritual rather than physical cleansing.

15. *before the throne*] Perhaps in a more favoured position than is given to *all*, even among Saints: as we have similar language about the most favoured Angels, Matt. xviii. 10; Luke i. 19.

serve Him] Cf. xxii. 3. The sense would be clearer if the word were rendered "worship:" it does not mean that they have active work to do for Him, but that they do what is the appropriate service of His Temple.

shall dwell among them] Rather, as R. V., **shall spread his tabernacle over them**: in xxi. 3 the verb is the same, but there the preposition

shall hunger no more, neither thirst any more; neither shall the sun light on them, nor any heat. 17 For the Lamb which is in the midst of the throne shall feed them, and shall lead them unto living fountains of waters: and God shall wipe away all tears from their eyes.

8 And when he had opened the seventh seal, there was silence in heaven about the space of half an hour.

"with" is right. The word is used in the N. T., and in Hellenistic writers generally, to express the dwelling of the Divine Presence in any of its manifestations: see esp. St John's Gospel, i. 14. The Greek word for "tabernacle," *scēnē*, was the more readily used in this sense because of its assonance with the late Hebrew word *Shěchīnāh* for "the cloud of glory shadowing the Mercy-seat." Here perhaps the thought is rather of that manifestation of God's Presence than of the fuller and later Presence in the Incarnation.

16, 17. Taken from Is. xlix. 10. We have again the solemn paradox, that the Lamb is Shepherd (of course we are reminded of St John x., but we ought to remember Ps. xxiii. as well, and its many O.T. imitations, including Is. l.c., in all of which the Shepherd is the Lord God of Israel), and the men are His flock—cf. Ezek. xxxiv. 31, xxxvi. 37, 38.

that is in the midst of the throne] See on v. 6.

living fountains of waters] Lit., **fountains of waters of life**, cf. xxii. 1: but the A.V. is right, in keeping the order of the words rather than the construction.

God shall wipe &c.] From Is. xxv. 8.

THE SEVENTH SEAL. CHAP. VIII. v. 1.

1. *there was silence*] All the promised signs of Christ's Coming have been fulfilled—everything has, apparently, been made ready for it: and we expect Him to come, and the world to come to an end: but the series of signs concludes—not with a catastrophe but—in silence. The same is the case, though less markedly, after the seventh trumpet in ch. xi. 15; and in fact, similar cases occur throughout the book. We have the choice between three explanations of this phenomenon. (I.) The preceding series of visions does describe the events leading up to Christ's Coming: when they are ended, He does come, but His Coming itself is not described. Here, it is passed over in silence, or only symbolised by the opening of the seventh seal: the half-hour's silence is, as St Victorinus grandly says, "*initium quietis aeternae.*" (II.) The previous series of visions describes events preparatory, indeed, to Christ's Coming, but not leading directly up to it: the events symbolised by these visions *have* been fulfilled, but those of the rest of the Book must be fulfilled also, before He really comes. (III.) These visions represent, *on a smaller scale*, the preparations for Christ's final Coming and Judgement: but they do not wait for their fulfilment

And I saw the seven angels which stood before God; 2
and to them were given seven trumpets. And another angel 3
came and stood at the altar, having a golden censer; and
there was given unto him much incense, that he should offer

till then, but have their proportionate fulfilment in any anticipatory
judgement which He executes on one nation or generation. The similar series of visions which follow are therefore not parallel with this,
but successive: again and again God executes His Judgements, fore-
shadowing the last Judgement of all, and leading men to expect it:
and at last He will execute that also. The last view is the one generally taken in these notes: see Introduction, p. lv. On any view it is
a pity that this verse is joined with this chapter rather than with the
preceding: the blowing of the seven trumpets can hardly be regarded
as the effect of the opening the seal.

THE SEVEN TRUMPETS. CHAP. VIII. 2—XI. 19.

2. *the seven angels which stood*] Should be, **which stand**. It is
probably a designation of seven Angels (commonly, perhaps correctly,
called Archangels) who permanently enjoy special nearness to God.
We have in Tobit xii. 15 an evidence of popular Jewish belief as to
these Angels; St John's vision is expressed in terms of that belief,
and, it may fairly be thought, sanctions it with his prophetic authority.

THE ANGEL WITH THE GOLDEN CENSER, vv. 3—6.

3. *another angel*] In Tobit, l.c. it is the seven Angels themselves
who present the prayers of the Saints before God: but, though the detail
varies, the passages agree in assigning a priestly word to Angels on
behalf of God's people on earth.

at the altar] More literally, **on the altar**, R. V. "over the altar."
The golden altar of Incense in the Tabernacle was only a cubit square
and two cubits high (Ex. xxx. 2), and we have no reason to suppose
that the analogous one either in the first or the second Temple was
larger: perhaps we may gather from 2 Chr. v. 5, that the altar in the
first Temple was identical with the one in the Tabernacle. But the
altar of burnt-offering was rather a large platform than what we commonly imagine an altar (see 1 Macc. i. 59, where the small Greek "idol
altar" stands *on* the "altar of God" as its basement—it cannot be substituted for it): in the Tabernacle it was 5 cubits square, in Solomon's
Temple 20, in Zerubbabel's probably the same, and in Herod's 50
according to Josephus, 32 according to the Mishna. In the Temple at
any rate, the height of the altar was such that the officiating priests had
to come up upon a ledge surrounding it (and such an ascent is contemplated in Ex. xx. 26). Probably here, though the Angel is offering
incense not burnt offering, the Altar where he officiates is conceived as
rather of the larger type: see on vi. 9.

censer] Plainly the sense here, though the Greek word properly
means "incense."

it with the prayers of all saints upon the golden altar which
4 was before the throne. And the smoke of the incense, *which came* with the prayers of the saints, ascended up be-
5 fore God out of the angel's hand. And the angel took the censer, and filled it with fire of the altar, and cast *it* into the earth: and there were voices, and thunderings, and
6 lightnings, and an earthquake. And the seven angels which had the seven trumpets prepared themselves to sound.

7 The first angel sounded, and there followed hail and fire

offer it with] Literally, **give** (i.e. add) **it to the prayers**; and if the literal translation requires a gloss, that of the A.V. can hardly be the right one. Apparently the image is, that the prayers of the Saints are already lying on the Altar, and the Angel, in modern liturgical phrase, "censes the holy things." Thus disappears the supposed theological necessity for identifying this Angel with the Lord Jesus: "the prayers of all saints" are presented by Him and by no one else, as is implied in v. 8, 9; where the incense *is* the prayers of the Saints, not something added to them. But here the Angels offer their own worship, as it is "given to them," in union, perhaps in subordination, to those of the redeemed. The prayers here spoken of are those of *all* saints, not of the Martyrs exclusively: still, it is well to notice that the Altar where *we* offer our prayers is apparently the same where *they* poured out their lives, vi. 9.

4. *which came with*] Again a misleading gloss: the most literal translation is, **and there went up the smoke of the incense for the prayers of the saints, out of the hand of the Angel, before God.** It went up for the prayers of the Saints, i.e. to consecrate and ratify them, to unite *all* His spiritual creation in the same supplication, which when thus united must prevail: or "for" may be equivalent only to "with."

5. *and cast it*] Probably cast the censer full of burning coals, but possibly only "scattered the fire," as Num. xvi. 37. The meaning must be, to represent the same instrument as obtaining God's mercy on His people, and executing His vengeance on His enemies: cf. Ezek. x. 2.

there were voices, &c.] "Voices" and "thunders" should be transposed. We have similar signs in xi. 19, xvi. 18, when the series of the seven trumpets and the seven vials respectively are ended: hence perhaps it is here rather than earlier that we are to look for the conclusion of the visions of the seven seals.

THE FIRST TRUMPET, v. 7.

7. *The first angel*] Read, **And the first.**
hail and fire mingled with blood] Cf. Ex. ix. 24: but here the *blood* marks the plague as more terrible, and more distinctly mira-

mingled with blood, and they were cast upon the earth: and the third *part* of trees was burnt up, and all green grass was burnt up.

And the second angel sounded, and as *it were* a great 8 mountain burning with fire was cast into the sea: and the third *part* of the sea became blood; and the third *part* of 9 the creatures which were in the sea, and had life, died; and the third *part* of the ships were destroyed.

And the third angel sounded, and there fell a great star 10 from heaven, burning as *it were* a lamp, and it fell upon the third *part* of the rivers, and upon the fountains of waters; and the name of the star is called Wormwood: and the third 11

culous. "The stones of hail and the balls of fire fell in a shower of blood, just as hail and fire balls commonly fall in a shower of rain." (Alford).

the third part] Read, **The third part of the earth was burnt up, and the third part of the trees was burnt up, and all green grass was burnt up.** It is certainly a feature to be noticed in the first four trumpets, as contrasted (see on vi. 9) with the last three, that they introduce plagues (i), on the powers of nature only, not on men, and (ii) that on these the plague stops short of entire destruction. But no plausible explanation has been given of the destruction of a *third part* (cf. vi. 8): still less can any reason be given why *all* green grass is destroyed, apparently not a third part only. The former feature is *perhaps* to be illustrated by Ezek. v. 2; Zech. xiii. 8, 9.

THE SECOND TRUMPET, vv. 8, 9.

8. *a great mountain burning with fire*] Cf. Jer. li. 25. It can hardly be said how far the image may have been suggested to either prophet by the natural phenomenon of a volcano: of the two, St John is likelier to have seen one than Jeremiah. Volcanoes are almost always near the sea.

became blood] This plague, like the last, reminds us of one of the plagues of Egypt, Ex. vii. 17 sqq.

THE THIRD TRUMPET, vv. 10, 11.

10. *burning as it were a lamp*] Rather, **like a torch**, with a flaring trail of fire. The same image is used of natural shooting stars, e.g. Verg. *Aen.* ii. 694.

11. *became wormwood*] We are perhaps to be reminded, as before, of the plagues in Egypt, so here of the mercy to Israel, Ex. xv. 25: here, as those are intensified, so that is reversed.

part of the waters became wormwood; and many men died of the waters, because they were made bitter. 12 And the fourth angel sounded, and the third *part* of the sun was smitten, and the third *part* of the moon, and the third *part* of the stars; so as the third *part* of them was darkened and the day shone not for a third *part* of it, and 13 the night likewise. And I beheld, and heard an angel flying through the midst of heaven, saying with a loud voice, Woe, woe, woe, to the inhabiters of the earth by reason of the other voices of the trumpet of the three angels, which are yet to sound.

many men died] Of course such water would be unwholesome for ordinary use, though wormwood is not exactly poisonous. But it may be a question whether St John means the name to indicate the herb now known as wormwood, or another more deadly one: *poison* seems to be meant in Deut. xxix. 18; Jer. ix. 15, xxiii. 15. The root of the Hebrew word there rendered "wormwood" seems to mean "noxious."

The Fourth Trumpet, vv. 12, 13.

12. *the third part of the sun*, &c.] Here we may think either of the Egyptian plague of darkness, Ex. x. 21 sqq., or of a *reversal* (as in the last case) of the blessing of Is. xxx. 26. There, as here, there seems to be no distinction made between an increase, or decrease, in the *intensity* of light and in its *duration*.

so as the third part of them was] More accurately, **that the third part of them might** (lit. **may**) "be darkened, and the day not shine, &c."

13. *an angel*] Read, **an eagle**: or more literally **one eagle**. But apparently there was a tendency in late Hebrew for the numeral to sink, as in modern languages, into a mere indefinite article; and here, and perhaps in one or two other places, we seem to have it so used in the N. T.: e.g. Matt. viii. 19, xxvi. 69, and probably ix. 18.

through the midst of heaven] Rather, **in mid-heaven**: it is a single compound word. It occurs again in xiv. 6, xix. 17, and nowhere else in the N. T.: but in the later classical Greek it is not uncommon for the position of the sun at noonday. Yet the last of the places cited from this book, where all natural birds are said to fly "in mid-heaven," seems rather as if St John used it of the *air*, the space between earth and sky.

Woe, woe, woe] We see by ix. 12, xi. 14 that three *distinct* woes are meant, one for each of the three trumpets.

And the fifth angel sounded, and I saw a star fall from 9
heaven unto the earth: and to him was given the key of the
bottomless pit. And he opened the bottomless pit; and 2
there arose a smoke out of the pit, as the smoke of a great
furnace; and the sun and the air were darkened by reason
of the smoke of the pit. And there came out of the smoke 3
locusts upon the earth: and unto them was given power,
as the scorpions of the earth have power. And it was com- 4
manded them that they should not hurt the grass of the
earth, neither any green *thing*, neither any tree; but only
those men which have not the seal of God in their foreheads.
And to them it was given that they should not kill them, but 5

THE FIFTH TRUMPET. FIRST WOE. CHAP. IX. vv. 1—12.

1. *fall from heaven*] Rather, **fallen.** St John does not say that he witnessed the actual fall.

to him was given] Clearly therefore the star is identified with a person: no doubt a "fallen angel," in the common sense of the term. For the identification of angels with stars, cf. i. 20, and Job xxxviii. 7: and of *fallen* angels in particular, Enoch xviii. 16, xxi. 3, &c. The fall of this star may legitimately be *illustrated*, as to the image by Is. xiv. 12, and as to the meaning by Luke x. 18, and xii. 9 in this book: but it is not to be assumed that this passage refers to the same event as either of the two last, still less that the first does.

of the bottomless pit] Lit. **of the pit** (or **well**) **of the abyss**: the depth of Hell, the home or penal prison of the demons (see Luke viii. 31, where the word translated "the deep" is the same), is conceived as a pit in the earth's surface, no doubt literally bottomless, but of finite area, so that it can be fitted with a cover which can be fastened down with a padlock or seal. Cf. xi. 7, xvii. 8, for the notion of evil beings issuing from the pit; xx. 1, 3, for their being confined there. But notice (i) that this pit is nowhere identified with the "lake of fire," the *final* destination of the Devil and his angels: (ii) that we are not told that the Devil himself is cast into it yet; rather the contrary is implied.

3. *the scorpions of the earth*] i.e. common natural scorpions: these infernal locusts are able to hurt men, as common scorpions are, but common locusts are not.

4. *that they should not hurt the grass*, &c.] i.e. *not* to do the damage that natural locusts do—these natural objects having been plagued already, viii. 7—but other damage, still more directly distressing the sinful world.

the seal of God] See vii. 3 and note.

that they should be tormented five months: and their torment *was* as the torment of a scorpion, when he striketh a
6 man. And in those days shall men seek death, and shall not find it; and shall desire to die, and death shall flee from
7 them. And the shapes of the locusts *were* like unto horses prepared unto battle; and on their heads *were* as *it were* crowns like gold, and their faces *were* as the faces of men.
8 And they had hair as the hair of women, and their teeth
9 were as *the teeth* of lions. And they had breastplates, as *it were* breastplates of iron; and the sound of their wings *was* as the sound of chariots of many horses running to battle.
10 And they had tails like unto scorpions, and there were stings in their tails: and their power *was* to hurt men five months.

5. *five months*] It has been conjectured that this period is named, as being the time for which a plague of the literal locusts is liable to last. But more probably the period is to be reckoned on the same principle—whatever that be—as the other periods of time indicated in this book.

6. *shall flee*] Lit. **fleeth**.

7. *like unto horses*] See Joel ii. 4. *Probably* that passage is only a highly idealised description of a natural swarm of locusts, and the verse cited refers to the resemblance in shape of the locust's head, and perhaps the legs, to a horse's. It is doubtful whether the words "**prepared unto battle**" (more accurately "**unto war**") suggest comparison between the frame of the locust and the plate-armour of a horse: such armour was rarely used in ancient times. More probably the comparison here is to the *discipline* of the locust host: as in Joel ii. 7, 8.

as it were crowns like gold] Lit. **as it were crowns like unto gold**—perhaps a mere golden mark, such as it is quite possible a real insect might have. But,

their faces were as the faces of men] Marks them distinctly as differing from real locusts. The word used for "men" means, in classical Greek at least, "human beings," not necessarily males. But in Hellenistic Greek it is not infrequently used in opposition to women, and probably the next clause marks it so here.

8. *as the hair of women*] It is said that, in Arabic poetry, the same comparison is used of the antennæ of the natural locust: but more probably this is one of the supernatural features of the description.

teeth of lions] Joel i. 6.

9. *breastplates of iron*] This probably *is* an idealisation of the structure of the natural locust.

chariots] Joel ii. 5.

10. *And they had...in their tails*] Read, **And they have tails like**

And they had a king over them, *which is* the angel of the 11
bottomless *pit*, whose name in the Hebrew tongue *is* Abaddon, but in the Greek *tongue* hath *his* name Apollyon. One 12
woe is past; *and* behold, there come two woes more hereafter.
And the sixth angel sounded, and I heard a voice from 13
the four horns of the golden altar which is before God, saying 14
to the sixth angel which had the trumpet, Loose the four

unto scorpions, and stings: and in their tails [is] their power, to hurt," &c.

11. *And they had a king*] Whereas "the (natural) locusts have no king," Prov. xxx. 27. In Amos vii. 1 the LXX. has the curious mistranslation or corrupt reading, "and behold one locust grub [was] Gog the king;" which possibly arose from, or suggested, a superstition that St John uses as an image.

the angel of the bottomless pit] Either the fallen star of *v.* 1, who opened the pit and let them out of it, or a spirit—presumably, if not quite certainly, a bad one—made the guardian of that lowest deep of God's creation. See Excursus I.

Abaddon] Properly an abstract noun, "destruction," but used apparently in the sense of "Hell" in Job xxvi. 6, &c. But

Apollyon] is a participle, "destroying," and so "Destroyer."

12. *One woe*] Of the three denounced by the eagle, viii. 13. A decided majority of orthodox commentators understand this vision as foretelling the Mahometan conquests—some taking the fallen star of *v.* 1 of Mahomet himself. The last is scarcely credible—unless one should adopt the view,—not perhaps inconsistent with the facts of Mahomet's career, but hardly in harmony with the general order of Revelation—that he really had a divine commission, but perverted it to serve his selfish ambition. It seems almost certain that the "star" is an angel, strictly speaking: but the interpretation as a whole seems worthy of respect. Perhaps the Mahometan conquest is to be regarded as at least a partial fulfilment of this prophecy: but the attempts to shew that it is in detail an exact fulfilment have not been very successful.

THE SIXTH TRUMPET. SECOND WOE, vv. 13—21.

13. *a voice*] Lit. **one voice**: see on viii. 13. The word "four" just afterwards should probably be omitted: else "one voice from the four horns" would give the numeral a special meaning.

14. *Loose the four angels*] We are reminded of the four angels of vii. 1, but it is hardly possible that they are the same as these. The plagues held back by them, on "the earth, the sea, and the trees," have come already, viii. 7—9: moreover, these angels do not stand "on the four corners of the earth," but in one not very remote part of it. No satisfactory explanation of their meaning has been

15 angels which are bound in the great river Euphrates. And the four angels were loosed, which were prepared for an hour, and a day, and a month, and a year, for to slay the 16 third *part* of men. And the number of the army of the horsemen *were* two hundred thousand thousand: and I 17 heard the number of them. And thus I saw the horses in the vision, and them that sat on them, having breastplates of fire, and of jacinth, and brimstone: and the heads of the horses *were* as the heads of lions; and out of their mouths

given: nor can we be sure whether the name Euphrates is to be taken literally. We hear of it again in xvi. 12, where the arguments for and against a literal interpretation seem almost equally balanced.

15. *for an hour*] Should be "for the hour." The article is not repeated, but plainly the one article belongs to all the nouns: they are "prepared for the hour, and day, and month, and year," when God has decreed to execute the vengeance here foretold.

16. *of the horsemen*] It is implied that the *way* the four angels will slay the third part of men will be by means of a vast invading army. The word rendered "horsemen" is not here plural but collective, as we should say "the cavalry." But it is not that he gives the number of one arm only of an army containing more: apparently this army consists of cavalry exclusively. This illustrates the use of the name Euphrates, just so far as to make it possible that the image was suggested to St John's mind by the fact that the Parthian cavalry were the most formidable barbarian force of his own day. More than this we can hardly say, as to the meaning of the vision, and any partial fulfilment that it may have had or be about to have.

two hundred thousand thousand] The number is perhaps suggested by Ps. lxviii. 17: still, it hardly seems as if these horsemen were celestial (like those of xix. 14), though they are not distinctly infernal, like the locusts of the previous visions.

and I heard] Omit "and."

17. *having breastplates*] This must be understood of the riders chiefly, but perhaps not exclusively: comparing ver. 9 we cannot be sure that St John would not use the word "breastplate" of the defensive armour of a horse, if he had such in his mind. In fact, the word is used in later Greek of defensive armour generally, not the breastplate only.

of fire, and of jacinth, and brimstone] All these are expressed in Greek by adjectives. The last means only "*like* brimstone;" and though the terminations of the two former would properly indicate the material, yet the "jacinth" seems so incongruous with the other two, that it is easiest to understand all three as referring to colour only: they had breastplates of fiery red, of smoky blue, and of sulphurous yellow. Whether all had tricoloured armour, or whether there were three divisions, each in a distinctive uniform, may be doubted: but the three plagues corresponding to these colours, which we hear of directly after,

issued fire and smoke and brimstone. By these three was 18
the third *part* of men killed, by the fire, and by the smoke,
and by the brimstone, which issued out of their mouths.
For their power is in their mouth, and in their tails: for 19
their tails *were* like unto serpents, and had heads, and with
them they do hurt. And the rest of the men which were 20
not killed by these plagues *yet* repented not of the works of
their hands, that they should not worship devils, and idols
of gold, and silver, and brass, and stone, and of wood:
which neither can see, nor hear, nor walk: neither repented 21
they of their murders, nor of their sorceries, nor of their
fornication, nor of their thefts.

And I saw another mighty angel come down from heaven, 10
clothed with a cloud: and a rainbow *was* upon *his* head,

are almost certainly inflicted by the whole army alike: and this affords some presumption that the attire of all was symbolical of all three.

18. *By these three*] Read, **by** (lit. *from*) **these three plagues were the third part of men killed, by the fire, and the smoke, and the brimstone,** &c.

19. *For their power*] Read, **for the power of the horses.** For the use of the word "power" (the same as is sometimes elsewhere translated "authority" or "licence"), cf. vi. 8, ver. 3: St Luke xxii. 53 illustrates the meaning of the word in such a context.

20. *that they should not worship.. idols*] This verse gives us the only clue we have to the interpretation. It is a plague on *idolaters* that is here described—neither on unfaithful Christians, nor on antichristian infidels of a more refined type—unless the latter shall in the last days, as in the age of the Roman persecutions, and one may almost say of the Renaissance and Reformation, ally itself against the Gospel with the vulgar or sensuous idolatry which it was its natural tendency to despise.

21. *sorceries*] Fitly mentioned between "murders" and "fornication," and in connexion with "idolatry;" cf. Gal. v. 20, and note on xxi. 8.

THE ANGEL WITH THE LITTLE BOOK. CHAP. X.

1. We are not told yet, as we might expect, that "the second woe is past," nor does the seventh trumpet and the third woe immediately follow: but just as in ch. vii. the two descriptions of the sealed Israelites and the palm-bearing multitude came after the sixth seal, so here the vision of the mighty angel, and the prophecy (passing insensibly into a vision) of the Two Witnesses, follow the sixth trumpet.

another mighty angel] "Another," probably, than the four mentioned

and his face *was* as *it were* the sun, and his feet as pillars
2 of fire : and he had in his hand a little book open : and he
set his right foot upon the sea, and *his* left *foot* on the earth,
3 and cried with a loud voice, as *when* a lion roareth : and
when he had cried, seven thunders uttered their voices.
4 And when the seven thunders had uttered their voices, I
was about to write : and I heard a voice from heaven saying
unto me, Seal *up those things* which the seven thunders
5 uttered, and write them not. And the angel which I saw

in ix. 15: cf. vii. 1, 2. Some suppose a reference back to v. 2, where we have heard of a "mighty angel" (the epithet is the same) before.

clothed with a cloud] And therefore with something of the state with which Christ will come to judgement: cf. i. 7, &c.

a rainbow] Lit. **the rainbow**: it is conceived as being the same bow of God that is seen every time that it appears.

his feet] i.e. his legs are as thick as the pillars of a temple, and their substance of fiery brightness.

2. *a little book*] The diminutive perhaps suggests comparison (but hardly contrast) with the book of v. 1 seqq.

3. *seven thunders*] Lit. **the seven thunders**. The only reason that we can imagine for the presence of the article is, that to St John's mind "the seven thunders" formed one element in the vision; as we might speak of "the seven seals," "the seven trumpets," "the seven vials"—these being known to us, as the thunders also were to him.

their voices] The possessive is emphatic, "*their own* voices." Perhaps the meaning is, "each uttered its own." It has been taken to imply that the voices of the thunders were not the voice of God: but comparing I's. xxix. *passim*; St John xii. 28—9, it is scarcely possible to doubt that these thunders, voices from heaven, are from God, or at least directed by Him.

4. *I was about to write*] See i. 19. It is useless to speculate how far the book was written at the same time that the vision was seen: possibly it may have been in part, but it is enough to suppose that, having been bidden to write, the seer seemed to himself to write, or (so to speak) saw himself writing, at appropriate points of the vision.

Seal up] Cf. Dan. xii. 4, 9. There the use of the words is more logical: Daniel is to write the vision, but not to let it be read: contrast in this book xxii. 10. Here the use of the word is suggested by the passage in Daniel—in the impassioned style of this book it is forgotten that what is not written cannot and need not be sealed. *Why* the voices of the thunders were not to be written it is idle to guess: it is worse than idle to guess what they were. And in our ignorance of this it is hardly possible that we should be able to identify the mission of this angel with any special dispensation of God yet known.

5. *lifted up his hand to heaven*] Read, "his **right** hand." Cf. Dan. xii. 7, where the angel lifts up *both* hands: here, his left is occupied

stand upon the sea and upon the earth lifted up his hand to heaven, and sware by him that liveth for ever and ever, who created heaven, and the *things* that therein are, and the earth, and the *things* that therein are, and the sea, and the *things* which are therein, that there should be time no longer: but in the days of the voice of the seventh angel, when he shall begin to sound, the mystery of God should be finished, as he hath declared to his servants the prophets.

And the voice which I heard from heaven spake unto me again, and said, Go *and* take the little book which is open in the hand of the angel which standeth upon the sea and upon the earth. And I went unto the angel, and said unto him, Give me the little book. And he said unto me, Take *it*, and eat it up; and it shall make thy belly bitter, but it

with the book. For the gesture symbolic of an oath see Gen. xiv. 22, &c.

6. *sware by him*] This angel therefore is in no sense a divine Person.

6, 7. *that there shall be time no longer: but*] i.e. as we say, "there shall be no more time *lost*, but"...: "there shall be delay no longer." It is not in harmony with the usual language of Scripture to suppose that finite "time" is meant to be opposed to eternity.

7. *when he shall begin to sound*] More accurately, "when he shall be **about to sound.**"

the mystery of God] Here Abp. Whately's paradox is hardly an exaggeration, that for "mystery" one might substitute "revelation," without altering the sense: see on i. 20.

shall be finished] The construction in the Greek is curious, but it is probably a mere Hebraism, and the sense of the A.V. right.

declared] The word is the characteristic *evangelical* one, "told the good news."

8. *spake unto me again*] The true reading is scarcely grammatical, but must mean "[I heard] again speaking unto me."

9. *I went*] Apparently from his place in heaven to the earth: but there are difficulties in tracing coherently the changes in the point of view.

and said unto him, Give me, &c.] Read, **saying unto him that he should give me.**

eat it up] Ezek. ii. 8, iii. 3.

it shall make thy belly bitter] This Ezekiel's roll did *not* do. We may presume that this little book, like the O.T. one, contained "lamentations, and mourning, and woe." To both prophets, the first result of absorbing the words of God and making them their own (Jer. xv. 16) is delight at communion with Him and enlightenment by Him: but the Priest of the Lord did not feel, as the Disciple of Jesus did, the afterthought of bitterness—the Christ-like sorrow for those against whom God's wrath is revealed, who "knew not the time of their visitation."

shall be in thy mouth sweet as honey. And I took the little book out of the angel's hand, and ate it up; and it was in my mouth sweet as honey: and as soon as I had eaten it, my belly was bitter. And he said unto me, Thou must prophesy again before many peoples, and nations, and tongues, and kings.

And there was given me a reed like unto a rod: and the angel stood, saying, Rise, and measure the temple of God,

"It grieves so sore his tender heart
To see God's ransom'd world in fear and wrath depart."

It is generally held, in one form or another, that this "little book" symbolises or contains "the mystery of God," the approaching completion of which has just been announced. Some needlessly combine with this the theory (see note on *v.* 1) that it contains the whole or part of this book of the Revelation. But really the surest clue to its meaning is the parallel passage in Ezekiel: if we say that the book contains "the Revelation of God's Judgement" (remembering how that Revelation is described in Rom. i. 18) we shall speak as definitely as is safe.

11. *And he said*] Read, **And they say.**

Thou must prophesy again] Some try to make out that there is here a new commission given to the Apostle, and that in the remainder of the book there are higher mysteries than in the foregoing part. But it is surely simpler to take it as a personal warning to the Apostle himself; he was to see the end of all things in vision, but his own earthly work and duties were not at an end. He had already "prophesied before many peoples and nations and tongues and kings" (whether Nero or Domitian was the last of these): and he would have to do the same "again."

THE MEASURING ANGEL AND THE TWO WITNESSES.
CHAP. XI. vv. 1—13.

1. *a reed*] Ezek. xl. 3; Zech. ii. 1.

like unto a rod] i.e. a walking-staff: probably not as long as the one in Ezek., l.c., but perhaps of six *feet:*—so that it would naturally, when carried, be grasped near the upper end, like a pilgrim's staff, or a modern alpenstock.

and the angel stood] These words should be omitted: they are no doubt inserted for grammatical completeness. "There was given unto me a reed like unto a staff,...saying" is of course easily understood to mean, "There was given unto me...he that gave it saying." It thus is not certain that it is the "mighty angel" of the preceding chapter who speaks in this.

the temple of God] The word used is not that for the whole "Temple-precinct," but the "Temple" in the narrowest sense—what in the O.T. is called "the house" or "the palace."

and the altar, and them that worship therein. But the court which is without the temple leave out, and measure it not;

the altar] Being *distinguished* from the Temple, we should naturally think of the Altar of Burnt-offering which stood outside it: besides that this was, and the Altar of Incense was not, large enough to be measured by something longer than a foot-rule. But we saw on vi. 9 that the Heavenly Temple apparently has *no* Altar of Burnt-offering distinct from the Altar of Incense: so the question only becomes important if we suppose the earthly Temple to be meant.
Is it then the heavenly or the earthly Temple that St John is bidden to measure? Probably the latter. Without pressing the argument from x. 9, that the seer is now on earth, it is hardly likely that, whereas in Ezekiel, Zechariah, and inf. xxi. 15 the measurement, not of the Temple only but of the Holy City, is the work of angels, it should here be ascribed to a man. But what is more decisive is, that the whole of this chapter describes God's *rebukes* and *correcting judgements* on the city, the fate of which is connected with that of the Temple here named. This proves that it is the earthly city of God that is meant—and therefore *probably* the literal Jerusalem: for the Christian Church, imperfectly as it realises its divine ideal, does not appear to be dissociated from it in Scriptural typology or prophecy: "Jerusalem which is above...is the Mother of us all," even now, and even now " our citizenship is in Heaven."
and them that worship therein] Lit. **in it**, not "in them," i.e. in the Temple, the mention of "the Altar" being parenthetical. But *neither* the Temple (in the narrower sense) *nor* the Altar was ordinarily a place of spiritual "worship," but only of the ritual "service of God." Therefore the meaning of the Temple and Altar must be *to some extent* spiritualised: even if the prophecy be concerned with God's judgements on Jerusalem and the Jewish people, we are not to understand that the actual Temple was to be spared (for we know it was not): but, most probably, that the true Israelites would not be cut off from communion with God, even when their city and the earthly splendours of their Temple were destroyed. Ezek. xi. 16 will thus illustrate the sense of the passage, though there does not appear to be a conscious reference to it.

2. *the court which is without the temple*] The words might be translated "the outer court of the Temple." It must be remembered that "the courts of the Lord's House" were the ordinary place for the worshippers to assemble, even before the outer and larger "Court of the Gentiles," with its magnificent colonnades, was added to Herod's Temple. Probably the latter is thought of, in its assignment to the Gentiles: but the meaning appears to be, that *all* the courts shall be profaned, up to the walls of the inmost Sanctuary.

leave out] Hardly a strong enough expression: the original is, "cast out outside." The sense must be, "leave out *for profanation.*" This excludes the hypothesis (otherwise not without plausibility) that the measurement of the Temple is for destruction, not for preservation: see

for it is given unto the Gentiles: and the holy city shall
3 they tread under foot forty *and* two months. And I will

2 Kings xxi. 13; Lam. ii. 8:—and for the destruction being regarded as the work of the prophet, cf. Ezek. xliii. 3.

tread under foot] So St Luke xxi. 24, which is no doubt referred to. Hitherto, the correspondences in this book with that Prophecy of our Lord's have been closest with St Matthew's version of it. Varying parallels like these serve to authenticate the reports of His words in the different Gospels—shewing that they are to be taken as mutually supplementary, not as more or less inaccurate. Of course, St John did not *use* our Gospels (though St Matthew's at least was in existence), but wrote independently from his own recollection.

forty and two months] So xiii. 5. This period is apparently identical with the "1260 days" of the next verse, and xii. 6: and with the "time, times, and half a time" (i.e. $3\frac{1}{2}$ years) of xii. 14. In Dan. vii. 25, xii. 7 we have this last measure of the period given, and the time indicated by Daniel must be either identical with or typical of that indicated by St John. It is to be noted, that in Dan. xii. 11, 12, we have the period extended to 1290 and 1335 days.

The key to these prophecies, that speak of definite periods of time, is generally sought in Ezek. iv. 6; It is supposed that each prophetical "day" stands for a year, and by consequence a "week" is equivalent to seven years, a "month" to 30, and a "year" to 360. This gives an *approximately* satisfactory explanation of the one prophecy of the "70 weeks" in Dan. ix.: they would naturally be understood to extend from B.C. 536 (the decree of Cyrus) to B.C. 5 (the Nativity), A.D. 29—30 (the Crucifixion), and A.D. 70 (the fall of Jerusalem); but the terms in which their beginning and end are described can with a little pressure be applied to B.C. 457 (the decree of Artaxerxes), A.D. 26 (the Baptism of St John), A.D. 29—30, and A.D. 33—*possibly* the date of the death of St Stephen, and so of the final rejection of the Gospel by the Jews and of the Jewish sacrifices by God. But in no other case has a prophecy been even tolerably interpreted on this principle. If it were admitted in this, we should naturally understand that Jerusalem was to have been restored in A.D. 1330—or at latest 1360 or 1405. Indeed, if the Saracen conquest instead of the Roman were taken as the starting-point, the restoration would not fall due till 1897, and it is humanly speaking quite possible that Palestine may pass into new hands then. But men ought to have learnt by this time to distrust such calculations: as we "know not the day nor the hour," so we know not the year nor the century. Two or three generations ago a number of *independent* calculations were made to converge to the year 1866 as the beginning of the end: but in that year nothing considerable happened except the Austrian war, which of all recent wars perhaps had least the character of a war between Christ and Antichrist. It was at worst an instance of the painful and not innocent way in which fallen human nature works out its best desires: the Austrians were technically in the right, while the victory of the Prussians has proved honourable and beneficial to both empires alike.

give *power* unto my two witnesses, and they shall prophesy a thousand two hundred *and* threescore days, clothed in sackcloth. These are the two olive trees, and the two 4 candlesticks standing before the God of the earth. And if 5 any *man* will hurt them, fire proceedeth out of their mouth,

3. *And I will give power*] Better, as in the margin, "I will give to My two Witnesses that they may prophesy"—the Hebrew idiom being literally reproduced.

my two witnesses] The traditional view of these, dating from the second century, is that they are Enoch and Elijah—the two prophets who, having (for a time) finished their work on earth, have left it without death: but who, since "it is appointed for all men once to die," will, as is here revealed, come on earth again, to prophesy and suffer death in the days of Antichrist.

As to Elijah, there seems to be little doubt that this view is true. The prophecy of Mal. iv. 5 has indeed received *a* fulfilment in the mission of the Baptist (St Luke i. 17). But St Matt. xvii. 11, 12 perhaps implies that this fulfilment is not the final one—especially when compared with St John i. 21. Really the plain sense of these passages seems to be, that Elijah will actually be sent before the second Coming of Christ, as one in his spirit and power was before His first.

But the personality of his colleague is more doubtful. Of Enoch we know so little, that internal evidence hardly applies either way: all we can say is, that he was recognised by popular Jewish belief as a seer of apocalypses, and that his character as a prophet and preacher of repentance is recognised by St Jude. This harmonises well enough with his being intended: but the internal evidence of Scripture itself points rather to *Moses* and Elijah being the two witnesses. Their names are coupled in the prophecy of Mal. iv. 4, 5, as well as in the history of the Transfiguration: and *v.* 6 ascribes to these prophets the plague actually inflicted by Moses, as well as that by Elijah. This modification of the traditional view was first suggested by the abbot Joachim, the great mediæval commentator on this book; but it has found wide acceptance in modern times. It may be observed, that as Elijah is doubtless still living a supernatural life in the body, so Moses must have been raised to such life for the Transfiguration: but he is not necessarily incapable of death, any more than were Lazarus and others who have been raised from the dead.

1260 *days*] See on *v.* 2.

4. *the two olive trees* &c.] See Zech. iv. *passim*. There apparently the "two Anointed Ones" are Zerubbabel and Jeshua, or rather perhaps the ideal King and Priest, conceived as types of Him Who is both: perhaps these two Witnesses similarly typify Him as King (cf. Deut. xxxiii. 5) and Prophet.

5. *will hurt them*] I.e. "*wishes*" or "*means* to hurt."

and devoureth their enemies: and if any *man* will hurt them,
6 he must in this manner be killed. These have power to
shut heaven, that it rain not in the days of their prophecy:
and have power over waters to turn them to blood, and to
7 smite the earth with all plagues, as often as they will. And
when they shall have finished their testimony, the beast that
ascendeth out of the bottomless *pit* shall make war against
8 them, and shall overcome them, and kill them. And their
dead bodies *shall lie* in the street of the great city, which
spiritually is called Sodom and Egypt, where also our Lord

fire proceedeth out of their mouth] Jer. v. 14 is a precedent for the image, 2 Kings i. 10, &c. for the sense.
6. *power to shut heaven*] Like Elijah: *over waters*, &c. like Moses.
7. *the beast*] Here first mentioned: probably that which appears in xiii. 1, not in xiii. 11: though neither of them makes his appearance immediately "out of the bottomless pit:" see, however, xvii. 8. But perhaps it is worth noticing that "the deep" in Rom. x. 7 (the word is the same as "the bottomless pit" here) corresponds to "the sea" of Deut. xxx. 13.
shall make war against them] Dan. vii. 21.
8. *the street*] For the sing. cf. xxi. 21, xxii. 2. The word in fact means a *broad* street, such as *the* principal street of a city would be. The modern Italian *piazza* is the same word; but xxii. 2 seems to shew that it is a street rather than a square—perhaps most accurately a "boulevard" in the modern sense, only running through the city, not round it.
the great city] Many commentators suppose this to be the Babylon of xiv. 8 and chaps. xvii. sqq.—i.e. Rome, whether literally or in an extended sense. But this seems hardly natural. If it were, why is it not *called* Babylon here, just as in the last verse the beast was called the beast? Besides, here the great majority of the inhabitants repent at God's judgement: contrast xvi. 9. The only other possible view is, that *this* great city is *Jerusalem:* and with this everything that is said about it seems to agree.
Sodom] Jerusalem is so *called* in Is. i. 10, and is *likened* to Sodom in Ezek. xvi. 46. For the licentiousness of the generation before the fall of Jerusalem, see comm. on Hos. iv. 14: Jos. *B. J.* IV. ix. 10 suggests a closer likeness.
Egypt] Jerusalem, it must be admitted, is never so called in the O. T. But New Testament facts made the name appropriate: comparing Acts ii. 47, v. 12, &c. with the Epistle to the Galatians, we see how Jerusalem was at first the refuge of the people of God, from which nevertheless they had at last to escape as from a house of bondage.
our Lord] Read, **their Lord**—i. e. of the two Witnesses. This clause seems almost certainly to identify "the great city" as Jerusalem: perhaps St John uses the title, as implying that its old one, "the Holy

was crucified. And *they* of the people and kindreds and 9
tongues and nations shall see their dead bodies three days
and a half, and shall not suffer their dead bodies to be put
in graves. And they that dwell upon the earth shall rejoice 10
over them, and make merry, and shall send gifts one to
another; because these two prophets tormented them that
dwelt on the earth. And after three days and a half the 11
spirit of life from God entered into them, and they stood
upon their feet; and great fear fell upon them which saw
them. And they heard a great voice from heaven saying 12
unto them, Come up hither. And they ascended up to
heaven in a cloud; and their enemies beheld them. And 13
the same hour was there a great earthquake, and the tenth
part of the city fell, and in the earthquake were slain of men

City," is forfeited. At the same time, if we *do* suppose the City meant to be Rome, these words can be explained, either by the responsibility of Pilate for the Lord's death, or on the principle of the beautiful legend, *Domine, quo vadis?*—that the Lord suffered in His Servants.

9. *shall see*] Read, **see**: and so "suffer not"…"rejoice…and make merry," but "shall send." The presents seem to make the transition from the prophecy to the narrative a little easier.

three days and a half] Should probably be "**the** three &c." The *half* day lends a certain support to the "year-day" hypothesis—that 3½ years are meant. But the traditional explanation takes the days literally—they rise, not on the third day like their Lord, but on the fourth—being like Him, though not equal to Him. Whether the *periods* named are to be taken literally or no, there seems no reason why we should not follow the traditional view, and understand this chapter as foretelling a sign which shall literally come to pass in the last days. The prophets Moses and Elijah will appear upon earth—or at the least two prophets will arise in their "spirit and power:" the scene of their prophecy will be Jerusalem, which will then be reoccupied by the Jewish nation. Antichrist (under whose patronage, it is believed, the restoration of the Jews will have taken place) will raise persecution against them, and kill them: but they will rise from the dead, and *then*, and not till then, the heart of Israel will turn to the Lord.

12. *they heard*] Probably not the two prophets only, but "they that beheld them."

in a cloud] Should be "in **the** cloud"—the same, perhaps, that received their Lord out of His Disciples' sight. Any way, "the cloud" is regarded as a permanently recurring phenomenon, like "the rainbow" in x. 1.

13. *of men*] Lit., **names of men**, as the margin: cf. iii. 4, and Acts i. 15 there quoted.

seven thousand: and the remnant were affrighted, and gave
14 glory to the God of heaven. The second woe is past; *and
behold, the third woe cometh quickly.*
15 And the seventh angel sounded; and there were great
voices in heaven, saying, The kingdoms of *this* world are
become *the kingdoms* of our Lord, and of his Christ; and he
16 shall reign for ever and ever. And the four and twenty
elders, which sat before God on their seats, fell upon their

seven thousand] Possibly this number is taken as approximately a tenth part of the population of Jerusalem. The city, which can never have extensive suburbs, being surrounded by ravines, can never hold a larger permanent population than 70,000; but in its highest prosperity it may have held as many, and perhaps it may again.

gave glory] Here and in xiv. 7, xvi. 9 these words seem to imply the *confession of sin*, as in Josh. vii. 19, and probably St John ix. 24. It was the predicted work of Elijah to "turn the hearts of the fathers to the children, and the heart of the children to their fathers:" this will be fulfilled by his posthumous success, uniting the original stock of God's People to the branches that now grow out of it (Rom. xi. 17, &c.).

the God of heaven] Seems to have been the way the Jews spoke of their God to heathens, see Jonah i. 9: Ezra i. 2 (which was probably written under Daniel's or other Jewish influence), v. 11, vi. 10. This accounts for the way that in later times heathens conceived of their religion. *Nil praeter nubes et* caeli numen *adorant* (Juv. XIV. 97).

14. *The second woe is past*] Having included the plagues inflicted by the two prophets, as well as the invasion of the terrible horsemen of chap. ix.

the third woe] In what does this consist? *Perhaps* we are to see the answer in xii. 12: but at any rate we have an instance of the way that, throughout this book, the last member of each series of signs disappoints us; we think (cf. x. 7) that the end of all things is come, but instead a new series begins.

THE SEVENTH TRUMPET, vv. 15—19. CHAP. XII. 7—12.

15. *great voices*] Cf. xvi. 17.

The kingdoms of this world &c.] Read, **The kingdom of the world is become our Lord's and His Christ's**. The phrase "*His* Christ" is founded on the O.T. phrase "the Lord's Anointed;" cf. St Luke ii. 26.

he shall reign] Who? Our Lord or His Christ? St John probably would have regarded the question as meaningless, though comparing v. 1 (see note on "therein") it is not likely that he used the sing. consciously to *imply* that Christ and His Father are One. It would be more to the point to compare "Christ the Lord" in St Luke ii. 11 with "the Lord's Christ" already quoted.

16. *which sat before God* &c.] Read, **which are before God, who sit upon their thrones**.

faces, and worshipped God, saying, We give thee thanks, 17
O Lord God Almighty, which art, and wast, and art to come;
because thou hast taken *to thee* thy great power, and hast
reigned. And the nations were angry, and thy wrath is 18
come, and the time of the dead, that *they* should be judged,
and that *thou* shouldest give reward unto thy servants the
prophets, and to the saints, and them that fear thy name,
small and great; and shouldest destroy them which destroy
the earth.

And the temple of God was opened in heaven, and there 19
was seen in his temple the ark of his testament: and there
were lightnings, and voices, and thunderings, and an earthquake, and great hail. And there appeared a great wonder 12
in heaven; a woman clothed with the sun, and the moon

17. *Lord God Almighty*] See on i. 8.
which art, and wast] Omit *and art to come*, as in xvi. 5. It is
not, however, likely that any importance is to be attached to the omission
of the full expression we had in i. 4, 8, iv. 8.

17, 18. *thou hast taken...thy wrath is come*] It is hypercritical in
the N.T., and in this book particularly, to attempt to distinguish
regularly between perfects and simple preterites: but here it is perhaps
worth observing that all the verbs (after the first) are in the same tense:
"Thou hast taken Thy great power, and didst reign: and the nations
were wroth, and Thy wrath came," &c. Cognate words are used to
express the *wrath* of the nations and of God.

18. *destroy them which destroy*] The verb used twice over is ambiguous, and perhaps has a meaning that we should express differently
in the two places; as in 1 Cor. iii. 17. Thus neither the marginal
rendering nor the text is wrong.

19. *the temple of God*] See on iv. 6, vi. 9.
the ark of his testament] Better **covenant**, as constantly in the
O.T.
there were lightnings &c.] So viii. 5, xvi. 18: in all three places,
they mark the end of the series of seven signs.

The Woman with the Man-Child. Chap. XII. vv. 1—6.

1. *a great wonder*] Should be **sign**, as in the margin, both here and
in *v.* 3.
a woman] Who is this? The two answers most commonly given
are (1) the Virgin Mary, (2) the Church. Neither seems quite satisfactory. There can indeed be little doubt that the Son born of this
woman is the Son of Mary: nor ought theological or ecclesiastical considerations to exclude the view that Mary is herself intended by the

under her feet, and upon her head a crown of twelve stars:
2 and she being with child cried, travailing in birth, and pained
3 to be delivered. And there appeared another wonder in
heaven; and behold a great red dragon, having seven heads

mother; the glory ascribed to her is no greater than that of a glorified saint (Dan. xii. 3; St Matt. xiii. 43), and St John was not bound to suppress a truth for fear of the false inference Pius V. or Pius IX. might seek to draw from it. But it is not in harmony with the usage of this book for a human being, even a glorified saint, to be introduced in his personal character: if St John saw (see on iv. 4, v. 5) *himself*, who was not yet glorified, sitting among the elders, it is plain that it is typical, not personal, glory or blessedness that this description indicates.

Who then, or what, is the typical or mystical Mother of Christ? Not the Christian Church, which in this book as elsewhere is represented as His wife: but *the Jewish Church*, the ideal Israel, "the daughter of Zion." See especially Mic. iv. 10, v. 3: where it is *her* travail from which He is to be born Who is born in Bethlehem. This accounts for the only features that support the other view, the appearance in her glory of the Sun, Moon, and stars of Cant. vi. 10, and the mention of "the remnant of her seed" in *v.* 17.

It may, however, perhaps be true that the ideal mother of the Lord is half identified in St John's mind, and intended to be so in his reader's, with His human mother: she embodies the ideal conception, just as the ideal of the false enemy of goodness in Ps. cix. received embodiment in Judas, or as the king of Israel who was to come is called "David," by Hosea and Ezekiel.

clothed with the sun &c.] There may be a reference to Cant. vi. 10, where however there is no mention of the stars. More certain is the reference, or at least similarity of imagery, to Gen. xxxvii. 9, where "the eleven stars," i.e. signs of the zodiac, represent Jacob's eleven sons, bowing down to Joseph, the twelfth. Here, the ideal Israel appears in the glory of all the patriarchs: Abraham, Isaac and Jacob, and their wives, are hers, and of the Twelve Tribes none is wanting. The whole description, in fact, is interpreted in Rom. ix. 5.

2. *and she...pained to be delivered*] There is probably a reminiscence of Gen. iii. 16, and perhaps of St John xvi. 21, as well as of Mic. iv. 10, to which the main reference is.

3. *dragon*] The word in classical Greek means simply "serpent," though perhaps it was always specially applied to the larger or more formidable kinds. But in St John's time the conception seems to have been familiar of a half-mythical kind of serpent, to which the name was appropriated: it had not gone so far as the mediæval type of "dragon," with legs and wings, but the dragon was supposed to "stand" (see the next verse), hardly perhaps "on his rear," as Milton imagines the Serpent of Eden to have done, before the curse of Gen. iii. 14, but erect from the middle upwards; see Verg. *Æn.* II. 206—8. Whether this dragon bore visibly on him the primæval curse or no, there is an undoubted

and ten horns, and seven crowns upon his heads. And his 4
tail drew the third *part* of the stars of heaven, and did cast
them to the earth: and the dragon stood before the woman
which was ready to be delivered, for to devour her child as
soon as it was born. And she brought forth a man child, 5
who was to rule all nations with a rod of iron: and her child
was caught up unto God, and *to* his throne. And the woman 6
fled into the wilderness, where she hath a place prepared of

reference to the story of the Fall in this picture of the woman, the
man, and the serpent. In Ps. lxxiv. 13, 14 (14, 15); Job xxvi. 13; Is.
xxvii. 1, li. 9, we seem to find references to a "war in heaven," either
past or future, like that which follows here.

seven heads] Probably the vision avails itself of the imagery furnished
by popular mythology: very likely Syria and Palestine had tales of
seven-headed serpents, like the hydra of Lerna, or the cobras of modern
Indian stories.

and ten horns] The only illustration of these is, that the beast of
chaps. xiii., xvii. and of Dan. vii. has the like. But we must remember that the dragon is the archetype, not a copy, of the beast: and
therefore the meaning here is probably more general: all unsanctified
power is embodied in him (cf. St Luke iv. 6), as all the power of
holiness in the Lamb (chap. v. 6).

4. *And his tail drew*] The great serpent crawls along the vault
of the sky, and the wrigglings of his tail remove the stars from their
places. "*Drew*" is literally **draweth**.

stood] Perhaps more accurately **standeth**.

for to devour her child] Symbolises the enmity of the serpent against
the seed of the woman, beginning with the intended treachery of Herod,
and massacre of the Innocents; but including also the malice that
pursued Him through life, the temptation, and at last the Cross.

5. *a man child*] Lit. **a son, a male**, the latter word being neuter.

who was to rule] Lit. **who is to rule**. This designation of the Son
proves beyond question who He is, see ii. 27 as proving, if there could
be any doubt about it, how Ps. ii. 9 is understood in this book.

to God, and to his throne] Cf. iii. 21. In the vision, "He that sat
on the throne" is still present, and no doubt St John *saw* the translation
of the child to His side.

6. *into the wilderness*] Did she descend to earth? she had appeared in heaven before. See on x. 9.

where she hath a place] Most of the historical interpretations that
have been advanced for this part of the vision proceed on the assumption that the Woman is the Christian Church. As interpretations,
they are excluded if we admit that she is the ancient Israel: though
applications and illustrations drawn from one may be appropriate to
the other. On the view taken here, the doctrine of this chapter is
analogous to that of Rom. xi., though the point of view is not quite the
same. St Paul distinguishes a double fulfilment of God's promises to

God, that they should feed her there a thousand two hundred *and* threescore days.

7 And there was war in heaven: Michael and his angels fought against the dragon; and the dragon fought and his 8 angels, and prevailed not; neither was their place found any 9 more in heaven. And the great dragon was cast *out, that* old serpent, called the devil, and Satan, which deceiveth

Israel—"the Election," the believing minority, receive them now, and "all Israel shall be saved" at last. St John does not distinguish the two, but uses language that covers both. The Daughter of Zion is kept alive by God, *both* in the continued quasi-national life of the Jewish people, and in the number (be it large or small) of Christians of Jewish race; who are known to God, though for 1500 years at least they have, as a community, disappeared in the mass of their Gentile fellow-believers. It is hardly necessary to contradict the utterly unhistorical theory, that any now existing Christian nation can be identified with a portion of Israel. The theory is perhaps most absurd when applied to the English, whose ancestors are mentioned as a pagan tribe of north Germany, within 30 years, if not within three of the date of this vision. (Tac. *Germ.* 40.)

1260 *days*] See on xi. 2, 3. Here, as in the earlier of those verses, the time defined is that of the humiliation of Israel: perhaps we may say that in the second it is conceived as that of their temporary rejection.

The War in Heaven, vv. 7—12.

7. *there was war in heaven*] This must refer to an event subsequent to the Incarnation—not, therefore, to the "Fall of the Angels," as readers of *Paradise Lost* are apt to assume. Milton may have been justified in using this description as *illustrating* or *suggesting* what may be supposed to have happened then: but we must not identify the two.

Michael] Dan. x. 13, 21, xii. 1. The two latter passages seem to tell us that he is the special patron or guardian angel of the people of Israel: and it may be in that character that he is introduced here.

his angels] He is called "the archangel" in Jude 9: the angels are "his," as well as "angels of the Lord," just as either a general or a king can talk of "*his* soldiers."

fought] Apparently the right reading is **to fight**—the sense is "there was war in Heaven, so that Michael and his angels made war with the Dragon." R.V. "*going forth* to war."

9. *cast out*] "Out" is not expressed—the sense is rather "cast down."

that old serpent] Gen. iii. 1. This is the only place in canonical Scripture (see, however, Wisd. ii. 24) where we are told that the Tempter in Eden was the Devil: but it cannot be doubted that we *are* so told here.

the Devil and Satan] The Greek word from which the former name

the whole world: he was cast *out* into the earth, and his angels were cast *out* with him. And I heard a loud voice 10 saying in heaven, Now is come salvation, and strength, and the kingdom of our God, and the power of his Christ: for the accuser of our brethren is cast down, which accused them before our God day and night. And they overcame 11 him by the blood of the Lamb, and by the word of their testimony; and they loved not their lives unto the death.

is derived is regularly used in the LXX. as the representative of the latter: though the two are not quite synonymous, the Hebrew name meaning "the Adversary," and the Greek "the Slanderer" (e.g. the same word is used in a general sense in 1 Tim. iii. 11). "Satan" has the article here, as always in the O.T., except in the Book of Job; it is still rather a designation than a proper name. In Enoch xl. 7 we have it used in the plural in a passage very like this: "The fourth voice I heard expelling the Satans, and prohibiting them from coming into the presence of the Lord of spirits, to prefer accusations against the inhabitants of the earth." The voice is afterwards explained to be that of Phanuel, the angel of penitence and hope.

he was cast out into the earth] St Luke x. 18, St John xii. 31 throw light on what must be meant—a breaking of the power of the Devil by that of the Incarnate Lord: but we cannot be quite sure that our Lord speaks of the *same* fall of Satan in both passages, or in either of the same that St John describes.

10. *a loud voice*] See on vi. 6: and cf. xi. 12: the word "loud" here is literally "great" as there. Here, "our brethren" seems to imply, that it is a number of angels that speak.

salvation, and strength] Rather, **the salvation and the might and the kingdom of...."**

power] Differs from the preceding word "strength" or "might" as implying that it is derivative—cf. 1 Cor. xv. 27, 28.

the accuser] In Jewish tradition, Satan is spoken of under this title, the Greek word here used being Hebraical, and here, though of course written in Greek letters, it has the Hebraical, not the classical form. St Michael was called by the correlative term, "the Advocate."

which accused] More literally **accuseth**, but the context shews that the meaning of the tense is to mark the act as habitual rather than as present. The "Prologue in Heaven" of the Book of Job, and Zech. iii. 1, of course illustrate the sense.

11. *by the blood*] More literally **because of the blood...and because of the word.**

they loved not their lives] St John xii. 25, St Luke xiv. 26 are the closest parallels among the similar sayings of our Lord. Here, as in all of them, the word for "life" is that elsewhere rendered "soul"—not the same as that used for "life eternal" in St John, l.c.

unto the death] They carried the temper of not loving life (not only to the renunciation of life's joys, but) even to death.

12 Therefore rejoice, ye heavens, and ye that dwell in them. Woe to the inhabiters of the earth and of the sea! for the devil is come down unto you, having great wrath, because he knoweth that he hath *but* a short time.
13 And when the dragon saw that he was cast unto the earth, he persecuted the woman which brought forth the man *child*.
14 And to the woman were given two wings of a great eagle, that she might fly into the wilderness, into her place, where she is nourished for a time, and times, and half a time, from
15 the face of the serpent. And the serpent cast out of his mouth water as a flood after the woman, that he might cause
16 her to be carried away of the flood. And the earth helped

12. *Therefore*] Because of the coming of "the salvation and might and kingdom," in which the victory of "our brethren" is included.
that dwell] Lit. **that tabernacle.**
Woe to the inhabiters of] We should read, **Woe to the earth and the sea!**—the sense is clear, though the construction is peculiar, which led to the alteration. *When* and *in what sense* the Devil's power was, or will be, at once lessened and brought into more terrible neighbourhood to earth, we can hardly venture to say. Perhaps it is to be illustrated by texts like St John ix. 39, xv. 22: the Incarnation, as it broke the otherwise invincible power of sin, so made sin more deadly, if it remains in spite of Christ's coming.
but a short time] viz. the time, apparently, between Christ's first coming, which broke his strength, and His second, which will destroy his kingdom for ever. It seems unlikely that the "little season" of xx. 3 is here referred to.

THE DELIVERANCE OF THE WOMAN, vv. 13—17.

13. *he persecuted the woman*] The reference is probably in the first instance to the Roman persecution of the Jews, in and after the wars of Titus and Hadrian: both the bitterness with which those wars were conducted (Josephus probably exaggerates the clemency of Titus), and the savage fanaticism which provoked it, were the Dragon's work. So also were the mediæval persecutions of the Jews by Christians: and so is the social or intellectual intolerance which is by no means extinct yet, and which is actually often bitterest against a *Christian* Jew who does not forget his nationality.
14. *two wings...eagle*] Should be "**the** two wings of **the** great eagle." The word is, however, no doubt used generically. Some suppose "the great eagle" to symbolise the Roman empire, but that did *not* protect the Jewish Church, though to some extent it did the Christian.
her place] v. 6.
15, 16. We have not means for interpreting this description in detail. All we can say certainly is, that it describes the providential foiling of Satanic attempts at the destruction of Israel. Perhaps the

the woman, and the earth opened her mouth, and swallowed up the flood which the dragon cast out of his mouth. And 17 the dragon was wroth with the woman, and went to make war with the remnant of her seed, which keep the commandments of God, and have the testimony of Jesus Christ.

And I stood upon the sand of the sea, and saw a beast 13 rise up out of the sea, having seven heads and ten horns,

most plausible suggestion of a definite meaning of the "flood" [better translated **river**] is that the Christians of Jerusalem, in their flight to "the mountains" (St Matt. xxiv. 16 &c.) of Pella, were delivered by a miracle or special providence from the dangers of the passage of Jordan: if they fled *immediately* before the siege was formed by Titus, this was just before the Passover, when the river was in flood (Josh. iii. 15). But of such an event we have no historical notice: and it is likely that the Christians fled when they had *first* "seen Jerusalem compassed with armies" (St Luke xxi. 20), in the unsuccessful assault of Cestius Gallus, three years before the fall of the city.

17. *the woman...the remnant of her seed*] Gen. iii. 15. The sense must be, that the Devil attempts to frustrate God's counsels, not now by attacking the old Israel, but the new "Israel of God." Titus, we are told, resolved to destroy the Temple, "in order that the religion of the Jews *and Christians* might be more completely abolished" (Sulp. Sev. ii. 30, supposed to embody a quotation from Tacitus). Hadrian, on the contrary, seeing that the Christians had separated their cause from that of the rebel Jews, extended to them a tolerance not merely contemptuous. But thenceforward the best and ablest emperors, from M. Aurelius to Diocletian, recognising the independent power of the Church, thought it necessary to persecute it. At last, Julian completely reversed the policy of Titus, seeking to discredit the Gospel by patronage to the Jews. This policy, apparently, will be carried out by Antichrist: but will be baffled when the Jews, whom he has restored to their land as unbelievers, are converted by the martyrdom and resurrection of the two prophets (see notes on the preceding chapter).

which keep the commandments] xiv. 12.
have the testimony] vi. 9. The word "Christ" should be omitted.

THE BEAST FROM THE SEA. CHAP. XIII. vv. 1—10.

1. *And I stood*] We should probably read "**and he** [the Dragon] **stood**"—the clause being connected with the preceding chapter.
and [I] saw...out of the sea] Dan. vii. 3.
seven heads and ten horns] Read, **ten horns and seven heads**. The ten horns are from Dan. vii. 7. But the beast seen by Daniel seems to have only one head, *v.* 20: and hence some have supposed that this beast is not the same as that, but a combination of all Daniel's four—and that the seven heads are obtained by adding together the four heads

and upon his horns ten crowns, and upon his heads the name of blasphemy. And the beast which I saw was like unto a leopard, and his feet *were* as *the feet* of a bear, and his mouth as the mouth of a lion: and the dragon gave him his power, and his seat, and great authority. And I saw one of his heads as *it were* wounded to death; and his deadly wound was healed: and all the world wondered after the beast. And they worshipped the dragon which gave power unto the beast: and they worshipped the beast, say-

of the leopard with the single ones of the other three beasts. But this seems far-fetched: it is better to remember (see on iv. 7) that God is not obliged always to reveal the same truth under the same image. St John's vision was like enough to Daniel's to indicate that it applied to the same thing, but it supplied details which Daniel's did not. For one thing, comparing this description with xii. 3, we learn that this beast has a special likeness to the Devil.

the name] Read, **names**, as in the margin. Cf. xvii. 3. The reference perhaps is to the blasphemous assumption of divine honours by the Roman emperors—most markedly (at least up to St John's time) by Gaius.

2. *like unto a leopard...bear...lion*] The fourth beast in Dan. vii. is not described as like any ordinary animal: here he is described as combining the likeness of the other three. We may draw the inference mentioned on *v.* 1, that this beast is not the fourth, but a combination of all four: but on the simpler view the description is not less appropriate. The Rome of St John's day *was* "like unto" a Greek empire, and at the same time embodied elements derived from Babylon and from Persia. And if we watch the "spirit of Antichrist" that is working in our day, we shall see it in the various forms of Hellenic aestheticism, of Persian luxury, and of Chaldean scientific necessarianism. It remains for this spirit to mount the imperial throne of Rome, when he who now letteth is taken out of the way.

the dragon gave him his power] It is the Devil's interest and policy to disguise his working under the forms of the world: at present, he has actually persuaded many to disbelieve in his existence.

seat] Better, **throne**. The words rendered "power" and "authority" here are the same as "strength" and "power" in xii. 10. Antichrist, or the Antichristian empire, bears just the same relation to the Devil as the true Christ to God.

3. *I saw*] Should be omitted from the Greek text, but of course must be supplied in sense.

one of his heads] Comparing xvii. 10, 11, it has been thought that this indicates the *death of Nero*, and his expected reappearance as Antichrist. See notes on ch. xvii. and Introduction pp. 47, 49.

his deadly wound] Lit., **the stroke of his death.**

4. *which gave power*] Rather, **because he gave his authority.**

ing, Who *is* like unto the beast? who is able to make war with him? And there was given unto him a mouth speaking great *things* and blasphemies; and power was given unto him to continue forty *and* two months. And he opened his mouth in blasphemy against God, to blaspheme his name, and his tabernacle, and them that dwell in heaven. And it was given unto him to make war with the saints, and to overcome them: and power was given him over all kindreds, and tongues, and nations. And all that dwell upon the earth shall worship him, whose names are not written in the book of life of the Lamb slain from the foundation of the world. If any *man* have an ear, let him hear. He that leadeth into

Who is like unto the beast?] A sort of blasphemous parody of sayings like Ex. xv. 11; Ps. xxxv. 10, lxxi. 19, lxxxix. 8, or of the name Michael, which is by interpretation "Who is like God?"

5. *a mouth* &c.] Dan. vii. 8.

to continue] Literally, **to make** or do. This may mean "to spend," so that the text will give the right sense: but perhaps rather, as in Dan viii. 24, xi. 28, 30, 32, "do" is used absolutely for "do exploits."

forty and two months] See on xi. 2.

6. *and them that dwell*] "And" should apparently be omitted, so that "them that tabernacle in Heaven" is in apposition with the "tabernacle" of God itself.

7. *And it was given unto him...to overcome them*] There is considerable authority for the omission of this clause: but the omission is no doubt merely accidental—it was left out in one or more very early copies, because scribes passed from one clause beginning "and there was given unto him" to another. For the sense cf. Dan. vii. 21 and ch. xi. 7: the latter proves that "the Saints" (i.e. the holy people of God) are to be understood as Christians, not as Israelites.

over all kindreds &c.] Lit., **over every tribe, and people, and tongue, and nation.** The Devil gives to Antichrist what he offered to Christ, St Luke iv. 6.

8. *whose names*] Read, **whose name**, the pronoun as well as the noun being singular.

the book of life of the Lamb] xxi. 27: see note on v. 1.

from the foundation of the world] Perhaps in Greek, as in English, it is most natural to connect these words with "slain:" and 1 Pet. i. 19, 20 works out what, on this view, would be the sense. But the similar clause xvii. 8 seems to prove that the words are to be taken with "written:" it is God's purpose of individual election, not of universal redemption, that is here dated "from the foundation of the world."

9. *If any man* &c.] See on ii. 7.

10. *He that leadeth into captivity*] Decidedly the best attested reading is, "If any into captivity, into captivity he goeth:" and there captivity *shall* go into captivity: he that killeth with the sword must be killed with the sword. Here is the patience and the faith of the saints.

And I beheld another beast coming up out of the earth; and he had two horns like a lamb, and he spake as a dragon. And he exerciseth all the power of the first beast before him,

being no verb expressed in the first clause, it is a question what verb is to be supplied. This will depend on the sense given to the rest of the sentence, and this on the reading adopted there. If the received text be right (it is, more literally than in the A.V., "if any will kill with the sword, he must be killed with the sword:" cf. St Matt. xxvi. 52), its reading in the earlier clause must be accepted as a correct gloss. But there is a reading—not so well attested, and which might have arisen accidentally—"if any to be killed by the sword, [he must]" (one important MS. omits this) "be killed by the sword." Inferior as this reading is in external evidence, it is supported by the parallel with Jer. xv. 2, xliii. 11. We have therefore the choice between the two versions, "If any man [be] for captivity, he goeth into captivity: if any [be] to be slain by the sword, he must be slain by the sword," and that of the A.V. with the word "leadeth" put in italics: and we shall choose between them, according as we think that St John is likelier to have had in his mind the text in Jeremiah or our Lord's saying. Perhaps the former suits the context best—"the patience and the faith of the saints" is to be *shewn* in submitting to death or captivity. But the other view, that their patience and faith is to be *sustained* by remembering the certainty of God's vengeance on their oppressors, is supported by the parallel passage, xiv. 12.

THE BEAST FROM THE LAND, vv. 11—16.

11. *another beast*] Afterwards called the False Prophet, xvi. 13, xix. 20, xx. 10. Some think that it is he, rather than the first Beast, who is to be identified with St Paul's "Man of Sin," the personal Antichrist—the first Beast being the antichristian Empire. But in xvii. 11 sqq. it seems plain that the seven-headed Beast, who is primarily a polity, at length becomes embodied in a person.

two horns] Perhaps *two*, only because that is the natural number for a lamb—the only significance of the number being, that they are *not* seven or ten.

like a lamb...as a dragon] No doubt the obvious view is right, that he *looks* like Christ and *is* like Satan. Alford well compares St Matt. vii. 15—though the resemblance is in the sense, not the language or even the image, so that perhaps there is no conscious reference.

12. *exerciseth*] Lit. **doeth**: the sense is, he does all that the Dragon has given the Beast power or authority to do.

before him] The relation of the False Prophet to the Beast is nearly the same as that of Aaron to Moses, Ex. iv. 16, vii. 9 sqq., or even of a true Prophet to God, 1 Kings xvii. 1.

and causeth the earth and them which dwell therein to worship the first beast, whose deadly wound was healed. And he doeth great wonders, so that he maketh fire come down from heaven on the earth in the sight of men, and deceiveth them that dwell on the earth by the means of *those* miracles which he had power to do in the sight of the beast; saying to them that dwell on the earth, that *they* should make an image to the beast, which had the wound by a sword, and did live. And he had power to give life unto the image of the beast, that the image of the beast should both speak, and cause that as many as would not worship the image of the beast should be killed. And he causeth all, *both* small and great, rich and poor, free and bond, to receive a mark in

13. *he doeth great wonders*] St Matt. xxiv. 24; 2 Thess. ii. 9.
maketh fire to come down] The similarity to 1 Kings xviii., 2 Kings i., is best explained by St Luke xii. 55. To reproduce the acts of Elijah *now* shews the spirit, not of the true Christ, but of the false.

14. *deceiveth*] xix. 20. There is still a reminiscence of St Matt. xxiv. 24.

an image] We cannot tell how, or how literally, this prophecy will be fulfilled in the last days: but it is certainly relevant to remember how the refusal of worship to the Emperor's image was made the test of Christianity in the primitive persecutions—perhaps especially by humane and reluctant persecutors like Pliny (see his famous letter to Trajan) who acted not from fanaticism, but from supposed political necessity. And the king-worship of the sixteenth and seventeenth centuries,—the maxim, earlier acted on than avowed, *cujus regio ejus religio*,—shews us the really Antichristian element in the persecutions of that age.—To the ingenious theory, that the second Beast is the Papacy, and "the image of the first Beast" the mediaeval Empire, it is a fatal objection that, though the Popes may be said to have *made* and *vivified* the "Holy Roman Empire," they certainly did not make the world worship it; they might more plausibly be charged with making it worship them.

15. *he had power*] Lit. **it was given to him.**
life] Lit. **breath** or **spirit.**

16. *to receive*] Lit. **that they give them.**

a mark] The word for "mark" is not the same as in Gal. vi. 17, but the image is, as there, that of the brand put upon slaves to identify them; pagan devotees sometimes received such a brand, marking them as the property of their god. In the so-called Third Book of Maccabees (which, stupid as it is, has perhaps some historical foundation) we are told that Ptolemy Philopator ordered the Jews of Alexandria to be branded with an ivy-leaf, the cognisance of Dionysus. One may compare also the sealing of the servants of God in chap. vii., and xiv. 1.

17 their right hand, or in their foreheads: and that no *man* might buy or sell, save he that had the mark, or the name 18 of the beast, or the number of his name. Here is wisdom. Let him that hath understanding count the number of the beast: for it is the number of a man; and his number *is* Six hundred threescore *and* six.

THE NUMBER OF THE NAME OF THE BEAST, vv. 17, 18.

17. *and that*] "And" should not improbably be omitted, the construction then, being, he causeth all...that they give them a mark,...that no man may..."

no man might buy or sell] Such disabilities seem to have been actually imposed, at least in the Diocletian persecution, by requiring business transactions to be preceded by pagan formulas.

the mark, or the name] Om. "or:" the true reading is, "the mark —the name of the Beast, or the number of his name."

the number of his name] In Hebrew and in Greek, *letters* were used for *numerals*, every letter having its own proper significance as a number. Among the Jews (and to some extent among early Christians, especially heretics) this suggested the possibility of finding numbers mystically corresponding to any word: the numerical value of all the letters might be added together, and the sum would represent the word. This process was called by the Jews *Gematria*, a corruption of the Greek *Geometria*. Ridiculous as were many of the attempts made to find mystical meanings in the words of Scripture by this process, it remains true that a Jew of St John's time would probably mean, by "the number of a name," the number formed by Gematria from its letters: and probably the numerous guesses, from St Irenaeus' time to our own, that have been based on this method are so far on the right track. But there are too many that are plausible for any one to be probable. There are in fact an indefinite number of proper names whose letters will amount to 666 (or 616, see below) either in Hebrew or Greek—at least when the names are *neither* Hebrew nor Greek, and so have to be arbitrarily transliterated. Thus neither *Lateinos*, i.e. *Latinus* (one of several mentioned by St Irenaeus) nor *Nerôn Kêsar* i.e. *Nero Caesar* (adopted by many modern interpreters) is convincing: and no other name (*Genseric, Mohammed*, and even *Napoleon* have been tried, with more or less violence) has any real chance of being right. The letters of *Lateinos* must be taken with their numeral value in Greek, those of *Neron Kesar* as Hebrew. If neither of these be the true one, we may be pretty certain it will not be discovered till Antichrist appears: and *then* believers will be able to identify him by this token.

18. *Here is wisdom. Let him that hath understanding* &c.] "The terms of the challenge serve at once to shew that the feat proposed is possible, and that it is difficult." (Alford.)

the number of a man] Comparing xxi. 17, it appears that these words mean "is reckoned simply, by an ordinary human method."

Six hundred threescore and six] The reading 616 is ancient, but

And I looked, and lo, a Lamb stood on the mount Sion, **14** and with him an hundred forty *and* four thousand, having his Father's name written in their foreheads. And I heard 2 a voice from heaven, as the voice of many waters, and as the voice of a great thunder: and I heard the voice of harpers harping with their harps: and they sung as *it were* a new 3 song before the throne, and before the four beasts, and the elders: and no *man* could learn *that* song but the hundred *and* forty *and* four thousand, which were redeemed from the earth. These are they which were not defiled with women; 4 for they are virgins. These are they which follow the Lamb

certainly wrong: and it is not impossible that the repetition (which must strike every one in the *words*, though the Greek *figures* do not suggest it like the Arabic) of the number 6 is significant: it approximates to, but falls short of, the sacred 7. Certainly we get no help by referring to 1 Kings x. 14—where the number is probably arrived at, by calculating that Solomon got 2000 talents every *three* years: cf. *v.* 22.

THE LAMB UPON MOUNT ZION. CHAP. XIV. vv. 1—5.

1. *a Lamb*] Read **the Lamb**: of course the same as in chap. v.
on the mount Sion] Probably the earthly one—the heavenly Jerusalem of chap. xxi. has not yet appeared. And in xi. 7, 8 we had an intimation that the seer's gaze was now directed to Jerusalem: Babylon, though *mentioned* in *v.* 8, is not *seen* till chap. xvii.
an hundred forty and four thousand] Cf. vii. 4.
his Father's name] Read, **His Name and His Father's Name**. Notice that it is assumed as understood, that the Lamb is the Son of God. See notes on iii. 12, vii. 3.
2. *as the voice...great thunder*] It was as loud and as *multitudinous* as these, but was harmonious, and apparently articulate.
3. *sung*] More accurately, **sing**.
as it were] Should perhaps be omitted, as in v. 9.
4. *for they are virgins*] The first instance of the use of the word as a masculine. It was adopted in ecclesiastical language, and applied e.g. to St John himself. It is best to understand the word literally. St Matt. xix. 12; 1 Cor. vii. prove, on any fair interpretation, that a devout and unselfish celibacy gives special means for serving God, and so we need not be surprised to learn here that it has a special reward from Him. No disparagement of holy matrimony is implied. Marriage is lowered by the Fall from what God meant it to be (Gen. iii. 16), and so, like other things which God made very good, has its own evils and dangers; but it does not follow that it is here conceived as in any sense defilement—they who are virgins *à fortiori* are "not defiled with women." It is noticeable that we owe to the two celibate apostles the highest con-

whithersoever he goeth. These were redeemed from among
5 men, *being* the firstfruits unto God and to the Lamb. And
in their mouth was found no guile: for they are without fault before the throne of God.
6 And I saw another angel fly in the midst of heaven, having
the everlasting gospel to preach unto them that dwell on the
earth, and to every nation, and kindred, and tongue, and
7 people, saying with a loud voice, Fear God, and give glory
to him; for the hour of his judgment is come: and worship
him that made heaven, and earth, and the sea, and the
8 fountains of waters. And there followed another angel,
saying, Babylon is fallen, is fallen, *that* great city, be-

secration of marriage, see Eph. v. 23—33, and the last two chapters of this Book.

being the firstfruits] This seems to imply, as is required by the view that "virgins" strictly speaking are meant, that the 144,000 do not represent the *whole* number of the Elect, but a specially sanctified number from among them. See on vii. 4.

5. *no guile*] Read, **no lie**.

before the throne of God] Should be omitted; and so perhaps should "for."

THE ANGEL WITH THE EVERLASTING GOSPEL, vv. 6, 7.

6. *another angel*] Different from the many mentioned before, *perhaps* especially distinguished from the one who appears in ch. x., but see *v.* 17, xviii. 1, where such a reference is hardly possible.

in the midst of heaven] See on viii. 13.

the everlasting gospel] Strictly speaking, these words have not the article, but neither has "[the] Gospel of God" in Rom. i. 1. Even if, therefore, the grammatical usage of this Book were more regular than it is, it would be needless to translate "an eternal piece of good news," in which, moreover, it would be hard to find a sense for the epithet. No doubt "gospel" is used in its constant N.T. sense; and the gospel is called "everlasting," as declaring the eternal truth of God. The preaching of the Gospel here stands in the same relation to God's Judgement as in St Matt. xxiv. 14. But notice, that the name is applied to the *whole* truth of God, not to what was revealed by Christ only: for the substance of the angel's message is pure natural theism.

7. *give glory to him*] See on xi. 13.

the sea, and the fountains of waters] Distinguished as (so to speak) different elements, as in viii. 8, 10, xvi. 3, 4.

ANGELS OF WARNING, vv. 8—11.

8. *another angel*] The correct text is **another angel a second**.

Babylon...that great city] Read **Babylon the great** as in xvii. 5. See also xviii. 10, 18 and 21 where we have "Babylon the great city," "the

cause she made all nations drink of the wine of the wrath of her fornication. And *the* third angel followed them, say- 9 ing with a loud voice, If any *man* worship the beast and his image, and receive *his* mark in his forehead, or in his hand, the same shall drink of the wine of the wrath of God, which 10 is poured out without mixture into the cup of his indignation; and he shall be tormented with fire and brimstone in the presence of the holy angels, and in the presence of the Lamb: and the smoke of their torment ascendeth up 11 for ever and ever: and they have no rest day nor night, who worship the beast and his image, and whosoever receiveth the mark of his name. Here is the patience of the saints: 12 here *are* they that keep the commandments of God, and the

great city" (meaning Babylon), and "**the** great city Babylon." The omission of city here makes the presumption less that "the great city" of xi. 8, xvi. 19 is the same.

is fallen, is fallen] Is. xxi. 9.
because she made] Read, **which hath made.**
the wine of the wrath of her fornication] There is a blending of the two views: she makes them drink of the cup of her fornication, xvii. 2, and she is made, and they are made with her, to drink of the cup of God's wrath: ver. 10, xvi. 19. In xviii. 6, as in Jer. li. 7, from which the image is taken, there is, as here, a combination of the two.

9. *the third angel*] Read, **another angel, a third.**
10. *drink of the wine of the wrath of God*] Ps. lxxv. 8 (9); Is. li. 17, 22; Jer. xxv. 15 sqq.

poured out without mixture] Lit. **mixed unmixed**: there is prob. nothing meant but the sense of the A.V., the "pouring out" of wine being *usually* a process of "mixing." But the paradoxical form of expression comes from the LXX. of Ps. lxxv. 8, where the word "red" (or perhaps "foaming," "fiery") is translated by "unmixed," proving that St John knows and uses the LXX. version, though he corrects it when necessary.

with fire and brimstone] Perhaps rather **in**. See xix. 20, xx. 15, xxi. 8.

in the presence, &c.] It is impossible to translate these words otherwise: they prove that the holy angels, and the Lamb Himself, acquiesce or something more in the justice and necessity of God's awful judgements. This being so, we dare not give weight to sentimental or *à priori* arguments against their possibility, though to our present faculties God's future treatment of sin may be as hard to reconcile with His known attributes as His permission of its origin in the past. We are *forced* to pass over the one difficulty: faith and humility will pass over the other.

12. *Here is the patience of the saints*] See xiii. 10, and the end of the note there.

here are *they*] Should be omitted, reading **of the saints that keep,**

13 faith of Jesus. And I heard a voice from heaven saying unto me, Write, Blessed *are* the dead which die in the Lord from henceforth: Yea, saith the Spirit, that they may rest from their labours; and their works do follow them.

14 And I looked, and behold a white cloud, and upon the cloud one sat like unto the Son of man, having on his head

&c. The construction, though not that of classical Greek, is that usual in cases of apposition in this Book.

Blessing on the Faithful Dead, and the Harvest and the Vintage of the Earth, vv. 13—20.

13. *Write*] See on x. 4.

Blessed are the dead &c.] Two questions arise as to this verse, though its touching associations make us unwilling to raise questions about it. What is its relevance *here*? and why are the holy dead blessed "*from henceforth*"?—i.e. probably, from the time foreshadowed by the last part of the vision. The answer to both probably is, that in those days a holy death will be the only escape from persecution and temptation, which "if it were possible should seduce even the Elect." Not only "for the Elect's sake the days shall be shortened," but even before they end, one and another of the Elect will be delivered from them. Even now it is a matter of thanksgiving when a Christian is delivered by death "from the miseries of this wretched world, from the body of death, and from all temptation," and much more then, when temptation is so much sorer that no Saint can dare wish to abide in the flesh.—This seems better than supposing that the special blessedness of the dead of those days consists only in the interval being shorter before their "perfect consummation and bliss."

that they may rest] The construction probably is, "who die that they may rest"—the sense is, "Yea, they are indeed blessed, for the result, and the providential end, of their dying is, to bring them to rest."

and their works] Read, **for their works.**

do follow them] More accurately, **follow with them**: there is therefore hardly any resemblance to 1 Tim. v. 24—5. The meaning of the passage is much the same as 1 Thess. iv. 15—we are not to think of the holy dead as if they missed (and as if the dead of the last days *only just* missed) the glories of the Lord's coming: for they and their good works are kept by Him safe against that day, ready to share in its glories.

14. *I looked*] Better, **beheld**, as iv. 1, &c.

one sat] More literally, [I saw] **One sitting.** It is scarcely possible to doubt that a vision of the Last Judgement is here interposed, to encourage "the patience of the Saints" that is to be so sorely tried. No one would have doubted that "One like unto the Son of Man" is the same Person as in i. 13, and that His coming with the clouds of heaven indicates the same as in i. 7, except from a desire to interpret the whole series of visions continuously, as fulfilled in chronological

a golden crown, and in his hand a sharp sickle. And another 15
angel came out of the temple, crying with a loud voice to
him that sat on the cloud, Thrust in thy sickle, and reap:
for the time is come for thee to reap; for the harvest of the
earth is ripe. And he that sat on the cloud thrust in his 16
sickle on the earth; and the earth was reaped.

order. Now it is probably right to regard the order of the visions as
always significant, and generally answering to the chronological order
of fulfilment. But exceptions to the latter rule must be admitted: xi. 7
plainly refers to the same events as chap. xiii., while chap. xii. goes
back to events earlier than, probably, any others indicated in the Book.
In this chapter itself, we have in *v.* 8 an anticipation of chap. xviii.:
we need not therefore hesitate to suppose that here we have an
anticipation of chap. xx. Those who wish to make the order of
visions strictly continuous put on the words "one like unto the [or
"a"—see on i. 13] Son of Man" the gloss "an Angel in the likeness
of the Messiah," and suppose that one of God's typical or anticipatory
judgements is described in terms suitable to the last.

a sharp sickle] The image of the harvest, combined with that of the
vintage, is from Joel iii. 13: see however also St Matt. xiii. 30 &c.

15. *another angel*] It is probably not relevant to argue that in
classical Greek this would not necessarily imply that the previously
named Person is an Angel, even if "another" is meant to distinguish
the Angel from Him. But comparing *v.* 6, it appears that the angel
may be called "another" simply to distinguish him from those of
vv. 6, 8, 9: and then no inference whatever can be drawn as to the
figure of *v.* 14.

out of the temple] See xi. 19, and note on iv. 6.

Thrust in] Lit. **send**, as in St Mark iv. 29, where "putteth in"
should be "sendeth forth" (the Greek word is not the same as here,
but there is hardly any difference in sense). It *may* be implied, that
the Son of Man does not reap Himself—cf. St Matt. xxiv. 31. See on
the next verse.

is ripe] Lit. **is dried**; hence R. V. "is over-ripe"; possibly a more
literal translation than St Mark's, l.c., of our Lord's words in the
parable, to which there is probably a reference.

16. *thrust in*] Lit. **cast**: but the word is used in much milder
senses, e. g. of the Lord "putting" His fingers in the deaf man's ears,
St Mark vii. 33. The A.V. can therefore be defended: but it is
perhaps likelier, that He Who sat on the cloud *threw down* the sickle,
for others (unnamed angels) to reap with.

the earth was reaped] Comparing the parables in SS. Matthew and
Mark, there is little doubt that the gathering of the harvest indicates the
gathering of the Elect. In Jer. li. 33, it is true, the image of harvest is
used of the time of God's *vengeance*, and so Joel iii. 13, where, as here,
it is combined with that of the vintage. But it would be pointless to
have the two images successively worked out, if they meant exactly the
same: while the *vengeance* of the other image is clearly defined in

17 And another angel came out of the temple which is in
18 heaven, he also having a sharp sickle. And another angel came out from the altar, which had power over fire; and cried with a loud cry to him that had the sharp sickle, saying, Thrust in thy sharp sickle, and gather the clusters of
19 the vine of the earth; for her grapes are fully ripe. And the angel thrust in his sickle into the earth, and gathered the vine of the earth, and cast *it* into the great winepress of
20 the wrath of God. And the winepress was trodden without the city, and blood came out of the winepress, *even* unto the horse bridles, by the space of a thousand *and* six hundred furlongs.

vv. 19, 20, and there is nothing (like the *threshing* of Jer., l.c.) to indicate it here.

18. *the altar*] vi. 9.

which had power over fire] Plainly the A.V. leads us to understand an elemental Angel, like "the Angel of the Waters" in xvi. 5. This is not impossible: the word "fire" has the article, but in Greek "the element of fire" would be naturally so expressed. It may therefore be, that "the Angel of Fire" is made to invoke the judgement on the wicked which will be executed by fire. But it is perhaps easiest to understand that this is the Angel "who had power over *the* fire" on the Altar—perhaps therefore the Angel whom we have already heard of, viii. 3—5.

Thrust in] **Send** as in *v.* 15.

19. *thrust in*] **Cast** as in *v.* 16: but here the Angel himself plainly gathers, as well as supplies the instrument for gathering.

the great winepress] Is. lxiii. 2, 3; Lam. i. 15.

20. *the city*] Probably Jerusalem, see on xiv. 1.

blood] Is. lxiii. 3.

even unto the horse bridles] Literally, **even unto the bridles of the horses**—though no horses are mentioned in the context. Probably the A.V. is right—that it is meant as a mere measure, that any horseman riding there finds his horse bridle-deep in blood; but some think of the horsemen of God's avenging army in xix. 14. There can hardly be a reference to the horses of chap. vi. or of ix. 17.

by the space of] Lit. **from**—perhaps best translated "from a distance of."

a thousand and six hundred furlongs] 200 Roman miles, or about 183 English. It is hardly likely that it is meant, that the blood covered a space of 40 furlongs *square*—more probably, that it extended 1600 (or perhaps 800) in every direction from the city. It has been imagined that the distance specified stands for the length of Palestine, which is estimated by St Jerome at 160 Roman miles, by modern surveys at about 140 English.

REVELATION, XV.

And I saw another sign in heaven, great and marvellous, 15
seven angels having the seven last plagues; for in them is
filled up the wrath of God. And I saw as *it were* a sea of 2
glass mingled with fire: and them that had gotten the victory
over the beast, and over his image, and over his mark, *and*
over the number of his name, stand on the sea of glass, having *the* harps of God. And they sing the song of Moses the 3

THE SEVEN VIALS. CHAPS. XV., XVI.

1. *another sign*] Besides those of xii. 1, 3. Here preparation is made (as in viii. 2) for another sevenfold series of visions. Some have attempted to see a sevenfold series in the three preceding chapters—its elements being the successively appearing figures of the Woman, the Dragon, the Man Child, Michael, the Beast, the False Prophet, and the Lamb. But this seems rather far-fetched: at any rate, it is not likely to have been consciously present to St John's mind.

the seven last plagues; for] Literally, **seven plagues, the last, for**: i.e. the fact that "in them is filled up [or rather "fulfilled, finished"] the wrath of God" is given as the reason why these plagues are the last.

THE TRIUMPH OF THE VICTORS OVER THE BEAST, vv. 2—8.

2. *a sea of glass mingled with fire*] Probably describes an optical appearance much like that of xxi. 18, 21. It gives no reason for doubting that this is the same sea of glass as in iv. 6: it is not till now that the Seer's attention is specially directed to it, and he now describes it in more detail than before.

them that had gotten the victory over] Lit. **them that overcame** [the same word as "him that overcometh" in chapters ii. iii.] **from**...: them that, as we might say, "fought their way clear of" all these dangers and temptations. R.V. "come victorious from."

and over his mark] Should be omitted.

stand] Lit. **standing**.

on the sea] Perhaps literally, for "a sea of glass" would of course be a solid support; or if not, they might walk upon the sea like their Lord, sustained by faith. But perhaps no more is meant than when we speak of a town lying "*on* the sea:" this is supported by the fact that Israel sung the song of Moses on the *shore*, after their passage. And the Greek preposition used, though naturally translated "on," is the same as in the phrase "stand *at* the door" in iii. 20.

harps] As v. 8, xiv. 2: though the harpers here are not the same as in the first place nor (probably) as in the second.

3. *the song of Moses*] Ex. xv.—the song of God's redeemed people, delivered from their enemies, and confident of coming, *but not come yet*, "unto the rest and to the inheritance which the Lord their God doth give unto them." There is probably no allusion to their coming

servant of God, and the song of the Lamb, saying, Great and marvellous *are* thy works, Lord God Almighty; just ⁴ and true *are* thy ways, thou King of saints. Who shall not fear thee, O Lord, and glorify thy name? for *thou* only *art* holy: for all nations shall come and worship before thee; for thy judgments are made manifest.

⁵ And after that I looked, and behold, the temple of the ⁶ tabernacle of the testimony in heaven was opened: and the seven angels came out of the temple, having the seven plagues, clothed in pure and white linen, and having their

from the "Red Sea" of martyrdom: that is a pretty conceit, but below the dignity of prophecy.

the servant of God] Ex. xiv. 31 is particularly referred to; but also in Num. xii. 7; Josh. i. 1, 2, 7, 13, 15, xxii. 5; Ps. cv. 26 "the servant of the Lord" is used as a special honourable title of Moses: cf. Heb. iii. 5.

the song of the Lamb] For the Lamb has redeemed them, as Moses redeemed Israel. "The song of the Lamb" is not a *different* song from "the song of Moses," but the same interpreted in a higher sense: well illustrated by the Christian use of Ps. cxiv., and the other Passover Psalms, in our Easter services.

Great and marvellous &c.] There *may* be references to Ps. cxi. 2, cxxxix. 14, cxlv. 17: but this psalm rather continues the spirit of those than combines their words. It is noticeable that this song, alone of those occurring in this book, has the *parallelism* or quasi-metrical structure of Hebrew poetry.

of saints] Read, **of the nations or of the ages**; the best editors are divided in their preference for one of these readings, but both are better attested than that of the received text. See Jer. x. 7, which no doubt is quoted, in these words and the clause following, and perhaps decides the balance of probability in favour of "nations."

4. *holy*] Not the same word as is applied to God in iv. 8 &c., but ordinarily used of human piety or holiness—and in that sense applied to our Lord, in His human character, in Heb. vii. 26. It is only used of God here and in xvi. 5 (the true text): in both places the sense is that God is "justified in His saying and clear when He is judged."

all nations shall come &c.] Ps. lxxxvi. 9; Is. lxvi. 23. לא יד׳ ל ג.

thy judgements] Rather, **righteous acts**. The word occurs only once besides in the N.T., Rom. v. 18.

5. *the Temple...was opened*] xi. 19. For the phrase "Tabernacle of the Testimony" (or "Witness"—the word is the same) cf. Acts vii. 44: see Num. i. 50). "Was opened in Heaven" would give the sense, more accurately than the order of the A.V.

6. *having*] We should probably read "which had": we see in v. 7 that they did *not* come out having them.

white] More accurately, **bright**.

linen] R.V. "arrayed with *precious* stone, pure *and* bright" follow-

breasts girded with golden girdles. And one of the four 7
beasts gave unto the seven angels seven golden vials full
of the wrath of God, who liveth for ever and ever. And 8
the temple was filled with smoke from the glory of God,
and from his power; and no *man* was able to enter into the
temple, till the seven plagues of the seven angels were fulfilled.

And I heard a great voice out of the temple saying to 16
the seven angels, Go your ways, and pour out the vials of
the wrath of God upon the earth. And the first went, and 2
poured out his vial upon the earth; and there fell a noisome
and grievous sore upon the men which had the mark of the
beast, and *upon* them which worshipped his image.

And the second angel poured out his vial upon the sea; 3

ing a strange reading "stone" (the Greek word differs only by one
letter), which is very strongly attested. If it be right, the nearest parallel
is Ezek. xxviii. 13—where, comparing the next two verses, it seems as
though the human "king of Tyrus" were identified with a fallen
Angel, perhaps the patron of the city. Therefore these holy Angels
may be here described as clothed in glory like his before his fall.

their breasts] As in i. 13, where see note.
7. *vials*] See on v. 8.
8. *smoke*] Is. vi. 4.
no man was able &c. Ex. xl. 35; 1 Kings viii. 11.

The First Vial. Chap. XVI. vv. 1, 2.

1. *the vials*] Read, **the seven vials.**
upon the earth] Lit., **into the earth,** here and in the next verse.
Here "the earth" seems to mean the lower world generally, there the
dry land only.
2. *went*] Lit., **went away,** from the Angels' place in Heaven
before the Temple to the *edge* or "window" whence they can look
down upon the earth.
a noisome and grievous sore] The plagues that accompany these
vials have a close analogy to those of the trumpets in ch. viii. sqq.,
and, like them, have some to the plagues of Egypt: here cf. Ex. ix. 9.
The epithets translated "noisome and grievous" are somewhat more
general: "bad and evil" would be perhaps their most exact equiva-
lents.

The Second Vial, v. 3.

3. *Angel*] Should be omitted, reading **the second, as** we had
"the first" before. So in *vv.* 4, 8, 10, 12, 17.

and it became as the blood of a dead *man*: and every living soul died in the sea.

4 And the third angel poured out his vial upon the rivers 5 and fountains of waters; and they became blood. And I heard the angel of the waters say, Thou art righteous, O Lord, which art, and wast, and shalt be, because thou hast 6 judged thus. For they have shed the blood of saints and prophets, and thou hast given them blood to drink; for they 7 are worthy. And I heard another out of the altar say, Even so, Lord God Almighty, true and righteous *are* thy judgments. 8 And the fourth angel poured out his vial upon the sun; and *power* was given unto him to scorch men with fire. 9 And men were scorched *with* great heat, and blasphemed

as the blood of a dead man] Lit., **blood as it were of a dead man.** See Ex. vii. 17 sqq., esp. 21. Compare in this Book ch. viii. 8; but here the plague has a wider reach.

The Third Vial, vv. 4—7.

4. *the rivers...waters*] viii. 10; see on xiv. 7.

5. *the angel of the waters*] Here at least there is no question (see on vii. 1, xiv. 18) that we have an elemental Angel; see Exc. I.

O Lord] Should be omitted.

which art, and wast, and shalt be] Read, **which art and wast, the Holy One**: the word for "holy" being the same as in xv. 4. As the phrase for "which art and wast" is ungrammatical (see on i. 4), it is perhaps better to render "which is and which was." For the omission of "which is to come," cf. xi. 17. Its virtual insertion here in the A.V. seems to be an oversight in translation, not a mistaken reading.

6. *of saints and prophets*] See xi. 18, xviii. 20.

for they are worthy] Omit "for:" but we may compare iii. 4, where a very different judgement is grounded on the same weighty words.

7. *another out of*] Should be omitted: St John "heard the Altar" itself "say" what follows. Why the unusual image should be used of the Altar speaking, instead of a voice only coming from it (cf. ix. 13), we cannot say: but perhaps vi. 9 sqq. suggests why the Altar utters its Amen to God's vengeance on the persecutors.

Even so] **Yea**, as in i. 7, &c.

The Fourth Vial, vv. 8, 9.

8. *the sun*] Cf. viii. 12; but there the light of the Sun is diminished, here his heat is increased. "Power" is not expressed in the original.

the name of God, which hath power over these plagues: and they repented not to give him glory.

And the fifth angel poured out his vial upon the seat of the beast; and his kingdom was full of darkness; and they gnawed their tongues for pain, and blasphemed the God of heaven because of their pains and their sores, and repented not of their deeds.

And the sixth angel poured out his vial upon the great river Euphrates; and the water thereof was dried up, that the way of the kings of the east might be prepared. And I

9. *repented not to give him glory*] Contrast xi. 13, which therefore cannot refer to the same judgements as here, nor (probably) to judgements on the same place or people.

THE FIFTH VIAL, vv. 10, 11.

10. *the seat*] Better **throne**: see xiii. 2. The word is best taken quite literally, not in the vague sense of the "seat" of his empire.
darkness] Ex. x. 21; ch. ix. 2.

THE SIXTH VIAL, vv. 12—16.

12. *Euphrates*] ix. 14 sqq. Where Babylon confessedly stands for Rome, we should naturally understand the Euphrates to be used also in a symbolical sense, possibly as meaning the Tiber. But the Tiber is not a very "great river:" and the mention of "the kings of the east" (lit., **the kings from the rising of the sun**) as needing to pass the Euphrates seems to mark it as meant literally.
the water thereof was dried up] Referring to the way that the ancient Babylon was actually captured by Cyrus, by drawing off the water of the Euphrates into a reservoir, so as to make its bed passable for a few hours. Though not mentioned in Dan. v., nor by Cyrus in his lately discovered account of the capture, there seems no doubt that this incident is historical: the details given in Hdt. I. 191 agree exactly with those of the predictions in Is. xliv. 27, xlv. 3; Jer. l. 38, 44, li. 30—32, 36.
that the way &c.] Compare the prophecies of Cyrus' advance in Is. xli. 2, 25. He is there spoken of as advancing on Babylon "from the East:" much more would any invader of Rome or the Roman Empire come from the East, if he had to cross the literal Euphrates.
the kings of the east] Rather, **from the east**. In xvii. 16 we hear of the kings of the earth combining to attack Babylon, and the Euphrates *may* be dried up, only that the kings from the east may be able to advance to bear their part in the assault. But why do they specially need their "way to be prepared"? The Euphrates is a far less impassable frontier than the Alps or the Mediterranean: it was

saw three unclean spirits like frogs *come* out of the mouth of

in fact in St John's day the weak side of the empire. And probably in this fact we may see the key to the prophecy. In Dan. viii. 8, xi. 4 we have the division of Alexander's empire described as "toward the four winds of heaven:" in xi. 5, 6 the Egyptian and Asiatic kingdoms are designated as "the kings of the south and of the north." It is implied therefore that the kings of Macedon are kings of the West: and it remains that the other great and *permanent* kingdom (of smaller ephemeral ones there were more than four) which arose from the dissolution of Alexander's shall be "the kings of the east." Now this designation obliges us to think of the *Parthians*, the longest-lived of all the Alexandrine kingdoms, and the only one surviving in St John's day. This differed from the others, in respect that its royal dynasty was native, not Macedonian, but it was not the less a portion of Alexander's empire, inheriting his traditions. (The veneer of Greek culture existing among the Arsacidae is well illustrated by the grim story of the performance of the *Bacchae* at the time of the death of Crassus: it is instructive also to look at the series of coins engraved in Smith's *Dictionary* s.v. *Arsacidae*, where we see Hellenic types gradually giving way to Assyrian.) In Enoch liv. 9 we hear of "the chiefs of the east among the Parthians and Medes:" that passage throws no real light on this, except as shewing who "the kings of the east" were understood to be, by a person familiar with the same ideas as St John. Now in St John's time (whether the earlier or later date be assigned to the vision) there were apprehensions of a Parthian invasion of the empire on behalf of a pseudo-Nero (Tac. *Hist.* I. ii. 3), i.e. a shadow of Antichrist: and it is likely that St John's prophecy is expressed (as so many O.T. prophecies are) *in terms of* the present political situation. But it had no immediate *fulfilment:* the danger from Parthia under Domitian passed off, and soon afterwards its power was broken for ever by Trajan. But its place was taken in time by the Sassanian kingdom of Persia, which remained for three centuries the most formidable enemy of Rome. Then, as Parthia had been broken by Trajan and fell before Persia, so Persia, broken by Heraclius, fell before the Arabs, who endangered the existence, and actually appropriated great part, of the Eastern Empire. To them succeeded the Turks, before whom it fell.

Now while no event in this series can be called a definite or precise fulfilment of St John's prophecy, we may hold that this habitual relation of "the kings of the east" to the Roman empire supplies a number of typical or partial fulfilments. A pseudo-Nero, made emperor by a Parthian conquest of Rome, and ruling (as might be expected) in Nero's spirit, would have been almost a real Antichrist: and for such a revelation of Antichrist St John's immediate readers were meant to be prepared. Again, in the conquests and persecutions of Sapor and Chosroes, of Omar, Mohammed, and Suleiman, it was intended that the Christians of the empire should see the approaches and threatenings of the kingdom of Antichrist. But the empire—whether Roman, Byzantine, or Austrian—continued to "withhold, that he may

the dragon, and out of the mouth of the beast, and out of the mouth of the false prophet. For they are the spirits of devils, 14 working miracles, which go forth unto the kings of the earth and of the whole world, to gather them to the battle of that great day of God Almighty. Behold, I come as a thief. Blessed *is* 15

be revealed in his season"; and its modern representatives will continue to do so "until it be taken out of the way: and then shall that Wicked be revealed."
It may be observed that Dan. xi. 40 sqq. seems to imply that the political situation in the East in the days of Antichrist will be not unlike that in the days of Antiochus: for while it is certain that the early part of that chapter applies to the latter, it is hard to regard the passage beginning at *v.* 36 as adequately fulfilled in him. Humanly speaking, it does not seem that the changes now going on in the east are as capable of producing a conquering empire, as they are of producing an antichristian fanaticism: but *qui vivra verra*.
13. *And I saw* &c.] Between the sixth and seventh vial, as between the sixth and seventh seal, and between the sixth and seventh trumpet, there appears a vision that has nothing to do with the series in which it is inserted, but which marks the near approach of the final conflict between the kingdoms of light and of darkness. But here we have the preparation for the conflict on the side of the latter, not, as in the two other places, of the former.
unclean spirits] This phrase is in the Gospels usually synonymous with "devils" or rather "demons." But here the term "spirit" seems to be rather used in the sense of "inspiring power,"—they are called in the next verse "spirits *of* demons." See St John's 1 Ep. iv. 3; 1 Tim. iv. 1, which probably refer to the same order of things as this: also 1 Sam. xvi. 14 &c. (note especially "he prophesied," xviii. 10), 1 Kings xxii. 21 sqq.
like frogs] There may be a reference to the plague of Egypt, Ex. viii. 2 sqq., but the parallel is not close. Frogs were proverbial for their constant and meaningless noise, which some think helps us to interpret the likeness. If so, one would be tempted to connect it with St Hippolytus' view mentioned on xvii. 12.
the false prophet] Identified by xix. 20 with the second beast of xiii. 11.
14. *devils*] Strictly **demons**: see on *v.* 13.
miracles] Strictly **signs**, as in xiii. 14. One may notice, that this is the word *always* used for miracles in St John's Gospel.
go forth unto the kings &c.] See xix. 19, and cf. xx. 3, 8.
the battle] xvii. 14, xix. 19—21.
15. *Behold, I come*] St John apparently hears, and writes down as he hears, the words of Christ spoken in the midst of his vision.
as a thief] See iii. 3 and references.
Blessed is he that watcheth] The *image* is that of St Matt. xxiv. 43, though in the *phrase* there may be a reminiscence of the different image of St Luke xii. 37.

he that watcheth, and keepeth his garments, lest he walk
16 naked, and they see his shame. And he gathered them together into a place called in the Hebrew tongue Armageddon.
17 And the seventh angel poured out his vial into the air; and there came a great voice out of the temple of heaven,

and keepeth his garments] The forewarned householder sits up with his clothes on, and the thief will decamp as soon as he sees him. If he were *not* forewarned, he might hear the thief at work, and start naked out of bed, but would be too late for anything but a fruitless chase in unseemly and ridiculous guise. It seems quite irrelevant to fancy an allusion to the curious Jewish custom, that if a priest fell asleep on night duty in the Temple, his clothes were set on fire—which of course would have the effect of making him throw them off, and run away naked.

his shame] Lit. **uncomeliness**, as 1 Cor. xii. 23.

THE MUSTER FOR THE BATTLE OF ARMAGEDDON, v. 16.

16. *And he gathered them*] More probably, **and they** [the unclean spirits] **gathered them**. The sentence goes on from the end of *v*. 14, *v*. 15 being strictly parenthetical.

Armageddon] The spelling which has the best authority is "Harmagedon." The meaning, according as we read *Ar* or *Har*, is "the City" or "the Mountain of Megiddo." But the insertion of "in the Hebrew tongue" *perhaps* indicates, that the *meaning* of the name Megiddo (which is apparently "cleaving") is more important than the geographical note. There is some truth (though some exaggeration) in the description of the plain of Esdraelon as "the battle-field of Palestine:" but the only occasions when *Megiddo* is mentioned in connexion with a battle are Judges v. 19, 2 Kings xxiii. 29 (cf. Zech. xii. 11). Of course Megiddo or its neighbourhood ("the Mountain of Megiddo" might be Tabor or that conventionally called Little Hermon) *may* be the destined scene of the gathering and overthrow of the Antichristian powers: but it is hardly to be assumed as certain. In Zech. xiv. 4, 5 the Mount of Olives, in Joel iii. 12 the Valley of Jehoshaphat (wherever that is: it must be a proper name, though a significant one, but it is a convention, and an improbable one, that identifies it with the gorge of the Kidron) seem to be represented as the scene of the Judgement.

THE SEVENTH VIAL. PRELIMINARIES OF JUDGEMENT, vv. 17—21.

17. *into the air*] Lit. **upon the air**, according to the best reading.

of heaven] Should be omitted, but of course it is the heavenly Temple that is meant. Here it seems that the Throne (that of iv. 2) is inside it: but see on iv. 6. Though coming from the Throne, this voice is not defined, like that of xxi. 5, as the voice of Him that sat on it: but comparing xxi. 6 it is possible we ought to take it so.

from the throne, saying, It is done. And there were voices, 18
and thunders, and lightnings; and there was a great earthquake, such as was not since men were upon the earth, so mighty an earthquake, *and* so great. And the great city 19 was *divided* into three parts, and the cities of the nations fell: and great Babylon came in remembrance before God, to give unto her the cup of the wine of the fierceness of his wrath. And every island fled *away*, and the mountains were 20 not found. And there fell upon men a great hail out of 21 heaven, *every stone* about the weight of a talent: and men

It is done] More literally, **it is come to pass**: but the same word is used in St Luke xiv. 22, where of course the A. V. is right. God's great Judgement has *not* come to pass yet, but everything has been done to prepare for it. "One who had fired a train would say 'It is done,' though the explosion had not yet taken place," and, we may add, might use the same words again when it *had*, as in xxi. 6.

18. *voices, and thunders, and lightnings*] viii. 5, xi. 19. Here the best reading is **lightnings and voices and thunders.**

earthquake] vi. 12, xi. 13: but this earthquake seems distinguished from those as surpassing them greatly in degree:—unless the second of those be the *local* aspect of this.

such as was not, &c.] Cf. Dan. xii. 1; St Matt. xxiv. 21.

19. *the great city*] Probably *Jerusalem*, as in chap. xi. 8. It seems pointless to suppose *Babylon* to be mentioned twice over: while on the other view there is a climax. Jerusalem is (or is to be) converted—she is the City of God again, yet even she is sorely shaken (cf. 1 St Peter iv. 17): other cities are wholly overthrown: while the City of God's Enemy is to receive something more than overthrow.

was divided into] There is probably a reminiscence of Zech. xiv. 4, 5.

three parts] It is just possible that there may be a reference to the three parties of John, Eleazar, and Simon, into which Jerusalem was divided at the time of its siege by Titus. We have seen (on xi. 13) that Jerusalem is to be converted at the very last: but xi. 7, 8 prove that this will not happen till the war with Antichrist is at least begun: consequently, this verse may be concerned with the judgement on Jerusalem still infidel.

the cities of the nations] Distinguished from Jerusalem on the one hand, and from Babylon on the other.

the cup of the wine &c.] See on xiv. 10.

20. *every island* &c.] See vi. 14.

great hail] viii. 7, xi. 19.

about the weight of a talent] While natural hailstones weighing the sixtieth part of one are noticed as extraordinary. Some notice, that the stones thrown by the engines at the siege of Jerusalem are said to have been of a talent weight: but it would be far-fetched to suppose these

blasphemed God, because of the plague of the hail; for the plague thereof was exceeding great.

17 And there came one of the seven angels which had the seven vials, and talked with me, saying unto me, *Come* hither; I will shew unto thee the judgment of the great whore 2 that sitteth upon many waters: with whom the kings of the earth have committed fornication, and the inhabiters of the earth have been made drunk with the wine of her fornication. 3 So he carried me away in the spirit into the wilderness: and

referred to. In this verse at least, the judgement described cannot be on Jerusalem—see on xi. 13 fin.

THE JUDGEMENT OF THE GREAT WHORE. HER POMP.
CHAP. XVII. vv. 1—6.

1. *one of the angels*] So xxi. 9: cf. v. 5.

I will shew unto thee the judgement &c.] Which had been exhibited, and described in general terms, in xvi. 19: but the seer is now to have a nearer view of it, and describe it in detail.

the great whore] The image of the *harlot* is taken from the Old Testament description, not of Babylon, which when personified is a virgin (Is. xlvii. 1), but of Tyre (Is. xxiii. 15 sqq.) and Nineveh (Nah. iii. 4). The truth is, the Antichristian Empire is conceived as embodying the various forms of evil that existed in previous earthly empires. They have existed and become great, in virtue of what was *good* in them: (see St Augustine's *City of God*, v. xii. 3, 5, xv. &c.; Epist. cxxxviii. 17: cf. Plat. *Rep.* I. xxiii. pp. 351—2); they are the divinely appointed protectors of God's people (Jer. xxix. 7; Rom. xiii. 1—7; 1 Tim. ii. 2) though their possible persecutors: and so they at once hinder (2 Thess. ii. 6, 7) the coming of Antichrist, and foreshadow his coming by acting in his spirit. The Babylon of Nebuchadnezzar had (as no one can read the Book of Daniel without seeing) something nobler in it than mere conquering pride, and to this nobler element Isaiah does justice: but St John sees (it does not follow that the natural man will see) that in the New Babylon the baser element is supreme.

on many waters] Jer. li. 13. Literally true of the old Babylon, it is explained of the new in v. 15.

2. *with whom the kings*, &c.] Is. xxiii. 17.

the inhabiters &c.] Jer. li. 7.

3. *in the spirit*] Cf. i. 10, iv. 2, xxi. 10.

into the wilderness] In Is. xxi. 1 the situation of the ancient Babylon is apparently conceived as in a desert: and in fact Babylonia has been reduced to one, despite its unsurpassed natural fertility. It *may* be relevant to compare the present desolation of the once populous Campagna of Rome.

I saw a woman sit upon a scarlet coloured beast, full of names of blasphemy, having seven heads and ten horns. And the woman was arrayed in purple and scarlet colour, 4

But another interpretation has been suggested. In xii. 6, 14 we found that the Woman, the City of God and the Mother of His Son, fled into the wilderness, and there was concealed through the time of the Beast's reign: and some have thought that the Woman in the Wilderness whom we meet with here is actually the same as the one we then parted with—the faithful City become an harlot (Is. i. 21.)

This view is an unpleasant one, and seems out of harmony with the tone either of chap. xii. or of this chapter. But it is supported by the argument, that the image of a harlot is most frequently, in the O. T. used of the unfaithful City of God: Is. i. 21; Jer. ii. 20, iii. 1 sqq., 6 sqq.; Ezek. xvi. xxiii.; Hos. i.—iii., iv. 15; Mic. i. 7: while it is applied to heathen cities only in Is. xxiii. fin.; Nah. iii. 4, already quoted.

On the other hand, in almost all those passages it is insisted on, more or less expressly, that the whoredoms of unfaithful Israel have the special guilt of *adultery*: and of that there is no hint here, the Lord does not say of Babylon as of Aholibah that she was "Mine." This seems to destroy the parallel with the former nine cases, which moreover is less close, as regards the details of language, than that with the two latter.

And further, the identification of the two Women is only possible on the assumption, that the Mother of chap. xii. is the true Christian Church, and the Harlot of this chapter the apostate Christian Church of Rome. Now we have seen reason to reject the former view: nor does the latter appear any more tenable. This subject is discussed in the Introduction: it may be enough to refer to St John's own words in 1 Ep. iv. 2, 3, as proving that the spirit of the theology (whatever may be said of the political attitude) of the existing Roman Church is, on the whole, of God—that it certainly is *not* the spirit of Antichrist.

Neither, on the other hand, is it possible to restrict the application of this chapter to the pagan Rome of the past. As to this the argument seems decisive, that though there was no lack of fornication, literal and spiritual, in the Rome of St John's day, yet she could not be said to commit fornication with *the kings of the earth*, whom it was her policy to enslave by force, rather than to entrap by blandishments.

a scarlet coloured beast] Undoubtedly the same as the Beast of xiii. 1—8, though there his colour was not mentioned. It is symbolic (compare that of the dragon, xii. 3), as being the colour of blood: perhaps also suggestive of the imperial purple.

full of names of blasphemy] So xiii. 1, but here the blasphemies are even more all-pervading. The construction in the Greek, according to the best text, is irregular and peculiar, but cannot alter the sense.

4. *arrayed in purple and scarlet colour*] Protestant interpreters have been fond of applying this description to the robes of Roman bishops and cardinals: and perhaps not altogether unjustly. See Introduction, pp. 57, 58.

and decked with gold and precious stone and pearls, having a golden cup in her hand full of abominations and filthiness of her fornication: and upon her forehead *was* a name written, MYSTERY, BABYLON THE GREAT, THE MOTHER OF HARLOTS AND ABOMINATIONS OF THE EARTH. And I saw the woman drunken with the blood of the saints, and with the blood of the martyrs of Jesus: and when I saw her, I wondered *with* great admiration. And the angel said unto me, Wherefore didst thou marvel? I will tell thee the mystery of the woman, and of the beast that carrieth her, which hath the seven heads and

decked with gold] Lit. **gilded with gold**: perhaps illustrated by the contemporary picture of the historical imperial harlot, Messalina.
precious stone] Lit. **stone**, used, of course, collectively. See on xv. 6.
a golden cup] See Jer. li. 7 already quoted. We can hardly say that the cup serves her to drink the blood of saints and martyrs (*v.* 6), but it is meant to suggest that she is drunken and invites to drunkenness, as well as to uncleanness.
5. *upon her forehead* was *a name written*] Probably not branded on the flesh, but tied on as a label, as Roman harlots actually did wear their names.
Mystery] Interpreters compare "the mystery of lawlessness" in 2 Thess. ii. 7. The use of the word in i. 20 may illustrate its meaning here: it indicates that "Babylon the Great" is to be understood in a mystical sense.
of harlots] Rather, **of the harlots**. She is the chief of these, and the cause of the rest being what they are. Therefore, though the fornications of Babylon are to be understood spiritually, yet her guilt includes the actual licentiousness of the Rome of Nero and Domitian, and in a wider sense "the sin of great cities" generally.
6. *with the blood of the saints* &c.] xviii. 24.
martyrs] See on ii. 13.
admiration] Better, **wonder**, the substantive used being cognate to the verb. Of course "admiration" is not meant in the modern sense of the word.

The Interpretation of the Mystery, vv. 7, 8.

7. *Wherefore didst thou marvel?*] Again the word should be **wonder**. For the angel's surprise at the seer not comprehending at once, see vii. 14.
I will tell thee] The "I" is emphatic: "*I* will tell thee, since *thou* findest it so strange."
the mystery] i.e. the mystical meaning: see on *v.* 5.
of the woman, and of the beast] The latter is explained first, *vv.* 8—14: the Woman is not clearly defined till *v.* 18.

ten horns. The beast that thou sawest was, and is not; 8
and shall ascend out of the bottomless *pit*, and go into perdition: and they that dwell on the earth shall wonder, whose names were not written in the book of life from the foundation of the world, when they behold the beast that was, and is not, and yet is. *And* here *is* the mind which 9

8. *was, and is not*] On the whole, ancient tradition where it speaks, and modern criticism, agree in the interpretation of these words. *Nero*, who killed himself in June A.D. 68, "had been, and was not" at the date of this vision: but his reappearance was looked for by many, with various feelings of hope and fear. When his dethronement and execution were imminent, it was said that he had talked of going to the East, and establishing his throne at Jerusalem (see on xi. 9): while one form (see on xvi. 12) of the belief that he survived, was that he had fled to the Parthians, and would return under their protection.

Now St John is not to be held responsible for all the opinions, superstitious or at least irrational, that were held by his pagan contemporaries about the return of Nero from the East. But when we find that the belief in Nero's destined return was held by Christians for the next four centuries, if not longer, when it had quite passed out of the minds of pagans, it becomes probable that St John *was* answerable for *their* belief; at any rate, they grounded it on his words. And it is possible that he means to tell us, that the Antichrist who is to come will actually be Nero risen from the dead (we notice, that in the words of the text his death, the reality of which is historically certain, is not denied, but affirmed): more probably, Antichrist will be a new Nero in the same way as he will be a new Antiochus, an enemy of God as they were, typified by them inasmuch as they were actuated by his spirit. It is needless to suppose with M. Renan that Nero is called "the Beast" in allusion to a loathsome atrocity said to be committed by him disguised as one: the analogy of Dan. vii. is what determines the image.

shall ascend out of the bottomless pit] xi. 7, where see note. Perhaps there is a distinction between the appearance of the Beast indicated here and that of xiii. 1. The persecuting Roman Empire, which was antichristian *in posse*, arose "out of the sea" like other Empires of the earth (Dan. vii. 3), out of the confused and often sinful, but not infra-natural, turmoil of the life of this world. But the *final* and *developed* antichristian and persecuting power, the Empire of Antichrist himself, will have a directly infernal source.

go into perdition] So v. 11: cf. 2 Thess. ii. 3. The fulfilment of this threat is indicated in xix. 20.

shall wonder] xiii. 3, 4.

whose names were not written] xiii. 8. We should almost certainly read, **are** [or **is**] **not written,** as there: and probably **name** for "names."

that was] Read, **that he was.**

and yet is] Read, **and shall come: lit. shall be here:** the word is cognate with that ordinarily used of the *Coming* of Christ.

9. *And here*] Omit "and." Compare xiii. 18. As there, the

10 hath wisdom. The seven heads are seven mountains, on which the woman sitteth. And there are seven kings: five

words seem to indicate that "the mind which hath wisdom" will recognise the meaning of the image, though it is obscurely expressed. But the "wisdom" required is not merely the faculty of guessing riddles—it is the wisdom enlightened from above; including however, we may suppose, an intelligent knowledge of the facts and principles of human history.

seven mountains] These words prove decisively that Babylon represents the City of *Rome*. It is needless to quote classical descriptions of Rome as the City of the Seven Mountains: the designation is as unmistakeable as the name would be. Nevertheless, it is curious that the number is rather conventionally than actually true. The *original* seven hills were the Palatium, the Germalus (virtually a part of the Palatine hill), the Velia (the low ridge crossing the Forum), the Cispius, Oppius, and Fagutal (three summits of the Esquiline), and the Suburra which is not a hill at all. But Rome in the days of its greatness covered the Palatine, Capitol, Aventine, Caelian, Esquiline (two of the ridges of which, though not very well defined, are yet as distinct as the two next), the Quirinal, the Viminal (these two, for some inexplicable reason, were never counted among the "seven mountains," though higher than any of them, but were always called "hills"), and the Janiculum and Vatican on the other side of the Tiber. In modern Rome, the buildings have spread over the Pincian Hill, but the Caelian, Palatine, Aventine, and much of the Esquiline are nearly uninhabited.

10. *And there are seven kings*] Rather, **and they** [the seven heads] **are seven kings**: they have a double significance—standing *both* for the seven mountains and the seven kings.

Who are these kings? According to the view mentioned on xiii. 2, that the Beast is not the Roman Empire, but an embodiment of the worldly imperial spirit, it is plausibly held that the kings are kingdoms or empires (like the "kings of Persia and Grecia" in Dan. viii.)—that they are the four kingdoms of Daniel ii. and vii., together with Egypt and Assyria that came before Babylon, and the kingdoms of modern Europe that come after Rome. On this view, the ten horns are all on one head: it is this ten-horned head which receives the deadly wound of xiii. 3: i.e. the Beast is nearly slain (the Empire *as an evil and persecuting power* overthrown) by the conversion, first of the later emperors, and then of the sovereigns of Europe, to Christianity: but he revives—e.g. in Julian after Constantine, and again in the neo-paganism of the Renaissance and the persecutions of the Reformation.

With all the elements of truth that must be acknowledged in this view, it seems hardly possible to doubt that the Beast, so closely united with the City of the Seven Hills, represents the *Roman* Empire particularly. On this view, the "kings" have been taken to represent *forms of government*—Rome having been successively governed, it is said, by kings, consuls, dictators, decemvirs, military tribunes, empe-

are fallen, and one is, *and* the other is not yet come; and

rors, and Christian emperors (the last being taken, as before, to be the *wounded* head: some however make the conversion of Constantine a wound to the *sixth* head, and count the Ostrogoth kings as the seventh). But considering that the dictatorship, the decemvirate, and even the tribunate, were transitory episodes in the Roman government —the first avowedly exceptional, the second both exceptional and ephemeral, and all three, as well as the primitive monarchy, probably unknown to St John's original readers,—this view does not appear even plausible.

It remains then that the kings be taken as individual Emperors of Rome: (it must be remembered that though these were never called "kings" in Latin, the Greek equivalent title was constantly applied to the Emperors: see e.g. 1 St Peter ii. 13, 17.) Who then were the first seven Emperors? According to the common reckoning, Julius Caesar, Augustus, Tiberius, Gaius (often called by modern writers by his nickname *Caligula*, "Little Boots"), Claudius, Nero, and Galba. But Julius Caesar, though he received the title of *Imperator* as the later Emperors did, cannot be considered, and is not considered by careful historians, as the first of the "Emperors," if the Empire be spoken of as a settled form of government. His authority in the state, so far as it was constitutional at all, lay in his Dictatorship: which office was legally abolished immediately after his death, and never revived. Augustus, and the later Emperors, ruled not as Dictator, but as Chief of the Senate with the power of Tribune.

five are fallen] Augustus, Tiberius, Gaius, Claudius, and Nero. (It is argued that the word "fallen" is not "appropriate to Augustus and Tiberius, who died in their beds:" but see Gen. xxv. 8, mar.) Is then the "one who is" Galba? So he is generally understood by those who adopt this scheme of interpretation: and if so, the date of the vision (see Introduction) is fixed at a time between June A.D. 68, and the 15th of January 69, when Galba was murdered. He was succeeded by Otho, who certainly "continued a short space," if he could be said to continue at all: he killed himself, on April 15th, when defeated by the army of Vitellius, who had revolted from Galba a few days before his murder by Otho.

But the rest of the prophecy, on this view, received nothing that can be reckoned as even a typical fulfilment. Vitellius, despite many contemptible vices, was a good-natured man, and not a bad ruler, so far as he had energy to rule at all. He could not be considered as an incarnation of the Antichristian power, nor even as a revival of Nero, though he, as well as Otho, treated Nero's memory with respect. And considering that Galba had only reigned in Rome for a few weeks before his death (though he had been acknowledged longer), that Otho *never* had an uncontested title, and Vitellius only from about the end of April to July 1st, it seems likelier that these three are passed over, as claimants of empire (and they had not been the only ones: see on *v.* 12) rather than actual emperors. Thus, the sixth king will be Vespasian, who was proclaimed emperor on July 1st, A.D. 69: his troops gained a decisive

11 when he cometh, he must continue a short *space*. And the beast that was, and is not, even he is the eighth, and is of 12 the seven, and goeth into perdition. And the ten horns
victory over those of Vitellius late in October, and Rome was taken, and Vitellius killed, on Dec. 21st.

Vespasian reigned well and peaceably, and was succeeded by his elder son Titus, in June 79: who "continued a short space," till Sept. 13th, A.D. 81, when he died, aged 40;—murdered, as some said, by his brother Domitian, who succeeded him, and who was regarded, by pagans and Christians alike, as a revival of Nero (Juv. iv. 38; Tert. *Apol.* c. 7). Like Nero, he persecuted the Christians: like Nero, he indulged in the most hideous vices: though unlike Nero, he had a strong sense of decorum, and was fanatically attached to the Roman religion. Further than this, the vision does not follow the fortunes of the Empire in detail. At the point where the type of Antichrist comes into the history, the prophecy introduces Antichrist himself: cf. Dan. xi., as understood by most orthodox interpreters.

must continue a short space] Both "continue" and "short" seem to be emphatic—his reign is to be short, but not ephemeral. Thus the designation seems more appropriate to Titus than to Otho. St Victorinus (in the present text) applies it to *Nerva*, who like Titus reigned mildly for only two years. But his successor Trajan (though he to a certain extent sanctioned the persecution of Christianity, and is said himself to have condemned St Ignatius) was anything but an Antichrist. It seems as though St Victorinus (or his editor) were making a rather clumsy attempt to reconcile the interpretation here given, which he was acquainted with as a tradition, with the general belief that St John was writing under Domitian.

11. *even he is the eighth*] Perhaps rather, **both is himself the eighth, and is of the seven.**

of the seven] is most easily understood "is one of the seven"—i.e. the eighth emperor of Rome, in whom the antichristian spirit of the empire finds its personal embodiment, will be a revival of one of his seven predecessors—viz. Nero, the fifth of them. The words can however be taken to mean "the successor and result of the seven, following and springing out of them;" if a scheme of interpretation be preferred with which this meaning harmonises better.

goeth into perdition] Implies something more than the "fall" of the other kings.

12. *the ten horns* &c.] Comparing Dan. vii. and viii., we can hardly doubt that these horns represent kingdoms related to the Roman Empire as the kingdoms of the Diadochi to that of Alexander. Such are the principal kingdoms of modern Europe: and in the recognition of this fact lies the key to mediaeval and to much of modern history. (See Sir F. Palgrave's *Normandy and England*, Intr. ch. 1, *English Commonwealth*, chh. 10, 11, 17, 18, 19, and Dr Bryce's *Holy Roman Empire*, passim). The number ten is probably to be taken as exact, but we cannot *yet* point to it as being definitely realised. It is remarkable that the kingdoms of Europe have (as is pointed out by Elliot, *Horae*

which thou sawest are ten kings, which have received no kingdom as yet; but receive power as kings one hour with the beast. These have one mind, and shall give 13 their power and strength unto the beast. These shall 14

Apoc. Part IV. ch. iv. § 2) tended at many periods to that number: but there are now more than ten sovereign states in Christendom, or even in Europe only. Judging from the analogy of the Macedonian kingdoms (see on xvi. 12) we may guess that only those are included which are of considerable size and power, and have some claim to continue the imperial tradition of the common predecessor. The existing states of Germany, France, Austria, and Russia have such a claim (which they assert, more or less constantly and more or less legitimately, by the use of the imperial title): so has our own country, which has claimed rank as an empire coordinate with continental ones since the days of Edgar the Peaceable: so (more doubtfully) have Spain and Portugal in virtue of their memories, and so have the new kingdoms of Greece and Italy in virtue of their hopes. A tenth can hardly be named, for Sweden though powerful was not imperial even under Gustavus Adolphus or Charles XII., and Turkey could hardly be thus coupled with the states of Christendom: but believers will watch the developement of "the Eastern Question" with a solemn interest.

receive power as kings] It is extraordinary that St Hippolytus, (*On Christ and Antichrist*, ch. 27) inferred, apparently not from this passage, but from Dan. ii. 42, that the ten powers of the last days, among which the Roman empire is partitioned, will pass from monarchies into *democracies*. Few things were humanly speaking less likely in his days, few more so in ours.

one hour] Presumably for a very short time: the end will be very near when the ten horns appear in their final and unmistakeable form. It therefore ought not to surprise us, that we cannot identify them all yet, that we only see them in process of developement.

Another explanation of the horns has been suggested (Renan, *L'Antechrist*, pp. 433, 4)—that they are *the claimants of the Empire* who appeared in the "long year" (Tac. *Dial.* 17) after the death of Nero. It is possible to enumerate ten of these, but unfortunately not without including both Galba and Vespasian, one of whom must be reckoned among the *heads*, and therefore not the *horns*. Else, both Rome and the Roman Empire were so severely shaken in the civil wars between the rival emperors, and their actual fall in the fifth century so nearly anticipated, that this interpretation harmonises well enough with *v.* 16. On the other hand, it fails to give meaning to *v.* 13, or to agree with the undoubted meaning of the same symbol in Daniel.

with the beast] Yet in Dan. vii. 7, 8 the ten horns appear *before* the little horn (which seems to correspond with this appearance of the Beast, no longer merely as a polity but as a person), and three of them are destroyed by him. I do not pretend to be able to reconcile the two.

13. *shall give their power and strength* &c.] Cf. xvi. 14, xix. 19, 20.
14. *These shall make war with the Lamb*] See the same passages.

make war with the Lamb, and the Lamb shall overcome them: for he is the Lord of lords, and King of kings: and they that are with him *are* called, and chosen, and faith-
15 ful. And he saith unto me, The waters which thou sawest, where the whore sitteth, are peoples, and multitudes, and
16 nations, and tongues. And the ten horns which thou sawest upon the beast, these shall hate the whore, and shall make her desolate and naked, and shall eat her flesh, and
17 burn her with fire. For God hath put in their hearts to

Lord of lords, and King of kings] xix. 16; Dan. ii. 47.
they that are with him] xix. 14.
called, and chosen, and faithful] All common titles of *Christians* applied even to the imperfect Churches on earth.
15. *The waters* &c.] Some compare Is. viii. 7 for the use of *waters* as an emblem of *multitudes*.
16. *upon the beast*] Read, **and the beast**: he (in his personal advent) and they will act together, against Babylon as well as against the Lamb.
shall hate the whore] Though she had been the object of their unchaste love, *v.* 2, and will be of their passionate regret, xviii. 9. Nero's treatment of his mistress or wife Poppaea cannot be alluded to, but is a good illustration of the image, and vindication of its consistency with vicious human nature.
naked] Cf. Is. xlvii. 2, 3; Ezek. xvi. 37—9.
eat her flesh, and burn her with fire] i.e. shall plunder and burn Rome. The threat was symbolised and almost fulfilled in the burning of the Capitol by the partisans of Vitellius, and the storming of Rome by those of Vespasian: it received a more complete fulfilment in the repeated disasters of the fifth century. The sack of Rome by Bourbon and the Germans was a less striking fulfilment: but the real and final one is no doubt still to come.
We should naturally understand from these words, that the judgement on Babylon described in the next chapter will be executed by the "kings of the earth," the ten States among which the Roman Empire is partitioned. But it is almost as remarkable as the view of Hippolytus noted on *v.* 12, that St Benedict is recorded (S. Greg. *Dial.* ii. 15) to have said, "Rome will not be destroyed by the nations, but be overthrown by thunderstorms, whirlwinds and *earthquakes.*" We know what he did not, that Rome stands, like Pompeii, on volcanic soil, within a few miles of volcanos that, though not active now, were so to the verge of historical times, and may be again. This book does not tell us positively how Babylon *will* fall, and no one has the right to pretend to say: but it is at least suggestive to know that it *might* fall by a convulsion which unbelievers would think quite "natural," while believers would see its place in the scheme of providence.
17. *For God hath put in their hearts* &c.] The very same "judicial blindness" is spoken of in 2 Thess. ii. 11.

fulfil his will, and to agree, and give their kingdom unto the beast, until the words of God shall be fulfilled. And the 18 woman which thou sawest is *that* great city, which reigneth over the kings of the earth.

And after these *things* I saw another angel come down 18 from heaven, having great power; and the earth was lightened with his glory. And he cried mightily with a strong voice, 2 saying,

Babylon the great is fallen, is fallen,
And is become the habitation of devils,

to agree] Lit., **to make,** (or **come to,**) **one mind,** (or **one will**): cf. *v.* 13.

and give their kingdom unto the beast] He therefore, though a representative of the Roman Empire, will not fall with the city of Rome: on the contrary, in the last days of the latter he will have appeared as its enemy. The gradual divorce of the Empire from the City, by Diocletian, Constantine, Charlemagne, the mediæval German Emperors, Charles V., Francis II., Napoleon, William, is significant as providing precedents for what Antichrist will do: though of course it would be absurd and unjust to think of all these as actuated by his spirit.

18. *that great city* &c.] Again as in *v.* 9 the designation of Rome is unmistakeable. The words cannot be glossed, "Babylon is (now represented by) Rome," but must mean "Babylon *is* Rome."

which reigneth] Lit., **which hath kingdom,** or **kingly power.**

THE JUDGEMENT ON BABYLON.

HER GLORY AND SUDDEN PLAGUES. CHAP. XVIII. vv. 1—8.

1. *another angel*] See on xiv. 6.

great power] Apparently for destruction: see note on the use of the word in ix. 19.

the earth was lightened with his glory] Ezek. xliii. 2, translated rather more literally than in the LXX.

2. *mightily with a strong voice*] We should read, **with a mighty voice.**

Babylon...is fallen] xiv. 8; Is. xxi. 9.

the habitation of devils] Better, **an habitation.** Similar vengeance is denounced on the literal Babylon, Is. xiii. 21—2, and on Edom, id. xxxiv. 13—15. It is not quite certain which of the words used in those passages are names of demons or goblins, and which of terrestrial birds and beasts: but there is little doubt that Isaiah, like St John, means to describe *both* as occupying the desolated city.

And the hold of every foul spirit,
And a cage of every unclean and hateful bird.
3 For all nations have drunk of the wine of the wrath of her fornication,
And the kings of the earth have committed fornication with her,
And the merchants of the earth are waxed rich through the abundance of her delicacies.
4 And I heard another voice from heaven, saying,
Come out of her, my people,
That ye be not partakers of her sins,
And that ye receive not of her plagues.
5 For her sins have reached unto heaven,
And God hath remembered her iniquities.
6 Reward her even as she rewarded you,

the hold] Probably a **prison**, not a fortress. It is the same word that is translated "cage" in the next clause, and "prison" in 1 St Peter Ep. iii. 19.

3. *the wine of*] Should perhaps be omitted: it *may* have come in from the parallel passage, xiv. 8.

the kings of the earth &c.] xvii. 2.

the merchants of the earth] Merchants are alluded to as frequenting the literal Babylon in Is. xlvii. 15; but the prominence given to them suggests the analogy, not of Babylon but of Tyre: see on xvii. 1. Rome was in St John's day a wealthy and luxurious city, not a commercial city *primarily*, in the same sense as ancient Tyre and modern London, but a city with an immense commerce, the commerce really belonging to the city, though the port of Ostia was considerably further from the Capitol than the Docks are from Westminster. What Rome was then it may, and probably will, be again: and there is thus no need to look elsewhere than at Rome for the literal fulfilment of St John's description, though some have thought it inappropriate to the geographical position of the city.

abundance of her delicacies] More literally, **power of her luxury**.

4. *Come out of her*] Is. xlviii. 20, lii. 11; Jer. l. 8, li. 6, 9, 45, all referring to the flight of Israel from the literal Babylon. This passage is nearest to the last of those cited: but in the second there is also the suggestion, that the Lord's people *must* depart to secure their purity, as well as that they *will* depart to secure their liberty. They are, however, presumably dwellers at Babylon as captives, not as citizens: it can hardly be meant that any of them really *belong to* Babylon, or are loth to quit her (like Lot in Sodom) till the very eve of her fall.

5. *have reached*] Lit., **have cleaved together**.

6. *rewarded you*] "You" should be omitted: a better translation

And double unto her double according to her works:
In the cup which she hath filled fill to her double.
How much she hath glorified herself, and lived deliciously, 7
So much torment and sorrow give her:
For she saith in her heart, I sit a queen,
And am no widow, and shall see no sorrow.
Therefore shall her plagues come in one day, 8
Death, and mourning, and famine;
And she shall be utterly burnt with fire:
For strong *is* the Lord God who judgeth her.
And the kings of the earth, who have committed fornica- 9
tion and lived deliciously with her,
Shall bewail her, and lament for her,
When they shall see the smoke of her burning,
Standing afar off for the fear of her torment, 10
Saying, Alas, alas, *that* great city Babylon, *that* mighty city!
For in one hour is thy judgment come.
And the merchants of the earth *shall* weep and mourn 11
over her;

would be, **Render to her as she herself rendered.** The thought is founded on Ps. cxxxvii. 8; Jer. l. 15, 29, and the expression on the former passage.

double unto her] See Jer. xvi. 18; where however the vengeance is on *Jerusalem*.

hath filled fill] Lit. **mixed mix**: cf. xiv. 10.

7. *for she saith in her heart* &c.] Is. xlvii. 7, 8: in *v.* 8 we have a reminiscence of the next verse of Isaiah, but less verbally close.

8. *she shall be utterly burnt with fire*] So xvii. 16. While literally true of the city, the doom may refer to that pronounced by the Law on certain cases of foul fornication, Lev. xxi. 9, &c.

for strong is the Lord God] Jer. l. 34.

that judgeth] Rather, **that hath judged.**

THE LAMENTATION OVER THEM ON EARTH, vv. 9—19.

9. *the kings of the earth*] Who bore a more or less immediately active part in her destruction, xvii. 16: see note there.

shall bewail her] Read simply, **shall weep.**

the smoke of her burning] Cf. Gen. xix. 28.

10. *for the fear*] i.e. because of *their* fear. Their regret for her destruction is sincere, but does not make them forget themselves.

Alas, alas] The interjection is the same as is elsewhere rendered "Woe." So in ver. 16.

11. *shall weep and mourn*] Read, **weep and mourn** (in the present tense).

For no *man* buyeth their merchandise any more:
12 The merchandise of gold, and silver,
And precious stones, and of pearls,
And fine linen, and purple, and silk, and scarlet,
And all thyine wood, and all *manner* vessels of ivory,
And all *manner* vessels of most precious wood,
And of brass, and iron, and marble,
13 And cinnamon, and odours,
And ointments, and frankincense,
And wine, and oil,
And fine flour, and wheat,
And beasts, and sheep, and horses, and chariots,
And slaves, and souls of men.
14 And the fruits that thy soul lusted after are departed from thee,

for no man buyeth &c.] Their sorrow is even more purely selfish than that of the kings.

merchandise] Strictly, **cargo**.

12. This whole passage should be compared with Ezek. xxvii., where the wealth and trade of Tyre is described in detail.

and scarlet] Thus far the goods enumerated have been expressed by genitives, "merchandise of gold...and of scarlet." Here they cease to be so, as far as the word "sheep."

thyine wood] Wood of the *thyia* or *thyion*, a kind of cypress or arbor vitae: apparently the same that was called *citrus* by the Romans, and used for the costliest furniture.

13. *and cinnamon*] Add "and amomum,"—a precious oriental ointment. The word was accidentally omitted by copyists, from its likeness to the latter part of the preceding one.

and horses] Lit., **of horses**,—the genitive dependent on "merchandise" is resumed.

chariots] Not war-chariots like those mentioned in the O.T., but luxurious carriages.

slaves] Comparing Ezek. xxvii. 14, perhaps we are to understand grooms or coachmen, attached to the horses and chariots. The word means literally **bodies**, but the sense "slaves" was recognised in Greek, though not strictly classical.

souls of men] Ezek. xxvii. 13. As "horses and chariots and bodies" are genitives, and "souls" accusative, we can hardly connect the last two words, "bodies and souls of men." But while we never find in the Bible an Englishman's horror of slavery as an institution, we are no doubt to understand that St John—perhaps even that Ezekiel—felt it to be cruel and unnatural to regard human beings as mere merchandise.

14. *fruits...lusted after*] Lit., **the fruit-harvest of the desire of thy soul**.

And all *things which were* dainty and goodly are departed from thee,
And thou shalt find them no more at all.
The merchants of these *things*, which were made rich by her, 15
Shall stand afar off for the fear of her torment,
Weeping and wailing, and saying, 16
Alas, alas, *that* great city,
That was clothed in fine linen, and purple, and scarlet,
And decked with gold, and precious stones, and pearls:
For in one hour so great riches is come to nought. 17

And every shipmaster, and all the company in ships,
And sailors, and as many as trade by sea,
Stood afar off, and cried 18
When they saw the smoke of her burning, saying,
What *city is* like unto *this* great city?
And they cast dust on their heads, 19
And cried, weeping and wailing, saying,
Alas, alas, *that* great city,
Wherein were made rich all that had ships in the sea by reason of her costliness:

thy...thee...thee...thou] It seems as though the writer had forgotten the construction with which the long sentence, *vv.* 11—13, began: this verse stands as if the lamentation of the merchants were being quoted. In the next verse, it is described again, and then is quoted more regularly.
goodly] Lit., **bright**. R.V. "sumptuous."
thou shalt find] Read, **they shall find**.
16. *Alas, alas*] See on *v.* 10.
decked] Lit., **gilded**, as at xvii. 4.
stones...pearls] Both these words should be collective singulars.
17. *is come to nought*] Lit., **is made desolate**.
all the company in ships] Read with R.V., **and everyone that saileth any whither**. The words will probably stand for the merchants travelling in ships with their own goods, which they intend to sell on arriving at their destination—Lat. *vectores*.
sailors] Cf. Ezek. xxvii. 29 sqq.
trade by sea] Lit., **work the sea**. The sense is more general than the A.V.: it will include all three classes, shipmasters, sailing merchants, and sailors.
18. *What city is like* &c.] Ezek. xxvii. 32.
19. *they cast dust* &c.] *Ibid.* 30.
had ships] Read, **had the ships** or **their ships**.

114 REVELATION, XVIII. [vv. 20—23.

For in one hour is she made desolate.
20 Rejoice over her, *thou* heaven,
And ye holy apostles and prophets;
For God hath avenged you on her.
21 And a mighty angel took up a stone like a great millstone, and cast *it* into the sea, saying,
Thus with violence shall *that* great city Babylon be thrown down, and shall be found no more at all.
22 And the voice of harpers, and musicians, and of pipers, and trumpeters, shall be heard no more at all in thee;
And no craftsman, of whatsoever craft *he be*, shall be found any more in thee;
And the sound of a millstone shall be heard no more at all in thee;
23 And the light of a candle shall shine no more at all in thee;
And the voice of the bridegroom and of the bride shall be heard no more at all in thee:

THE REJOICING OVER THEM IN HEAVEN, vv. 20—24.

20. *Rejoice over her*] xii. 12. There may be a reminiscence of Jer. li. 48. We cannot tell if the words are those of the angel of v. 1, of the voice of v. 4, or of the seer himself: perhaps the second is most likely.

holy apostles and prophets] Read, **the saints and the apostles and the prophets.**

avenged you] Lit., **judged your judgement**, condemned her for her condemnation of you. Notice the mention of "apostles" as well as other "saints," as proving that apostles suffered in Rome; and so confirming the unanimous tradition as to the martyrdom there of SS. Peter and Paul. Notice also (in reference to the theory mentioned on ii. 2) St John's recognition of the latter as an apostle. Whether he had himself been condemned to death at Rome cannot be determined: the tradition to that effect was ancient, but not demonstrably *so* ancient, nor so wide-spread or so confirmed by scriptural evidence (see on St John's Gospel xxi. 18, 19).

21. *a mighty angel*] Lit., **one strong angel.**
cast it into the sea &c.] Jer. li. 63—4.
with violence] Lit., **with a rush** or **dash.** R.V. "with a mighty fall."

22. *the voice of harpers* &c.] Is. xiv. 11, of Babylon, Ezek. xxvi. 13, of Tyre, are certainly parallels: compare also Is. xxiv. 8, which is as similar as the passages of Jeremiah referred to on the following passage, and apparently, like them, spoken of the unfaithful Jerusalem.

the sound of a millstone &c.] Jer. xxv. 10.

23. *the voice of the bridegroom* &c.] Jer. vii. 34, xvi. 9.

For thy merchants were the great men of the earth;
For by thy sorceries were all nations deceived.
And in her was found the blood of prophets, and of saints, 2
And of all that were slain upon the earth.

And after these *things* I heard a great voice of much 1
people in heaven, saying, Alleluia; Salvation, and glory, and
honour, and power, unto the Lord our God: for true and 2
righteous *are* his judgments: for he hath judged the great
whore, which did corrupt the earth with her fornication, and
hath avenged the blood of his servants at her hand. And 3
again they said, Alleluia. And her smoke rose up for ever
and ever. And the four and twenty elders and the four 4
beasts fell down and worshipped God that sat on the throne,
saying, Amen; Alleluia. And a voice came out of the 5
throne, saying, Praise our God, all ye his servants, and ye

for thy merchants &c.] Is. xxiii. 8, of Tyre. Some read "for the great men of the earth were thy merchants," which makes the resemblance less close, but does not forbid our seeing a reference.

by thy sorceries] Compare especially Nah. iii. 4.

24. *And in her*] St John passes from recording the angel's denunciation to the impression made on his own mind by the judgement he witnessed.

of all that were slain upon the earth] Cf. Jer. li. 49, where however, if the A.V. be right, the sense is rather different. "The slain of all the earth" *here* seem to mean "the slain of (the spiritual) Israel," *there*, the allies of Babylon who share in her fall.

FURTHER THANKSGIVINGS. CHAP. XIX. vv. 1—6.

1. *And after*] Omit "and."
a great voice] Read, **as it were a great voice**.
Salvation &c.] Cf. vii. 10; also iv. 11, v. 12, 13, vii. 12.
and honour] Should be omitted.
unto the Lord our God] Read, [are] our God's.

2. For the joy of the Saints in sympathy with God's judgement, see on xiv. 10. There is a passage somewhat like this in Enoch xlvii. 4: "Then were the hearts of the saints full of joy, because the number of righteousness was arrived, the supplication of the saints heard, and the blood of the righteous appreciated by the Lord of Spirits."

3. *And her smoke* &c.] Perhaps best taken as a part of the anthem. For the word "rose up" should be "riseth."

4. *And the four and twenty* &c.] Cf. v. 14.

5. *Praise our God* &c.] Compare the opening of Pss. cxxxiv., cxxxv.

6 that fear him, both small and great. And I heard as *it were* the voice of a great multitude, and as the voice of many waters, and as the voice of mighty thunderings, saying, 7 Alleluia: for the Lord God Omnipotent reigneth. Let us be glad and rejoice, and give honour to him: for the marriage of the Lamb is come, and his wife hath made herself ready. 8 And to her was granted that she should be arrayed in fine linen, clean and white: for the fine linen is the righteousness

both small and great] Ps. cxv. 13. "Both" should perhaps be omitted.
6. *great multitude*] *v.* 1, where the words rendered "much people" are the same.
many waters] i. 15, xiv. 2.
mighty thunderings] vi. 1, xiv. 2.
the Lord God Omnipotent] Read, **the Lord our God**: and the last word is that usually rendered "Almighty"—rather a name "the Almighty" than an epithet—see on i. 8.
reigneth] The only translation that will give the sense without cumbrousness; though "hath taken the kingdom" might express the tense of the original more accurately.

THE MARRIAGE OF THE LAMB, vv. 7—9.

7. *honour*] Better, **the glory.**
the marriage of the Lamb] The first suggestion of this image in the N.T. is in our Lord's parables, St Matt. xxii. 2, xxv. 1—10: it is more fully worked out by St Paul, Eph. v. 22—32. But men's minds were prepared for it by the language of all the Prophets about the spiritual marriage of the Lord and Israel: still more, perhaps, by that of the 45th Psalm, rising so far above the royal marriage that no doubt furnished its occasion. And there is little doubt that the Song of Songs was already mystically interpreted among the Jews, though its claim to a place in the Canon was still disputed.
his wife] Called by St John the New Jerusalem, xxi. 2, by St Paul both by that name, Gal. iv. 26, and more simply the Church, Eph. v. 23 sqq.
8. *And to her was granted*] Better, **it was given to her**—the form is the same as recurs so often throughout the vision, from vi. 2 onwards. This being so, it is not likely that this clause still forms part of the proclamation of the voice: it is the Seer's description of the "making herself ready" which the voice proclaimed.
clean and white] The epithets should be transposed, and "and" omitted, **bright clean fine linen.**
the righteousness] Rather, **the righteous acts.** Every good work done by every single saint goes to make up the perfect glory of the Church as it shall be when at last complete. The doctrine of the Communion of Saints is contained in, or follows from, that of the holy Catholic Church.

of saints. And he saith unto me, Write, Blessed *are* they 9 which are called unto the marriage supper of the Lamb. And he saith unto me, These are the true sayings of God. And I fell at his feet to worship him. And he said unto me, 10 See *thou do it* not: I am thy fellowservant, and of thy brethren that have the testimony of Jesus: worship God: for the testimony of Jesus is the spirit of prophecy.

9. *And he saith*] Who speaks? Plainly an angel (see *v.* 10), presumably the angel of xvii. 1.
Blessed are *they*, &c.] St John, and "they that hear the words of this prophecy, and keep those things which are written therein" (i. 3) are made to realise heartily what our Lord's fellow-guest (St Luke xiv. 15) said without seeing the full force of his own words. Of course, when we reduce the image to plain prose, "they that are called" are the same as the Bride: while St Paul again speaks of them as her children.
These are the true sayings of God] More literally, **These words are** [some add "the"] **true** (words) **of God**.

THE ERROR OF THE SEER, v. 10.

10. *to worship him*] Perhaps understanding from the last words that the speaker was God Himself. In the O.T. God had revealed Himself to men by means of angels, and men had, by falling at the feet of angels, rightly worshipped the God Who was present in them (see esp. Hos. xii. 4 compared with Gen. xxxii. 30). But since a more perfect revelation of God has been given by the Incarnation, no such divine presence in an angel is to be looked for. (So Jer. Taylor, *Dissuasive from Popery*, Part II. II. viii. 3.) We have therefore no need to suppose that the holy apostle was in intent guilty of idolatry; he meant the worship for God in the angel, but *this* being an angel and nothing more, it follows of course that he ought not to be honoured as God. See xxii. 8.
I am thy fellowservant] In a sense, the angels are even servants to the elect on earth, Heb. i. 14.
and of thy brethren that have, &c.] In the parallel passage, xxii. 9, we have "thy brethren the prophets," and the sense seems to be the same here, from the last words of the verse.
have the testimony of Jesus] i. 2, 9, vi. 9, and, closest of all, xii. 17. In all these the word rendered "testimony" comes near to the sense that became technical, of "martyrdom."
for the testimony, &c.] Comparing xxii. 9 with the passages last cited, it seems that the sense of the passage is, " Martyrdom like thine " (the seer was at least a confessor, i. 2, perhaps, as tradition says, a *proved* martyr in will) "and thy brethren's involves in it the grace of prophecy, and so places the martyrs in so close communion with God that they need no angel mediator." But what is said to St John as a prophet is in its measure true of all Christians. All in their measure are witnesses

11   And I saw heaven opened, and behold a white horse; and he that sat upon him *was* called Faithful and True, and
12 in righteousness he doth judge and make war. His eyes *were* as a flame of fire, and on his head *were* many crowns; and he had a name written, that no *man* knew, but he him-
13 self. And he *was* clothed with a vesture dipt in blood: and

for Christ, and all partakers of His Spirit; and therefore all are prophets in the same sense that they are all priests and kings. Thus all, if not *yet* "equal with the angels" (St Luke xx. 36), are brought too near to God to need angels to bring Him near to them.

THE VICTORY OF THE RIDER ON THE WHITE HORSE, vv. 11—21.

11. *heaven opened*] Ezek. i. 1; St Matt. iii. 16, and parallels, St John i. 51; Acts vii. 56, x. 11. Something more seems to be implied than in iv. 1; the "door" through which the seer was called up is not sufficient to let out this mounted army, or "the chariot of paternal Deity" which appeared to Ezekiel.

a white horse] vi. 2, where see notes. Here, at least, there is no doubt about the interpretation.

and he that sat upon him] Had better not be separated in punctuation from the previous clause: "behold a white horse, and he that sat upon him, [who was] called," &c.

called] There is some, but not sufficient, authority for omitting this word.

Faithful and True] iii. 14; also i. 5, iii. 7.
in righteousness] Is. xi. 4.
make war] In Ps. xlv. 3—5 (4—6) we have the same mixture as here of the Bridegroom with the triumphant Warrior. Compare St Chrysostom on Rom. xiii. 12, "Fear not at hearing of array and arms.... for it is of light that the arms are....As the bridegroom goes forth with joyous looks from His chamber, so doth he too who is defended with these arms; for he is at once soldier and bridegroom."

12. *His eyes*, &c.] i. 14.
many crowns] These are distinctively *kingly* crowns, see on iv. 4, vi. 2. Their *number* marks Him as King of kings, *v.* 16: perhaps also as both King and Priest, as in Zech. vi. 11 sqq., and in the use of the triple crown by modern popes.

a name written] Probably on the forehead, as xiv. 1. There is some authority for the remarkable reading, "names written, and a name written which," &c.

that no man knew, &c.] ii. 17: for the Lord having such a name, see iii. 12, and notes on both places.

13. *vesture*] Or, **cloak**: it is the *outer* garment that is so described.

dipt in blood] There is almost equal authority for this reading, "dipped," or "dyed," and for "sprinkled." Either is almost equally supported by the language of Is. lxiii. 1, 3, "With *dyed* garments... their blood shall be *sprinkled* upon My garments." The reference to

his name is called The Word of God. And the armies which 14
were in heaven followed him upon white horses, clothed in
fine linen, white and clean. And out of his mouth goeth a 15
sharp sword, that with it he should smite the nations: and
he shall rule them with a rod of iron: and he treadeth the
winepress of the fierceness and wrath of Almighty God.

that passage is unquestionable, and so the *primary* meaning must be,
as there, to describe the Conqueror as stained with the blood of *His
enemies*. But no doubt it is legitimate for the Christian to remember,
in interpreting both passages, that the *way* that Christ overcomes His
enemies is by shedding, not their blood, but His own.

The Word of God] The only place in Scripture (unless Heb. iv. 12
be so interpreted, which is not probable) where this exact phrase is used
of the *personal* Word, the Son of God. But of course the use of "the
Word" in St John i. 1 is the same in principle and meaning.

14. *the armies which were in heaven*] According to ordinary O.T.
usage (e.g. 1 Kings xxii. 19) this would mean the holy Angels exclusively,
or at least primarily. But some think that the glorified Saints are at
least included: it seems in harmony with the ideas of this Book to represent them, not indeed as executing Christ's vengeance (which the
angels do, xiv. 19; St Matt. xiii. 39—42), but as spectators of His
triumph, which is all that these armies seem to be.

fine linen, white and clean] The dress of Angels in St Matt. xxviii. 3
and parallels, Acts i. 10; but of Saints in this Book, iii. 4, vii. 9, and
probably iv. 4: compare the almost exactly similar words of *v*. 8. Here
this costume contrasts with the blood-dyed one of their Leader. The
probable meaning is, that they have no need to take part in the work of
slaughter, see *v*. 21. We cannot argue that Martyrs who shed their own
blood for their Lord are not included, nor yet that these are not of those
for whom His Blood was shed; for vii. 14 shews that *that* Blood does
not leave a stain.

15. *out of his mouth*] So i. 16, proving, if proof were needed, the
identity of the "Son of Man" of that passage with "the Word of God"
of this. For the meaning, see the notes there.

sharp] Some ancient authorities insert "two-edged," from the parallel
passage in ch. i.

smite the nations] God is said to smite men with plagues, e.g.
Zech. xiv. 18, but nowhere else with a sword. Are we to infer from
1 Chron. xxi. 12 what this sword will be? Certainly the ascription to
the Lord of the fierce struggles of a human warrior is markedly avoided.

shall rule them] Lit. **shall be their shepherd**, as in ii. 27, xii. 5
Of course in all three places the reference is to Ps. ii. 9.

and he treadeth] Is. lxiii. 3. The pronoun "he" is emphatic—He
Himself, by Himself, as is there expressed.

the winepress] So we are obliged to translate the single word, e.g.
at xiv. 19; while here we have the fuller phrase, "the winepress of the
wine of," &c.

fierceness and wrath] Read, **fierceness of the wrath**.

16 And he hath on *his* vesture and on his thigh a name written, KING OF KINGS, AND LORD OF LORDS.
17 And I saw an angel standing in the sun; and he cried with a loud voice, saying to all the fowls that fly in the midst of heaven, Come and gather yourselves together unto the
18 supper of the great God; that ye may eat the flesh of kings, and the flesh of captains, and the flesh of mighty *men*, and the flesh of horses, and of them that sit on them, and the flesh of all *men*, both free and bond, both small and great.
19 And I saw the beast, and the kings of the earth, and their armies, gathered together to make war against him that sat
20 on the horse, and against his army. And the beast was taken, and with him the false prophet that wrought miracles before him, with which he deceived them that had received the mark of the beast, and them that worshipped his image. *These* both were cast alive into a lake of fire burning with

16. *on his vesture and on his thigh*] i.e, probably, beginning on the lower part of the cloak, and continued where the thigh projected from it as He rode—whether this continuation was on the bare flesh, or (as seems likelier) on the skirt of the tunic.

King of Kings and Lord of Lords] xvii. 14. Cf. Dan. ii. 47, vii. 14; also 1 Tim. vi. 15, where a title substantially (not verbally) the same as this is given to God the Father.

17. *an angel*] Lit. **one angel.**

in the sun] Perhaps he is the Angel of the Sun (like the other elemental angels in xvi. 5 and perhaps xiv. 18): but the "one" makes this less likely. Probably he is stationed there only as a position commanding the "mid-heaven" (on this word see on viii. 13).

to all the fowls] Ezek. xxxix. 17 sqq., of the slaughter of Gog and Magog: from which however this slaughter seems to be distinguished, see xx. 8, 9.

the supper of the great God] Read, **the great supper of God.** In Ezek. l.c. it is called a *sacrifice*, sacrifices being the only ordinary occasion for a feast of flesh: cf. Is. xxxiv. 6, which was probably in Ezekiel's mind.

18. *captains*] Lit. **captains of a thousand;** see on vi. 15.

19. *the beast, and the kings*] Their confederacy under his leadership has been already intimated, xvi. 14, 16, xvii. 12—14. The so-called battle of Armageddon, there foretold, is here described.

20. *was taken*] Scarcely a strong enough word—"was seized" or "overpowered."

the false prophet] So called in xvi. 13: see xiii. 11 sqq.

miracles] Should be "the signs"—those described in xiii. 13 sqq.

were cast alive &c.] In Dan. vii. 11 the Beast is slain and his body

brimstone. And the remnant were slain with the sword of him that sat upon the horse, which *sword* proceeded out of his mouth: and all the fowls were filled with their flesh.

And I saw an angel come down from heaven, having the key of the bottomless *pit* and a great chain in his hand. And he laid hold on the dragon, *that* old serpent, which is the devil, and Satan, and bound him a thousand years, and cast him into the bottomless *pit*, and shut him up, and set a seal upon him, that he should deceive the nations no more, till the thousand years should be fulfilled: and after that he must be loosed a little season.

And I saw thrones, and they sat upon them, and judgment was given unto them: and *I saw* the souls of them

burnt. Perhaps the one indicates the fate of the empire, the other of its personal ruler.

21. *And the remnant were slain*] They are not, at least at once, consigned to the same eternal torment as their leaders: but see xiv. 10, xx. 15.

with the sword of him &c.] None of His followers have need to bear part in the battle: indeed they seem to bear no arms, *v.* 14. Compare the grand passage of St Chrysostom, in his 24th Homily on the Epistle to the Romans—(on xiii. 12), already partly quoted on *v.* 11. "What then, is there no necessity for thee to fight? Yea, needful is it to fight, yet not to be distressed and toil. For it is not in fact war, but a solemn dance and feast-day, such is the nature of the arms, such the power of the Commander." The victory is so plainly designated as one to be gained by purely spiritual means, that it is by no means certain that the armies to be overthrown are to be understood of an actual military confederacy. More probably, the confederacy of the powers of the world, under the leadership of Antichrist, will be primarily intellectual and spiritual.

THE BINDING OF SATAN. THE FIRST RESURRECTION.
CHAP. XX. vv. 1—6.

1. *the bottomless pit*]   See on ix. 1.
in his hand] Lit. **on his hand**—hung over it.
2. *that old serpent*] xii. 9.
3. *and shut him up...upon him*]   Read, **and shut and sealed [it] over him**: the opening of ix. 2 is undone.
he must be loosed] *v.* 7.
4. *thrones*] Dan. vii. 9. "They" who sat upon them, to whom judgement (i.e. the right of judging: see 1 Cor. vi. 2, 3) was given are identified by Dan. vii. 22 as "the saints of the Most High"—saints, plainly, in the modern sense, as distinguished from angels.
[*I saw*] *the souls*]   Cf. vi. 9.

that were beheaded for the witness of Jesus, and for the word of God, and which had not worshipped the beast, neither his image, neither had received *his* mark upon their foreheads, or in their hands; and they lived and reigned with

beheaded] Lit. **struck with the axe**, the old Roman mode of execution by sentence of the supreme magistrate. Capital punishment of citizens had been virtually abolished for the last years of the Republic: and when the emperors assumed the right of executing men for treason, it was done as though by military law (cf. St Mark vi. 27), by a soldier with a sword. But the old constitutional punishment was inflicted on provincials down to the fall of the Republic (Cic. *Phil.* XIII. xvi. 33): and it is not impossible that it was revived when it was desired that a citizen should be executed in due form of law. Thus it is not unlikely that St Paul will be included among those thus designated.

which had not worshipped &c.] xiii. 12, 15, 16.

reigned with Christ] 2 Tim. ii. 12. This "reign" was foretold in v. 10. "The nations" of the world continue to exist as usual (*v.* 2), so it is no doubt over them that the saints and martyrs reign.

a thousand years] Only in this passage is the kingdom of Christ on earth (which is of course one of the most frequent subjects of prophecy) designated as a millennium or period of 1000 years. It may be added, that this is the only prophecy where there is at all good reason for supposing that the Millennium of popular belief is indicated, as distinct on the one hand from the Kingdom of God which already exists in the Christian Church, and on the other from that which will be set up at the last day.

Nevertheless, this passage is quite sufficient foundation for the doctrine, even if it stood alone: and there are many other prophecies which, if not teaching it so plainly, may fairly be understood to refer to it, if the doctrine be admitted to be according to the mind of the Spirit. We therefore have to consider the question, Is this prophecy to be understood literally? Is it meant that, for a period of a thousand years (or more), before the general Resurrection and the end of this world, this earth will be the scene of a blessed visible Kingdom of God, wherein the power of the Devil will have vanished, and that of Christ be supreme and unopposed? wherein Christ shall either reign visibly on earth, or at least shall make His presence felt far more unmistakeably than at present; while the martyrs and other great saints of all past time shall rise, and, whether on earth or in heaven, share in the glory of His reign?

Down to the fourth century, the decidedly dominant belief of Christendom was in favour of this literal interpretation of the prophecy: since then, at least till the Reformation, it has been still more decidedly against it. In the second century, Papias, who seems to have been more or less personally acquainted with St John himself, taught Millenarian doctrine decidedly: and St Irenaeus and others derived it from him. In the same age St Justin accepted the doctrine, though admitting that Christians were not unanimous on the subject: but he considers St John's authority, in this passage, decisive.

Christ a thousand years. But the rest of the dead lived not 5

And in fact, the rejection of the doctrine was usually on the part of those who rejected or questioned the authority of the Revelation as a whole: it was held to discredit the book, that it taught the doctrine. Thus in the third century, Caius the Roman Presbyter seems unmistakeably to ascribe the book, not to St John but to his adversary Cerinthus; on the ground of its teaching this carnal and Jewish doctrine of an earthly kingdom of Christ. And St Dionysius of Alexandria, who, though not admitting the book to be the work of St John the Apostle, yet on the whole recognises its inspiration and authority, thinks it necessary to refute a suffragan bishop of his own, who adopted Millenarian views, as though he were at least on the verge of heresy.

The case seems to have stood thus. The doctrine of the Millennium was current in the Church, but was most insisted on in that section of the Church whose Jewish affinities were strongest : and it is asserted— it is very likely true—that the heretical Judaizers expressed their millennial hopes in a coarse and carnal form. Orthodox Christians condemned their language : but while some of them, like Justin, felt bound, in obedience to the plain teaching of St John, to believe in a Millennium of spiritual blessedness on earth, others, like Caius, rejected altogether the doctrine of the Millennium, and rejected, if necessary, the Apocalypse as teaching it.

But when St Dionysius proposed to reject millennial doctrine without rejecting the authority of the Apocalypse, a course was suggested which, if less critically and logically defensible, was theologically safer than either. The Apocalypse was declared not really to foretell a millennium, but only such a kingdom of Christ as all prophecy does foretell, viz. a Church such as now exists. To expect His more perfect kingdom to be an earthly and temporal one was pronounced a heresy, a falling back to Judaism.

St Jerome who, living in Palestine, knew more than most men of the Judaizing heresies which still existed in his time, and had once been formidable, spoke very strongly (as his manner was) in condemnation of the *Milliarii* (this, not *Millenarii*, is the ancient Latin name of the sect). He apparently grouped together all believers in the earthly kingdom, whether they regarded its delights as carnal or not : and it seems that his strong language frightened the Church of his time into giving it up. St Augustine had held and taught the doctrine, of course in a pure and spiritual form: but towards the close of his life he abandoned it, and though admitting his old belief to be tolerable, he echoes Jerome's condemnation of the Judaizing caricature of it. The opinion of these two great Fathers was adopted by the Church down to the Reformation, not formally or synodically, but as a matter of popular tradition.

At the Reformation, the Anabaptists proclaimed an earthly kingdom of Christ in the Millenarian sense, and certainly did all they could to discredit the doctrine, by the carnal form in which they held it. There was a tendency to revive the doctrine, among sober Protestants : but the alarm raised by the Anabaptists at first went far to counteract it ;

again until the thousand years were finished. This *is* the

e.g. in England one of the 42 Articles of A.D. 1552 condemned it as "Jewish dotage." But when the controversies of the Reformation quieted down, and both the Romanist and the Protestant Churches formulated their own beliefs, the former adhered to the tradition of SS. Jerome and Augustine, while the latter, for the most part, as was natural, went back to the literal sense of Scripture and the older tradition.

It thus appears, that Catholic consent cannot fairly be alleged either for or against the literal interpretation. Catholic feeling does of course condemn a Judaizing or carnal view of the nature of Christ's Kingdom: but whether He will have a kingdom on earth more perfect, or reign more visibly, than is the case now, is a point on which Christians may lawfully differ; the Church has not pronounced either way.

If the question be theologically open, it appears that, as a matter of opinion, the literal sense is to be preferred: "when the literal sense will stand, that furthest from the letter is the worst." Can anyone honestly say, that Satan has been bound during the time (already far more than a thousand years) that the kingdom of Christ on earth has already existed? that he deceives the nations no more till the present dispensation approaches its end in the days of Antichrist? It is far easier to hold that he *will* be bound for a long time (probably more rather than less than a thousand literal years), after Antichrist has been overthrown, but before the actual end of the world.

5. *But*] Should be omitted; there is more authority for reading "and."

This is the first resurrection] Here, as with the Millennium, there is the question whether these words are to be understood literally. In fact, the interpretation of these words, literally or otherwise, is the turning-point of the Millenarian controversy.

The plain meaning of the words is, that after the overthrow of Antichrist, the Martyrs and other most excellent Saints will rise from the dead and have their part in the Millennial kingdom: the rest of the dead, even those finally saved, will not rise till later. But at last, after the Millennium, and after the last short-lived assault of Satan, all the dead, good and wicked, will rise.

Now no Christian doubts, that the second or general Resurrection described in *v.* 12 will be literally realised.. It is therefore very harsh to suppose that the first is of a different kind. Such is, however, the view which since St Augustine's time has been usually adopted by Catholic theologians. The first Resurrection is understood to be the resurrection "from the death of sin unto the life of righteousness." It admits men into the kingdom of Christ, i.e. the Church, *within which* the power of the Devil is restrained, so that, if he can seduce some to sin, he cannot seduce them to actual idolatry or denial of God. This state of things will last through the whole course of the present dispensation, which, whatever its actual chronological length, is symbolically described as a thousand years. When that ends, there will ensue the three and a half years' struggle with Antichrist—*vv.* 7—16 being regarded

first resurrection. Blessed and holy *is* he that hath part in 6
the first resurrection: on such the second death hath no
power, but they shall be priests of God and of Christ, and
shall reign with him a thousand years.

And when the thousand years are expired, Satan shall be 7
loosed out of his prison, and shall go out to deceive the 8
nations which are in the four quarters of the earth, Gog and

as a new description of that period. If anyone can think this a legitimate interpretation of St John's words, he may: and for the coupling of a spiritual with a literal resurrection, St Augustine, and those who follow him, compare St John v. 25, 28. But it seems straining the view of "resumptions" very far, not to take the whole of this chapter as chronologically subsequent to the preceding: and really any view but the literal one seems exposed to insuperable exegetical difficulties.

If the true sense be *not* the literal one, it is safest to regard it as being as yet undiscovered.

6. *Blessed and holy* &c.] He is sure of eternal blessedness, absolutely and indefeasibly consecrated to God. "Holy" refers to the relation to God into which this brings him, not to the foregoing faithfulness that is implied in his being admitted into it.

the second death] See ii. 11, and v. 14. Cf. Rom. vi. 9, 10.

they shall be priests] Cf. i. 6, v. 10.

of God and of Christ] The strongest proof, perhaps, in the book of the doctrine of Christ's coequal Deity. If we read these words in the light of St John's Gospel, or of the Nicene Creed, they suggest no difficulty, but without the doctrine there taught, they make salvation to consist in the deadly sin which the Moslems call "association"—the worshipping the creature by the side of the Creator. Notice, however, that the *word* "God" in this book always means the Father; and so throughout the N.T., with few exceptions.

thousand years] We should probably read, "**the** thousand years."

THE LOOSING OF SATAN, THE WAR OF GOG AND MAGOG, THE JUDGEMENT ON THE DEVIL, THE BEAST, AND THE FALSE PROPHET, vv. 7—10.

7. *Satan shall be loosed*] "for a little season," as we heard in v. 3. The words are different from the "short time" of xii. 12, and we have no reason to understand that they refer to the same period: still the two passages to a certain extent illustrate one another.

8. *the nations which are* &c.] It almost seems as though the kingdom of Christ and of His Saints had not been world-wide, but had been, like the Roman empire of St John's day, or the Christendom of our own, a wide but limited region of light in the midst of a barbarous world. It is not therefore certain that the coming of the kingdom must be postponed till Christianity has gained its victory over the compact mass of nations which, from China to Guinea, still hold out against it: and we ought to remember the possibility, that they may

Magog, to gather them together to battle: the number of
9 whom *is* as the sand of the sea. And they went up on the
breadth of the earth, and compassed the camp of the saints
about, and the beloved city: and fire came down from

prove as dangerous to the fabric of modern civilisation as the barbarians of Scythia, Germany, and Arabia proved to the ancient. But it is possible that this prediction refers, not to an incursion from outlying heathens, but to an apostasy of outlying Christians. If so, this may be illustrated by the way that the remoter provinces of Christendom fell into heresy in the fifth and following centuries, and were, in great measure as a consequence, absorbed in Islam afterwards. We may also think of the many wild and unchristian sects rising in our own time in America and in Russia—the countries of Christendom remotest from its centres of intellectual life.

quarters] Better, **corners**.

Gog and Magog] See Ezek. xxxviii., xxxix.—a prophecy which *may*, for aught we know, have had some nearly contemporary fulfilment, but which the Jewish traditions interpret of a war in the days of the Messiah, nearly as here. Magog is given in Gen. x. 2 as the name of a son of Japhet, the eponymus, there is no doubt, of one of the nations lying near the Black Sea, and called by Europeans Scythian in the wide sense. Gog appears in Ezek. l.c. to be not a national name, but the name, whether personal or dynastic, of the king of Magog and the neighbouring or kindred tribes of Rosh, Meshech, and Tubal. The resemblance of two of these names to the modern *Russia* and *Muscovy* is merely accidental: but it would be rash to deny the possibility, that the geographical or ethnological suggestion is to be taken literally, and that St John does foretell an invasion, something like that of the Huns, or Tartars, and falling on Christendom from the same quarter.

to gather them &c.] Nearly a repetition of xvi. 14, xvii. 12, 14, xix. 19. Yet it can hardly describe the same event: it seems plain that, whatever be the meaning of the first resurrection and the thousand years' reign, they intervene between that war and this. Moreover, the former war was on the part of the rulers of the civilised world, this on the part of the outer barbarians.

9. *And they went up* &c.] The Seer does not pass easily over the immense space of time during which the world is too happy to have a history. He *sees* the establishment of the earthly kingdom of Christ, and *foretells* its end: it is only gradually that he comes to see the end also brought before his view as present.

the breadth of the earth] Perhaps rather, **of the land;** they overspread the whole land of Israel, against which, as we see from the next clause, their attack is directed.

the camp of the saints] God's people assemble in military array, and stand on their defence against His enemies. They are probably prepared to fight, but as in xix. 21, they have no need.

the beloved city] i.e. Jerusalem, which, it appears from this place only, will be the seat and capital of the millennial kingdom. It

God out of heaven, and devoured them. And the devil 10
that deceived them was cast into the lake of fire and brimstone, where the beast and the false prophet *are*, and shall be tormented day and night for ever and ever.

And I saw a great white throne, and him that sat on it, 11

appears that in the popular millennial anticipations, which discredited the literal interpretation of this prophecy, this localisation of the kingdom was much insisted on, and it was even thought that the Jewish law and the sacrificial worship would be revived. This of course is utterly incredible to most Christians: but there is no difficulty in supposing that the Kingdom of God may literally have an earthly centre in the Holy City and the Holy Land. Even if the literal view be not taken, the prophecy can hardly imply less than a future purity of the Church far exceeding the present; and it may be that this purified Church will recognise a better Papacy at Jerusalem, one not too proud to learn either from the excellences or from the faults of the Roman.

and fire came down &c.] Cf. 2 Kings i. 10, and ch. xi. 5, and even xiii. 13. This does not agree with the description of Gog's overthrow in Ezek. xxxix., where the army lie slain till they are buried, and their weapons are broken up for firewood.

from God] Should probably be omitted.

10. *And the devil that deceived them*] Lit. **that deceiveth**, but the sense is general: as if we were to say "their deceiver."

into the lake &c.] xix. 20.

where] Read, **where also**.

the beast and the false prophet are] It might be better to supply **were cast**. That they are there still, not consumed by their more than thousand years of torment, is not stated in this clause but is in the next.

shall be &c.] To prevent ambiguity we should render, **they shall be**, all three of them.

for ever and ever] Lit. **to the ages of the ages**, as strong an expression for absolute endlessness as Biblical language affords. The expression "day and night" seems hardly consistent with the view often expressed, that the eternity here spoken of is unaccompanied with a sense of duration like that which we call time.

THE GREAT WHITE THRONE, THE GENERAL RESURRECTION, THE JUDGEMENT ON ALL THE DEAD AND ON DEATH AND HELL,
VV. 11—15.

11. *a great white throne*] Probably not absolutely the same as that of iv. 2 &c.: the King is to sit now not as Lawgiver or Administrator but as Judge. Possibly it is called "great" as compared with the thrones of *v.* 4; "white," of course, as symbolical of the holiness and purity of the judgement to be administered.

and him that sat on it] This has throughout, from iv. 2 onwards,

from whose face the earth and the heaven fled *away*; and
12 there was found no place for them. And I saw the dead, small and great, stand before God; and the books were

been universally the title of God the Father. Moreover, the description of the Great Assize here is substantially the same as that of Dan. vii. 9, 10: and there the Ancient of Days, Who sits on the throne, is plainly distinguished from the Son of Man. Therefore we are no doubt to understand the presence of the Father here, in spite of St John v. 22, 27. There is no contradiction, if we take a duly high view of the relation between the Father and the Son. St Paul's doctrine, Acts xvii. 31; Rom. ii. 16 (allowing that Tit. ii. 13 is ambiguous), shews the accurate relation between the two sides of the truth: and iii. 21, compared with our Lord's own words in St Matt. xvi. 27 and parallels, shews the propriety of this image.

from whose face &c.] The passing away of earth and heaven is spoken of in Is. li. 6, St Matt. xxiv. 35 and parallels; but the strong expression of their fleeing before God's presence is peculiar to this place: Ps. civ. 32, however, is something of a precedent. That the destruction will be by fire is not stated here, or anywhere but in 2 Pet. iii. 10, 12, and perhaps 2 Thess. i. 7, 8. In St Peter l.c. we have this destruction of the world by fire compared with the destruction by the Flood, and this parallel seems to have been recognised in popular Jewish belief. Popular Christian belief continued the series, by interpolating between the two a purely mythical "flood of wind;" an idea also found, curiously enough, in the Mexican mythology, which completed the elemental series with a destruction by earthquakes. The lesson of all this seems to be, that the Deluge is a matter of universal tradition, and that the destructibility of the world is recognised by a universal instinct: but that the *manner* of its destruction is not so revealed, that it can safely be conceived by us in picturesque detail. The destruction of our globe, perhaps of the whole solar system, by fire is quite within the bounds of possibility, even according to the known laws of nature; but those laws more naturally suggest the world literally "waxing old like a garment, and them that dwell therein dying like a moth," and the elements rather congealing with cold than "melting with fervent heat." On the other hand, passages like Acts x. 42; 1 Thess. iv. 15; 2 Tim. iv. 1; 1 Pet. iv. 5 seem plainly to prove that the human race will not be extinct when that Day comes, but that there will be "the quick" as well as "the dead" ready to undergo the Judgement. But the judgement of the dead only is described here. St John had learnt, as St Paul had not, that the dead would be the larger class of the two: whether he learnt it from his own longer life, or from the length of time implied in this vision.

and there was found no place for them] The phrase is a reminiscence of Dan. ii. 35; we had a similar one in xii. 8.

12. *small and great*] Read **the great and the small.** The sense, as in xix. 5, is probably to indicate the nothingness of human dis-

opened: and another book was opened, which is *the book of life*: and the dead were judged out of those *things* which were written in the books, according to their works. And 13 the sea gave up the dead which were in it; and death and hell delivered up the dead which were in them: and they were judged every man according to their works. And 14 death and hell were cast into the lake of fire. This is the

tinctions before God. Those who are "great in the Kingdom of Heaven" have been raised already, *vv.* 4, 5.
before God] Read, **before the throne.** This verse therefore does not absolutely prove Who it is that sits on the throne, but shews how it was understood by the Church, in which the common text grew up and was received.
the books were opened] Rather, simply **books**: see Dan. vii. 13, where also the article (or equivalent form) is wanting.
and another book was opened] The salvation of those who are saved is not due to their own works, but to God's electing love, which (however we punctuate xiii. 8) preceded any work of theirs. Yet reference to their works is not ignored, but the "books would be as it were vouchers for the book of life" (Alford); shewing that those written in that book had lived as became the grace given to them.
the book *of life*] See iii. 5, xiii. 8, xxi. 27: also note on v. 1. The image is used exactly in this sense in Dan. xii. 1, though the phrase "Book of Life" is not used. We have a near approach to that in Ps. lxix. 28, but there and in Ex. xxxii. 32, 33 it is not equally certain that *eternal* life is meant. Words and meaning are exactly the same in this book as in Phil. iv. 3.
the dead were judged &c.] We see then that "the books" contained the record of "their works." Thus this passage justifies, in some measure, the modern popular myth of "the recording Angel."
according to their works] St Matt. xvi. 27; Rom. ii. 6.
13. *death and hell*] See vi. 8. *Sheol*, the Hebrew equivalent of *Hades*, seems not quite determined in meaning between the receptacle of the bodies of the dead and of their souls, but is sometimes translateable as "the grave." Here it seems implied that those who died in the sea are not in Hades, as those who were buried are: but all, whether buried or unburied, are raised and judged.
14. *And death and hell were cast* &c.] They are enemies of God, 1 Cor. xv. 26, and to be destroyed at Christ's triumph, *ib.* 54. But though no doubt presented to St John as individual demon figures (see vi. 8), we are probably not to understand that they are real persons, like the Devil and those represented by the Beast and the False Prophet: and hence we are not told that, like them, they continue to exist in torment in the lake of fire.
This is the second death] Add, **the Lake of Fire.** We have learnt already, that temporal death does not hinder eternal life, nay, may secure a better and an earlier resurrection thereto. We now

15 second death. And whosoever was not found written in the book of life was cast into the lake of fire.

21 And I saw a new heaven and a new earth: for the first heaven and the first earth were passed away; and there was 2 no more sea. And I John saw the holy city, new Jerusalem, coming down from God out of heaven, prepared as a bride

learn the opposite doctrine, that there is a resurrection not to life, but to a death far more terrible than that which ends this life. Cf. St John v. 29. It is quite true, however, that both in popular Jewish belief, and in the language of the N.T., when the Resurrection is spoken of, it is ordinarily conceived as one to life. This does not prevent the more terrible side of the doctrine from being also taught in the Gospel, but it does indicate which side is the healthier, as well as the pleasanter, for our thoughts to dwell on.

15. *And whosoever* &c.] "By the works of the Law shall no flesh be justified." Any who are not in the number of those saved by God's free grace, are sure to have sins recorded against them, sufficient for a judgement "out of those things which were written in the books" to end in this terrible sentence. Cf. St Matt. xxv. 41.

THE NEW HEAVEN AND EARTH. CHAP. XXI. 1.

1. *a new heaven and a new earth*] Is. lxv. 17, lxvi. 22; referred to, as here, in 2 Pet. iii. 13. It is idle to ask, what amount of change in the physical constitution of the universe is implied: the destruction of the earth, as a seat of life, and its renewal, would imply a complete change of the visible heavens. But a world "wherein dwelleth righteousness" would be a new world, even without any physical change at all.

there was no more sea] More literally, **the sea is no more.** We cannot be sure that this is to be taken literally; we hear of a river in the next chapter, and a perennial stream implies an abundant reservoir of water somewhere. To us, the absence of sea seems, so to speak, a defect in the landscape, while to the ancients it seemed a pledge of security and of unfettered intercourse between all nations: see Is. xxxiii. 21.

THE NEW JERUSALEM, v. 2.

2. *And I John saw*] Read simply, **and I saw.**

new Jerusalem] For the old Jerusalem, though we saw (xx. 9, and note) that it is to be again "a holy city" in the last days as of old, will have passed away with "the first earth."

coming down from God out of heaven] Transpose the two clauses, **out of heaven from God.** This is the New Jerusalem of which the earthly city is an imperfect copy; see on iv. 6, vi. 9 for the heavenly Temple. While this world lasts, this true Jerusalem is above (Gal. iv. 26); and we only know its nature from the earthly copy of it, before

adorned for her husband. And I heard a great voice out of 3
heaven saying, Behold, the tabernacle of God *is* with men,
and he will dwell with them, and they shall be his people,
and God himself shall be with them, *and be* their God. And 4
God shall wipe away all tears from their eyes; and there
shall be no more death, neither sorrow, nor crying, neither

Christ came, and the spiritual approach to it (Heb. xii. 22) since.
But in the days here described, it will be realised on earth in all its
perfection.
prepared] The building and arrangements of the city serve the
same purpose as the dress and ornaments of a bride. Cf. Is. lxi. 10.
as a bride] See xix. 7, and notes thereon.
adorned &c.] Is. lxi. 10.

A VOICE FROM HEAVEN OF BLESSING AND JUDGEMENT, vv. 3—8.

3. *out of heaven*] Read, **out of the Throne**; cf. xix. 5.
the tabernacle of God] i.e. the Shechinah, the divine Presence, see
on vii. 15. So in the next words,
he will dwell with them] Lit., **have His tabernacle with them**, the
verb being the same as in St John's Gospel i. 14; though the prepositions "among" and "with" are different.
his people] The word is a plural: **peoples**, though used in modern English, at least as a Gallicism, is scarcely (see however x. 11,
xvii. 15) admitted in the English of the A.V. It would not do to translate "His nations," for in Hellenistic language, representing O.T.
usage, "the nations" means Gentiles, and "the people" Israel. Here
therefore the use of this word in the plural has a special significance:
all nations shall be God's people, in the sense that one nation only has
been hitherto.
(and be) their God] There is considerable authority for the omission
of this clause. If it be retained, it is a question of taste whether to
insert the words in brackets, or to render "God Himself, their own
God, shall be with them"—something like Ps. lxvii. 6. There may be a
reminiscence of the name *Immanuel:* there certainly is of Jer. xxiv. 7
&c.; Ezek. xi. 20 &c.; Zech. viii. 8, whether on St John's part or only
on that of his copyists.
4. *God shall wipe*] Read simply, **and shall wipe**, or, **and He
shall wipe**, according as it is thought necessary or not to begin a
new sentence. The name of "God" is introduced from the parallel
passage, vii. 17: in Is. xxv. 8 the names used are those traditionally
represented by "the Lord GOD."
there shall be no more death] More exactly, **death shall be no more**,
having been destroyed in the Lake of Fire, xx. 14: not that the personification is put forward here.
neither sorrow...any more pain] Better, **neither shall there be
sorrow, nor crying, nor pain any more**. See Is. xxxv. 10, li. 11,
lxv. 19.

shall there be any more pain: for the former *things* are
5 passed away. And he that sat upon the throne said, Behold, I make all *things* new. And he said unto me, Write:
6 for these words are true and faithful. And he said unto
me, It is done. I am Alpha and Omega, the beginning and
the end. I will give unto him that is athirst of the fountain
7 of the water of life freely. He that overcometh shall inherit

for the former things are passed away] **for** should probably be omitted; and the word for "former" is literally, **first**.

5. *And he that sat upon the throne said*] The first time that He speaks. The reference is rather to the eternal throne of iv. 2 than to the judgement-throne of xx. 11, so far as the two can be distinguished.

Behold, I make all things new] Some O.T. parallels are alleged, e.g. Is. xliii. 19; Jer. xxxi. 22; but really the only close parallel is 2 Cor. v. 17; and the meaning of this passage is, of course, even fuller than of that.

he said unto me] Read only, **he saith**. It is doubtful whether the speaker is still "He that sat on the throne;" for a similar command to "write" has been given already,—xiv. 13, xix. 9; cf. x. 4—either by an impersonal "voice from heaven" or by the revealing angel. The question is best left open. The repetition of the words "He said unto me" in the next verse is a reason against ascribing all three speeches to Him that sat on the throne; the fresh mention of a revealing angel in *v.* 9 is perhaps a stronger one against supposing an angel to be speaking here; and the form of the words themselves against their referring to an impersonal voice.

Write: for] Or perhaps, "Write, 'These words are'" &c.: lit. **that these words are**"....

true and faithful] Read, **faithful and true**, as at iii. 14, xix. 11, and still more exactly xxii. 6.

6. *It is done*] We should read the plural: the word therefore is not an *exact* repetition of that in xvi. 17. If we ask, what is the subject to this verb, "*They* are come into being," perhaps the best answer is "all things." The new universe of which the creating Word has just gone forth, has now been made, "and God sees that it is good."

Alpha and Omega] As in i. 8 (not 11), xxii. 13. Here, as in the former passage, it is God the Father that speaks.

of the fountain of the water of life] See vii. 17 and note, xxii. 1: also our Lord's words in St John's Gospel, iv. 14, vii. 38. The last quoted passage is, with a touching grotesqueness confounded with this in the Epistle describing the Martyrs of Gaul (Eus. *H. E.* v. i. 18).

freely] i.e. not "abundantly," but *gratis*: cf. Is. lv. 1.

7. *He that overcometh*] Carries back our thoughts to the promises at the beginning of the book, ii. 7, &c. There is perhaps some significance in the Father thus taking up and repeating the language of the Son.

all *things;* and I will be his God, and he shall be my son. But the fearful, and unbelieving, and the abominable, and 8 murderers, and whoremongers, and sorcerers, and idolaters, and all liars, shall have their part in the lake which burneth with fire and brimstone: which is the second death.

And there came unto me one of the seven angels which 9 had the seven vials full of the seven last plagues, and talked

all things] Read, **these things**; viz. the new heavens and earth, and the things in them which, like them, have just "come into being."
I will be...my son] Lit. **I will be to him a God, and he shall be to Me a son.** The form of the promise therefore resembles 2 Sam. vii. 14, at least as closely as Jer. xxiv. 7, &c.: and the sense combines that of both. The finally victorious share in the privileges, not only of God's people, but of the Only-begotten: see iii. 21.

8. *But the fearful*] **The cowards** would express the sense more accurately, at least in modern English. Those condemned are those who are afraid to do their duty, not those who do it, though timidly and in spite of the fears of nature: still less those who do it "with fear and trembling" in St Paul's sense.

unbelieving] It is, as usual, questionable whether this word or "unfaithful" expresses the sense most accurately. He who believes God's Word is "faithful" to God: the character here condemned is the exact opposite.

abominable] Lit. **abominated**; probably alluding to crimes yet fouler than those named.

sorcerers] Not the same word as that applied to Simon and Bar-jesus in the Acts, but cognate with that used above, ix. 21, and rendered "witchcrafts" in Gal. v. 20. The natural meaning of the word would rather be "poisoners;" and in fact in St John's days the two generally went together, and no line could be drawn between them. It is therefore no wonder that both the Apostles speak of it as a real crime connected with murder and other "works of the flesh," as well as with idolatry. For of course professed sorcery involved devil-worship, the basest idolatry of all, even if the devil had no more direct communication with the sorcerers than he has with all liars and impostors.

liars] The word is a little more general, **all the false.**
shall have] Lit. **But to the fearful,** &c. **their portion [shall be] in the lake** &c.

THE VISION OF THE NEW JERUSALEM, XXI. 9—XXII. 5.
THE MEASURE OF THE CITY, vv. 9—17.

9. *And there came unto me* &c.] As in xvii. 1. "unto me" should be omitted, so that the sentence as far as "vials" is *verbatim* the same as there. The identical form of introduction emphasizes the contrast between Babylon and Jerusalem, the harlot and the bride.

full] According to the correct text, this word is made to agree not with "the seven bowls" but with "the seven angels." But probably it

with me, saying, *Come* hither, I will shew thee the bride,
10 the Lamb's wife. And he carried me away in the spirit to
a great and high mountain, and shewed me *that* great city,
the holy Jerusalem, descending out of heaven from God,
11 having the glory of God: and her light *was* like unto a
stone most precious, *even* like a jasper stone, clear as crystal;
12 and had a wall great and high, and had twelve gates, and at
the gates twelve angels, and names written *there*on, which
are *the names* of the twelve tribes of the children of Israel:
13 on the east three gates; on the north three gates; on the

is a merely accidental grammatical inaccuracy of St John's. There is a much worse "false concord" in xiv. 19.
in the Spirit] xvii. 3, i. 10. Cf. Ezek. iii. 14.
to a great and high mountain] Ezek. xl. 2. The preposition rendered "to" plainly implies that St John was set *on* the mountain; whether the city occupied the mountain itself, or another site within view. In Ezek. l.c. the city apparently occupies the southern slope of the mountain, whence the seer views it.
that great city, the holy Jerusalem] Read, **the holy city Jerusalem**.
descending...from God] Verbatim the same as in *v.* 2, according to the true text. The descent described here is no doubt the same as there, but St John's vision of the descent is not exactly the same. He has seen, as it were in the distance, the appearance of the city: but his attention was absorbed in listening to the sayings of *vv.* 3—8. Now, he is summoned to attend to the other, and finds it at the same stage where he noticed it in passing before.
11. *Having the glory of God*] i.e. the visible cloud of glory (cf. Heb. ix. 5), the Shechinah of the divine Presence. See *v.* 23.
and her light] Omit "and". The word for **light** is peculiar—it would properly be used of a star, as we say "luminary."
a jasper stone] See on iv. 3.
clear as crystal] Expressed by one word, and that strictly a participle, **crystallizing**. Are we to understand that the comparison is not with an ordinary jasper, but with a stone combining the pure and full colours of this with the crystalline structure of other more precious jewels?
12. *and had*] Lit. **having**; but there is a break in the construction, at least as marked as that given by the A.V.
a wall great and high] Its exact height is stated in *v.* 17.
twelve gates...Israel] So Ezek. xlviii. 31—34. Probably the order of the names on the gates would be the same as there; but the order can hardly be pressed as important, since it is quite different from that of the foursquare encampment in the wilderness, Num. ii. The 12 gates *of heaven* in Enoch xxxiii.—xxxv. do not really present a very close parallel to these.
twelve angels] As porters and sentinels. Such officers are in keeping with the image of a well-ordered city, though in fact neither they, nor walls and gates, are practically needed in this City of Peace.
13. *east...north...south...west*] The order of enumeration in Numbers

south three gates; and on the west three gates. And the 14
wall of the city had twelve foundations, and in them the
names of the twelve apostles of the Lamb. And he that 15
talked with me had a golden reed to measure the city, and
the gates thereof, and the wall thereof. And the city lieth 16
foursquare, and the length is as large as the breadth: and
he measured the city with the reed, twelve thousand furlongs.

is E. S. W. N., in Ezekiel N. E. S. W. in Enoch N. W. S. E., as in each of them the surveyor goes round methodically in order: in this more ecstatic book, the whole is apprehended simultaneously, perhaps rather confusedly.

14. *And the wall...twelve foundations*] Probably each of the twelve sections into which the wall is divided by the gates rests on an enormous jewel, reaching from gate to gate. This symbolises the solidity as well as the beauty of the divine structure: and was itself symbolised by the enormous size of the stones used in the foundations of the earthly temple. See St Mark xiii. 1 and parallels. *Had* is literally **having**, a solecism like that of *v.* 12.

twelve names of the twelve apostles] Expressing the same doctrine as St Paul in Eph. ii. 20, and (probably) our Lord in St Matt. xvi. 18. It is absurd to suppose that there is any pointed insistance on the Apostles being *only* twelve, St Paul being excluded: to introduce thirteen or fourteen would have spoilt the symmetry characteristic of the whole vision. We might just as well say, that there ought to be thirteen gates for the thirteen tribes; counting Ephraim, Manasseh and Levi all as coordinate with the rest. Really, it is idle to ask whether the twelfth name was that of St Paul or St Matthias. St John does not notice his own name being written there, though of course it was (cf. St Luke x. 20); the Apostles are here mentioned in their collective and official, not in their individual character. (See on v. 5.)

of the Lamb] His identity is taken for granted with the Jesus of the earthly ministry, as in xiv. 1 with the Son of God.

15. *a golden reed*] So xi. 1; this is more closely parallel to Ezek. xl. 3, 5. See also Zech. ii. 1.

the gates] As it happens, we are not actually told of their measurement.

16. *he measured the city*] It is doubtful whether this is the measurement of the *side* of the square, or of the whole circumference. The twelve-fold measure is in favour of the former view: thus from each gate to the next would be 1000 furlongs; the outmost gate on each side being 500 from the angle.

with the reed] He has not, as in the parallel passages of Ezekiel and Zechariah, a *line* for the long measurements (like our "chains" and "poles").

twelve thousand furlongs] The construction is peculiar, but the sense clear. The measure would be about 1378 English miles, making the City 344 miles square, according to the lower computation.

The length and the breadth and the height of it are equal. 17 And he measured the wall thereof, an hundred *and* forty *and* four cubits, *according to* the measure of a man, that is, 18 of *the* angel. And the building of the wall of it was *of* jasper: and the city *was* pure gold, like unto clear glass. 19 And the foundations of the wall of the city *were* garnished

the length and the breadth and the height of it are equal] It seems inconsistent with the pictorial vividness of this book, to imagine that the City is described as forming a *cube* of over 300 miles each way; and we are told in the next verse that the wall was of a great but not unimaginable or disproportionate height. Yet no other interpretation has been proposed that seems fairly reconcileable with the words; and passages are quoted from the Rabbis, that seem to prove that this notion, of Jerusalem being elevated to an enormous height, did commend itself to Jewish habits of thought. Would it be admissible to suppose that the City, which almost certainly lies on a mountain, forms not a *cube* but a *pyramid?* The height of it, equal to one side of the base, may then be conceived to be measured along the slope, either at the angle, or at the centre of one side: the conception of *vertical* height is rather too abstruse to be looked for, and it could not be measured with the reed. The vertical height would on one view be about 2121 stadia, or 243 miles: on the other, about 2598 stadia, or 298 miles.

17. *he measured the wall*] We should naturally understand, the height of it. The walls of the historical Babylon are differently stated as having been 200, 300, or nearly 340 feet high. But we are told that they were about 80 feet in breadth (Hdt. 1. clxxviii. 5: cf. Jer. li. 58): so if we do admit that the City here is conceived as 340 miles high, there is a sort of proportion in making its walls not less than 73 yards thick.

according to...the angel] Rather, **of an angel**. Angels use, he means, a cubit of the same length as men—viz. the average length of the forearm, from the elbow to the finger-tip. It is perhaps implied, that angels are not of superhuman stature.

THE BUILDING FOUNDATIONS AND STREET, vv. 18—21.

18. *And the building*] The word is a half-technical one, as it were "the superstructure," as distinct from the foundations.

jasper] See on iv. 3.

the city was pure gold] i.e. the houses included within the wall.

like...glass] *This* gold is transparent, not like the earthly: see note on ver. 11. The epithet of the glass is the same as that of the gold: both should be rendered **pure.**

19. *garnished*] The same word that is rendered "adorned" in *v.* 2. From the next sentence we are to understand that they are adorned by being *constructed* of these stones, not that stones are fastened on *merely* for ornament.

with all *manner of* precious stones. The first foundation *was* jasper; the second, sapphire; the third, a chalcedony; the fourth, an emerald; the fifth, sardonyx; the sixth, sardius; the seventh, chrysolite; the eighth, beryl; the ninth, a topaz; the tenth, a chrysoprasus; the eleventh, a jacinth; the twelfth, an amethyst. And the twelve gates 20 21

precious stones] See Is. liv. 11, 12; where however there is less detail than here, and what there is is not quite the same: a warning against expecting too minute a symbolism in the details. It is true that contemporary superstition ascribed mystical meanings and magical virtues to the various stones, and it is possible that the revelation made to St John was given in terms of these beliefs, which he and his readers may have known of or even have held. But though not *a priori* incredible, this is hardly likely: these superstitions had, it seems, much less hold on the popular mind in St John's day than some centuries later: and at all times they were too vague and too variable to give us a key to the interpretation. There may be a definite meaning in each of the stones named, but the general meaning of the whole is all that we can be sure of. As St Hildebert says,

Quis chalcedon, quis jacinthus,
Norunt *illi qui sunt intus.*

The first foundation] The enumeration probably begins from one of the angles, and goes round the wall in order. It is useless to guess which Apostle's name was on which stone, but it may be presumed that St Peter's would be on the first. But in no two of the canonical lists of the Apostles are their names given in the same order; and, so far as there is any order among them, they are arranged in three groups of four, not, as is here required, in four groups of three.

jasper] Like the superstructure of the wall, *v.* 18. But it can hardly be meant, that the Church is built more solidly on to St Peter than to any other of the Twelve.

sapphire] The Greek and Hebrew words are (as with "jasper") the same as the English. Yet it is almost certain that the stone so called in St John's day was not our sapphire, but the far less precious lapis lazuli.

chalcedony] Apparently not the stone now so called, but one closely resembling the emerald.

20. *chrysolite...topaz*] According to the best authorities, the ancient application of these names was the reverse of the modern. Chrysolite ought, according to the etymology, to be a "golden stone," while the modern chrysolite is green. Perhaps the ancient chrysolite included the modern jacinth as well as the true "Oriental topaz."

chrysoprasus] A variety of the beryl, of a more yellowish-green: probably that now called chrysolite.

jacinth] Probably *our* sapphire, the "sapphire" above being lapis lazuli. The modern jacinth is a crystalline stone, usually red.

amethyst] This, the emerald, sardius, and beryl are undoubtedly the stones now so called.

were twelve pearls; every several gate was of one pearl: and the street of the city *was* pure gold, as *it were* transparent glass. And I saw no temple therein: for the Lord God Almighty and the Lamb are the temple of it. And the city had no need of the sun, neither of the moon, to shine in it: for the glory of God did lighten it, and the Lamb *is* the light thereof. And the nations of them which are saved shall walk in the light of it: and the kings of the

21. *pearls*] Contrast Is. liv. 12, where they are carbuncles.
the street] Or "square:" see on xi. 8. The City has one great space in the midst of it, like an Agora or Forum: but the word Agora would have associations, commercial or political, that would be incongruous with the repose of this city. It is probably the pavement of the street which, like the walls of the houses, is of transparent gold.

The Temple, the Light, the Riches, and the Inhabitants of the City, vv. 22—27.

22. *And I saw no temple*] The New Jerusalem is on earth, though on the *new* earth: this does not therefore prove that the heavenly temple of xi. 19 &c. has ceased to exist. But He Who dwells from all eternity in that Temple will dwell to all eternity in the New Jerusalem; and will dwell there so manifestly, that there will be no need of an earthly figure of that Temple to symbolise His presence, or aid men to realise it.
the Lord God Almighty] See on i. 8, iv. 8.
and the Lamb are] More accurately, **the Lord God the Almighty is the Temple of it, and the Lamb.** But the coupling of the Lamb with the Eternal is scarcely the less significant: see on xx. 6.

23. *no need of the sun* &c.] Is. lx. 19. It is impossible to say whether it is here meant that the sun and moon do not shine, or only that the city is not dependent on them.
the light thereof] The word is that commonly rendered **candle** or **lamp.** This makes it unlikely that the analogy is meant to be suggested, that the Lord God is the Sun of the city, and the Lamb the Moon.

24. *of them which are saved*] Should be omitted. Notice that the new Jerusalem is not the only inhabited part of the new earth, but only its centre and capital, as the earthly Jerusalem was in chap. xx. It follows from xx. 15, that *all* the dwellers in the new earth are those who were written in the Lamb's Book of Life; but it does not appear who among them have the further privilege of citizenship in the Holy City. That there *is* such a further privilege, above the lot of all the Elect, has been already suggested by vii. 4, 9, xiv. 1—5.
in the light] Read, **by or through the light.**
and the kings of the earth &c.] Apparently, civic government is still

vv. 25—27; 1, 2.] REVELATION, XXI. XXII.   139

earth do bring their glory and honour into it. And the 25
gates of it shall not be shut at all by day: for there shall be
no night there. And they shall bring the glory and honour 26
of the nations into it. And there shall in no wise enter into 27
it any *thing* that defileth, neither *whatsoever* worketh abomination, or *maketh* a lie: but they which are written in the
Lamb's book of life. And he shewed me a pure river of 22
water of life, clear as crystal, proceeding out of the throne
of God and of the Lamb. In the midst of the street of it, 2

needed, or at any rate still exists, among "the nations" of the regenerate earth. But probably this is only a part of the imagery:
Jerusalem is conceived (as in Is. xlv. 14, xlix. 23, lx. 10, 11) as an
imperial city receiving the tribute of the world, simply because that was
the form of world-wide sovereignty recognised and understood in the
prophets' times.
 and honour] Should be omitted: the words come in from *v.* 26.
 25. *And the gates* &c.] Is. lx. 11. But the later prophet speaks
of a further glory than the earlier: Isaiah recognises the succession
of day and night, while St John sees that in that perpetual day the gates
cannot need to be closed. In an earthly city they are not closed by
day except in time of war; but even in perfect peace they are closed
every night (cf. Neh. xiii. 19); here the daylight is as perpetual as the
peace.
 27. *that defileth*] Read **unclean**, lit. **common.**
 whatsoever *worketh*] Read, **he that worketh**, or rather **doeth**.
 the Lamb's book of life] So xiii. 8.

THE WATER AND THE TREE OF LIFE; THE SERVICE AND THE
 KINGDOM OF GOD'S SERVANTS. CHAP. XXII. vv. 1—5.

 1. *pure*] Should be omitted.
 river of water of life] See vii. 17, xxi. 6.
 clear] **Bright** would perhaps be more accurate.
 proceeding out of the throne &c.] In Ezekiel's vision (chap. xlvii.)
the River proceeded out of the Temple, here out of the Temple's antitype. We are also meant to think of the River that watered the ancient
paradise, Gen. ii. 10, and of such parallels to Ezekiel's vision as
Pss. xlvi. 4, lxv. 9; Zech. xiv. 8. The original type, of which these
Prophecies are developments, is the fact that there was a natural
spring, that of Siloam, in the precincts of the Temple at Jerusalem.
We are not told here, as in the old Paradise, that the River is fourfold:
but if the City stands on a pyramidal mountain (see on xxi. 16) it is
likely enough that there is a stream running down each of its four
faces, the throne which is the source being at the summit.
 2. *In the midst...of the river*] The picture is, almost certainly,
that the river runs along the broad high-street or piazza (see on xi.

and of either side of the river, *was there* the tree of life, which bare twelve *manner of* fruits, *and* yielded her fruit every month: and the leaves of the tree *were* for the healing 3 of the nations. And there shall be no more curse: but the

8, xxi. 21, and note that, if the mountain be pyramidal, the "street" is cruciform), and rows or plantations, all of the one tree, stand along the banks on either side. But the exact construction and punctuation is not quite certain: that assumed in the A.V. is not very likely. Either we may punctuate as the Revised Version, connecting "in the midst of the street thereof" with the preceding sentence, or else we should probably translate, "Midway between the street of it and the river, on this side and on that:" i.e. there is a "street" or boulevard on each side of the river, and parted from the river by a sort of quay, in the midst of which is a row of the trees. It can hardly be meant that there is a *single* plant of the tree, as in the old Paradise (Gen. ii. 9), for how could one tree grow "on this side and on that of the river?" and the words would hardly bear the sense "in the midst of the street thereof and of the river, *with them running* on this side and on that *of it*." It would be awkward to represent the tree as growing in the midst of the river: and though there is a difference between this Paradise and the old in the multiplication of the tree, it is all, as it should be, in favour of the new.

the tree of life] Gen. ii. 9, cp. chap. ii. 7; where the likeness, not the difference, between the arrangement of this Paradise and the old is brought out.

every month] Yet there can hardly be months and years when there is no moon nor sun. It is not, however, certain that this is the case here: see on xxi. 23. But the real meaning is, that the fruit is always in season, and never cloys.

and the leaves...healing] Ezek. xlvii. 12.

the nations] Those outside the city: see on xxi. 24. This is perhaps the only passage in Scripture which suggests that, *even after the Day of Judgement*, there may be a process of purification for those whom that Day finds in a state of salvation, but imperfectly sanctified. But though it cannot be denied that this passage suggests this, it would be very rash to say that it proves it. It is quite possible that it is only at their first admission to the new earth that "the nations" have any need of "healing." Surely no one can doubt, that this need will be felt by almost all, perhaps by all, who are saved at the last. Even if they were what we rightly account to be saints on earth they need a "healing" of their surviving sins before they are fit for heaven. They may receive this at the moment of death, as most Protestants suppose, or between death and judgement, as (in different forms) was supposed by some of the fathers and by the modern Roman Church. But apparently the oldest belief was that the work would be done at the moment of Judgement; see Comm. on 1 Cor. iii. 13—15: and this passage is quite in harmony with that view.

3. *no more curse*] The word for "curse" is rather peculiar; it is

throne of God and of the Lamb shall be in it; and his servants shall serve him: and they shall see his face; and his 4 name *shall be* in their foreheads. And there shall be no 5 night there; and they need no candle, neither light of the sun; for the Lord God giveth them light: and they shall reign for ever and ever.

And he said unto me, These sayings *are* faithful and true: 6 and the Lord God of the holy prophets sent his angel to shew unto his servants *the things* which must shortly be

no doubt meant as a translation of that rendered "utter destruction" in Zech. xiv. 11, of which this verse is a reminiscence.

the throne &c.] Implied already in xxi. 23 and *v.* 1. Interpreters compare the last words of Ezekiel's cognate prophecy.

his servants] Note the singular pronoun, implying the Unity of the Persons-named.

shall serve him] See vii. 15, and note there.

4. *shall see his face*] This is the *locus classicus* for what constitutes the blessedness of heaven, the "Beatific Vision." It is intimated in Job xix. 26 and in Is. lii. 8, where there may be an allusion to the privilege of Moses, Ex. xxxiii. 11; Num. xii. 8; Deut. xxxiv. 10. In the last verse of Ps. xvii. it may be questioned whether the final and immediate vision, or an earthly foretaste, is intended; but Job xlii. 5, 6; Is. vi. 5 shew that it is only to "the spirits of just men made perfect" that the vision is endurable. In the N.T. we have the promise in St Matt. v. 8; 1 Cor. xiii. 12; St John's 1 Ep. iii. 2.

his name [shall be] *in their foreheads*] So in xiv. 1, where, according to the true text, we see that "*His*" still means the Name of God, both the Father and the Son.

5. *there*] Read, **any more.** See xxi. 25.

they need no candle &c.] Read, **they have no need of light of lamp, neither of light of sun.**

giveth them light] Read, **shall give light upon them.** Here end the visions.

THE CONFIRMATION OF THE PROMISE; THE ERROR OF THE SEER, vv. 6—11.

6. *And he said unto me*] Who speaks? the angel of xxi. 9, or "He that sitteth upon the throne," as in xxi. 5—8, or Christ as in *v.* 16? Probably, an angel speaks in the name of Christ: and this leads St John to fancy, as once before, that the angel is himself a divine person.

These sayings] Better, **words**—the phrase (except that the copula "are" is not expressed) is *verbatim* the same as in xxi. 5.

of the holy prophets] Read, **of the spirits of the prophets**: for the phrase, cf. 1 Cor. xiv. 32.

to shew unto his servants &c.] i. 1.

7 done. Behold, I come quickly: blessed *is* he that keepeth the sayings of the prophecy of this book.

8 And I John saw these *things*, and heard *them*. And when I had heard and seen, I fell down to worship before the feet 9 of the angel which shewed me these *things*. Then saith he unto me, See *thou do it* not: for I am thy fellowservant, and of thy brethren the prophets, and of them which keep the 10 sayings of this book: worship God. And he saith unto me, Seal not the sayings of the prophecy of this book: for the

7. *Behold*] Read, **And behold**.
I come quickly] Spoken no doubt in the *name* of Christ, though hardly by Him. Cf. iii. 11, and *vv*. 12, 20.
blessed is *he that keepeth* &c.] i. 3. "Sayings" should again be **words**, as in the parallel passage.

8. *And I John saw* &c.] Lit. **and I John [am] he that saw and heard** (or "heard and saw") **these things**. It is possible to connect these words with the immediately preceding sentence, regarding it, not as a continuation of the angel's speech, but as the beginning of St John's reflexion, "Blessed is he that keepeth the words, &c., and [blessed am] I John, who see and hear these things." It was so understood by St Dionysius of Alexandria in the third century, and this construction is the easiest and smoothest grammatically. But few modern commentators accept this view: it seems inappropriate to the context.

I fell down to worship] As at xix. 10. Some suppose that St John is here repeating his statement of what he did then, but it is far more natural to understand that he did the same again. The words "I come quickly" would even more naturally lead him to think that this angel was "He that is to come," than the words of that angel (who may or may not have been the same as this) led him to think that he was the God Whose "true sayings" he communicated.

9. *for*] should be omitted.
thy brethren the prophets] It has been recognised in *vv*. 6, 7, that St John is a prophet, and shares in the special blessedness given to prophets. But at the same time "they which keep the words of this book," though not prophets, share that blessedness with them. St Matt. x. 41 implies the same, though the form of statement is somewhat different.

10. *he saith*] Still, probably, the same angel. He speaks still more unmistakeably in Christ's person, now that St John understands beyond mistake that he is not Christ Himself.

Seal not &c.] Pointedly contrasted with Dan. xii. 4, 9. In Daniel's time, both the coming of Antichrist and the deliverance from him were far off: Daniel was bidden to write what he saw and heard, but not to make it public, for it would be unintelligible till long after his own generation:—at least till the typical persecution of Antiochus, and the typical day of vengeance and deliverance of the Maccabees. But to St John's readers, all was to be as plain as an unfulfilled prophecy ever can be: except one detail (x. 4) the whole vision is to be laid before the

time is at hand. He that is unjust, let him be unjust still: 11
and he which is filthy, let him be filthy still: and *he that is*
righteous, let him be righteous still: and *he that is* holy, let
him be holy still. And behold, I come quickly; and my 12
reward *is* with me, to give every man according as his work
shall be. I am Alpha and Omega, the beginning and the 13

Church. It *may* be meant further, that the typical persecution of Nero was already within the Church's experience, and that its typical revival under Domitian was to fall within the present generation.

for the time is at hand] So i. 3. Besides the fact that partial and typical fulfilments were nearer to St John's age than to Daniel's, it is intimated that the same age, the same dispensation under which St John and his readers lived was to last till the time of the end; while the Jewish age in which Daniel lived passed away long before the end. For in mere chronology the difference is slight: from St John's day to the end is, as we know, more than 1800 years, and from Daniel's more than 2400: in comparison with the longer period, the shorter can hardly be spoken of as short.

11. *He that is unjust* &c.] The sense is generally understood to be, "The time is so short, that it is too late to change: for good or evil, you must go on as you are;" a solemn and terrible irony, like "Sleep on now, and take your rest," to the Disciples who had missed their opportunity. As that was followed by "Rise, let us be going," so there is nothing inconsistent with this in the Church continuing to preach repentance to the unjust and the filthy. But in the Epistle of the Churches of Gaul (Eus. *H. E.* v. i. 53) the passage is quoted (not quite accurately, it is true) as though the sense were, 'Let the unrighteous do *more* unrighteousness" &c.; a possible rendering of the Greek. Then the sense will be, that the world "must be worse before it is better"—that sin must come to its height, in order that the righteous may be made perfect. For "unjust" it would be better to render "unrighteousness," or else "just" for "righteous" below, as the two words are the exact opposites of each other.

be righteous] Read, **do righteousness**.
be holy] More literally, **be sanctified**.

THE WITNESS OF THE LORD, vv. 12—18.

12. *I come quickly*] Of course He Who "comes" is the Lord Jesus: but we are probably not to imagine that He is personally present—the angel still speaks in His name.

my reward is *with me*] Is. xl. 10, lxii. 11.

to give every man] Better, **to render to every man**. The source of the expression is in Job xxxiv. 11; Ps. lxii. 12. In the N.T. this retribution is ascribed to God in Rom. ii. 6, to the Son in His own words in St Matt. xvi. 27.

shall be] Read, **is**.

13. *I am Alpha* &c.] So i. 8 (not 11). The words there, are those of the Father, here, of the Son.

14 end, the first and the last. Blessed *are* they that do his commandments, that they may have right to the tree of life,
15 and may enter in through the gates into the city. For without *are* dogs, and sorcerers, and whoremongers, and murderers, and idolaters, and whosoever loveth and maketh a lie.
16 I Jesus have sent mine angel to testify unto you these

the beginning &c.] The true order seems to be **the first and the last, the beginning and the end**.

14. *that do his commandments*] Read, **that wash their robes**: cf. vii. 14. The change from one reading to the other is in the Greek only one of a few letters; it seems uncalled for to charge the copyists who introduced the received reading with a wish to substitute justification by works for justification by faith. There are plenty of Scriptural parallels for the sentence, read either way: but there seems to be no doubt which way St John in fact wrote it.

that they may have right] Lit. **that the right** (or **power**, or **license**) **may be theirs**. The right of approaching the Tree of Life is a definite privilege, granted to a certain class, viz. those who "wash their robes."

15. *For*] should be omitted.

dogs &c.] The articles should be expressed, "*the* dogs, and the sorcerers (see on ix. 21, xxi. 8), and the fornicators, and the murderers and the idolaters, and everyone that loveth &c."

maketh] Or **doeth**: the word is the same as in St John's 1 Ep. i. 6. To *do* the truth or a lie is a great deal more, for good or evil, than merely to *say* it. In that passage, the false Christian's falsehood lies altogether in what he does, not in the privileges he claims, which would be truly his, if not belied by his life.

16. *I Jesus*] Here only does our Lord reveal His Name, though from i. 13, 18 onwards, it has been obvious that He is the revealer; as was expressed in the title, i. 1. Whether He is *personally* present, however, is doubtful: the words are His, but it is probably still the angel that speaks them.

mine angel] Would our Lord say this of any angel of the Lord, because "all things that the Father hath are His." Or has our Lord, as Man, an angel of His own in the same way that His saints have? St Luke xxii. 43 seems as if He needed and had, in the days of His flesh, such angelic guardianship as is implied in St Matt. xviii. 10: and this passage is at least consistent with the view, that His angel appears in His form, as St Peter's was supposed to do, Acts xii. 15. It is very ably argued by St Augustine (*de Cura pro Mortuis*), that if any apparitions after death or at the moment of death are really objective and supernatural, they must be ascribed to angels, not to the spirits of the dead. But we must remember that our Lord's state is not the same as that of His departed servants. He is already in the body of the Resurrection, and so conceivably visible. And there can be no doubt that He appeared in His own risen body to St Paul, and probably to St Stephen. It may be, therefore, that He now

things in the churches. I am the root and the offspring of David, *and* the bright and morning star. And the Spirit 17 and the bride say, Come. And let him that heareth say, Come. And let him that is athirst come. And whosoever will, let him take the water of life freely. For I testify unto 18

appears personally to St John, at once superseding and authenticating the previous ministry of the angel.

the root and the offspring of David] He bears the former title in v. 5, where see note. The latter is substantially the same as the familiar one, "the Son of David."

and *the bright and morning star*] Both "and"s should be omitted. There may be a reference to Num. xxiv. 17, or to the title of "the Day-spring," St Luke i. 78, and perhaps Zech. iii. 8, vi. 12. In ii. 28, though the words are more nearly the same as here, the sense is different: see note there.

THE SPIRIT AND THE BRIDE, v. 17.

17. *And the Spirit* &c.] "The Bride" is, it is here implied, the Church on earth, imploring her Lord about to come to her. But the Bride throughout this book has been the perfect or heavenly Church; notice the identification of the Church in both states. Notice also the identity of St Paul's doctrine, and in part of his imagery, Gal. iv. 26: Eph. v. 25 sqq. "The Spirit" is, as in Rom. viii. 26, the Spirit dwelling in or inspiring the faithful: the Spirit says, "Come!" when He teaches the Bride to say it.

Come] The word is (in the true text) the same here as in vi. 1, 3, 5, 7.

let him that heareth say, Come] The prayers of the Church are prayed, not preached; yet they do serve for instruction to those who only "hear" them: by hearing they are educated to join in them. Cf. Col. iii. 16.

let him that is athirst] Is. lv. 1.

come] Correlative to the "coming" of Christ to us is our "coming" to Him. The invocation "Come!" in the earlier clauses is certainly addressed to Him, so that this does not express the answer to it. But it is evident (even more evident in the Greek than in the English) that the thought is present of the one coming being correlative to the other. We come to Christ, that we may learn to "love His appearing," and be able to cry to Him "Come," instead of fearing it.

and whosoever &c.] Omit "and": the last clause of the verse is rather explanatory of the preceding one than coordinate with it.

freely] i.e. "without money and without price:" see on xxi. 6.

THE FINAL TESTIMONY OF THE SEER AND HIS BENEDICTION, vv. 18—21.

18. *For I testify*] Omit "for."

every *man* that heareth the words of the prophecy of this book, If any *man* shall add unto these *things*, God shall
19 add unto him the plagues that are written in this book: and if any *man* shall take away from the words of the book of this prophecy, God shall take away his part out of the book of life, and out of the holy city, and *from* the *things* which
20 are written in this book. He which testifieth these *things* saith, Surely I come quickly. Amen. Even, so, come,
21 Lord Jesus. The grace of our Lord Jesus Christ *be* with you all. Amen.

If any man *shall add* &c.] Deut. iv. 2, xii. 32. The parallel of those passages proves, that the curse denounced is on those who interpolate unauthorised *doctrines* in the prophecy, or who neglect essential ones; not on transcribers who might unadvisedly interpolate or omit something in the true text. The curse, if understood in the latter sense, has been remarkably ineffective, for the common text of this book is more corrupt, and the true text oftener doubtful, than in any other part of the N.T. But it may be feared that additions and omissions in the more serious sense have also been frequently made by rash interpreters. It is certain that the curse is designed to guard the integrity of *this* Book of the Revelation, not to close the N.T. canon. It is not even certain that this was the last written of the canonical books.

unto these things] Better simply **unto them**: an unemphatic pronoun being used. Though it cannot grammatically refer to "the words of the prophecy," i.e. it no doubt does so refer ungrammatically.

19. *out of the book of life*] Read **from the tree of life**.

and from &c.] "and" should be omitted, the sense being, "from the Tree of Life, out of the Holy City, in short, from all the good things written &c."

20. *Surely*] The word is that rendered **Even so** in i. 7, and in the next clause here, and which might be better rendered **Yea**. It should be omitted in the next clause, so that the whole will read, "He that testifieth these things saith, 'Yea [in answer to the prayers of *v*. 17] I come quickly.' Amen: come, Lord Jesus.

21. *our Lord Jesus Christ*] Read only, **the Lord Jesus**.

with you all] We should read either only **with all**, or more probably **with the saints**. Many authorities omit "Amen" here, as after the benedictions ending many of St Paul's Epistles.

APPENDIX.

EXCURSUS I.

THE ANGELS OF THE CHURCHES: ELEMENTAL ANGELS: THE LIVING CREATURES.

THERE are two views of the angels of the Churches. According to one they are simply the bishops of the Churches; according to the other they are superhuman beings standing in some intimate relation to the Churches: more intimate than the relation to Nature of the angels who hold the four winds, vii. 1, the angel who hath power over the fire, xiv. 18, and presumably the angel of the waters, xvi. 5. The first view, which at present is perhaps the most widely received, rests upon the following considerations. In Haggai i. 13 a prophet, in Mal. ii. 7 the priest is 'the angel of "THE LORD,"' and it is generally agreed (see note in *Cambridge Bible for Schools*, *ad loc.*) that 'the angel,' Ecc. v. 6, means simply the priest. Hence as in St Ignatius the bishop is always the chief minister of the Christian Sacrifice it might seem that he is a priest and mystically an 'angel.' Again, as Westcott and Hort, *ad loc.* Greek Testament, ii. 137, point out, there is an analogy between what we may call the 'style and title' of the 'angels' and the style and title of the pagan high-priests of Asia. Moreover, if Jezebel be the wife of the 'angel' in Thyatira he must be a man, as she is a woman. No inference can be drawn from the name, which in Greek would be the same as 'angel,' of an officer in the synagogue who may have been established in St John's time: for he was in no sense a ruler; in the Christian hierarchy he corresponded to an acolyte, not to a bishop.

The great difficulty in the way of this view is that the 'angels' seem to be more completely identified with the Churches than human bishops can be: take for instance the messages to Sardis or Laodicea, can we suppose that the Church had all the faults of the bishop or the bishop all the faults of the Church? Take even the message to Ephesus: can we suppose that the fervour of the Church and the bishop has been declining *pari passu* for exactly the same time? Nor can we infer from the way in which Old Testament saints from Jeremiah to Nehemiah confess the sins of their people as if they were their own, nor even from Is. liii. 6 that the Lord lays the iniquity of the Church upon the bishop as a matter of course. Again, the seven candlesticks are the seven Churches, the seven stars are the 'angels.' One would expect an impenitent bishop to perish with his Church, yet the threat to the 'angel' at Ephesus is 'except thou repent I will take away thy candlestick,' not 'I will cast thee out of My hand.' This cannot be pressed: both the threat and the counsel to the 'angel' at Laodicea suggest a human rather than a superhuman recipient, though the former at least must be metaphorical. It is rather an evasion than a solution to regard the 'angels' as mere personifications of the prevailing spirit of the Churches: such a view would be at bottom unreal and unmeaning, but on the surface it has fewer difficulties than either the view that the 'angels' are human bishops, or that they are perfect, blessed, faultless spirits charged with the oversight of communities which may be imperfect, faulty, miserable. This view indeed depends entirely upon a doctrine of angels which perhaps would only be found in Holy Scripture by readers who bring it there with them. Those who were praying in the house of Mary the mother of John, whose surname was Mark, clearly believed that Peter's angel would speak with Peter's voice: did they believe that he was, so to speak, a heavenly double of Peter who came into the world with him? It is important to remember that they were familiar with the whole body of thought at which we have to guess mainly from the incidental notices and hints of sacred writers who appear in some measure to share, and therefore to sanction, the beliefs of their own day. While the 'little ones' keep their innocency their 'angels' see the Father's face. When they seek out many inventions it may be that their 'angels' are charged 'with folly' because they too have failed to keep 'the first estate.' Again in Ezek. xxviii. 11—19, we seem to have a prophecy against the superhuman 'king of Tyrus,' parallel to the prophecy in xxviii. 1—10 against the human prince who thinks himself God. If so, the 'king of Tyrus,' who for all his superhuman attributes is to perish with the city with which he has been created, must be something like the 'spiritual form' of the city, a spirit with a personality of his own, yet wise with its wisdom, rich with its wealth, proud with its pride. The book of Daniel gives us no reason to think that the 'princes' of Persia and of Grecia belong to a higher order. If there be such spirits of nations, certainly it is simplest to think that the 'angels' stand in the same relation to 'Churches,' in the eternal order of grace and glory, as that in which 'princes' stand to nations, in the temporal order of secular providence. But since the time of St Victorinus no interpreter has ventured to maintain that elect angels can have real need of repentance as the 'angels' of the churches certainly have.

In the Old Testament angels seem to be identified in some sense with stars, e.g. Job iv. 18, xxv. 3, 5; and with fire and wind, Ps. civ. 4; and Longfellow's lines:

'The angels of wind and of fire
Breathe each but one song and expire.'

are true to one aspect of Rabbinical speculation in which angels seem to forestall the 'metaphysical' conception of 'forces.' There is no trace that either line of thought influenced the seer of Patmos. The elemental angels, so to call them, are apparently pure spirits, who neither impart their characters to what they act upon nor are influenced in their own character by the sphere of their action. The angel of the waters no more suffers loss when they who are worthy have blood given them to drink than the angels who withhold the four winds from blowing. Still the energy of the material universe seems like the giving of the law to be committed to the disposition of angels. So far as this goes we might suppose that even the Angel of the Bottomless Pit was like the evil angels of Ps. lxxviii. 49, a not unwilling minister of God's anger, but unless he is the same as the fallen star he is himself a prisoner in the Pit with those over whom he rules; in this he is like the four angels bound in the river Euphrates, who also are held ready to execute a work of vengeance at a time appointed. It may be added that though the writer of the Ascent of Isaiah x. 8, who seems to imitate this passage, distinguishes the 'angel who is in hell' from 'Destruction,' i.e. 'Abaddon,' he clearly assumes that hell is the permanent dwelling of the angel.

The four living creatures certainly correspond to the cherubim in Ezekiel. The resemblances outweigh the differences, and it is to be supposed that St John, like Ezekiel, could only see the 'appearance' of spiritual forms. The throne in his vision is immoveable: it reminds us not of Him Who bowed the heavens and came down, but of the Father of Lights without variableness or shadow of turning. Instead of wheels full of eyes the living creatures are full of eyes themselves. If the eyes are stars, we might say that if the cherubim in Ezekiel are spirits in a sense, of the storm, the living creatures are spirits of constellations, the true power behind the starry shapes that men have traced in the sky. The two do not exclude each other. Heavenly princes of the east, of the west, of the north, of the south, might be manifested in vision under either shape.

The four riders who appear one by one as each of the first four seals is opened recall not only sword, famine and pestilence among the four sore judgements in Ezekiel, but the four chariots in Zechariah, which seem expressly identified with the four winds. This makes it more remarkable that the four living creatures cry 'Come,' one by one, before the riders appear. The riders come (? from the four ends of heaven) in answer to this cry, even if we suppose that in its deepest meaning the cry is for the coming of the Judge Himself, Whose heralds all judgements are.

In Daniel the four beasts who symbolise the four kingdoms are raised up by the strife of the four winds upon the great deep, as if the first thing shewed to the prophet was four world-wide kingdoms, each arising from one of the four ends of the earth. As all four are in rebellion against the Ancient of Days, Who allows no dominion but the fifth monarchy of one like unto the Son of Man, we cannot follow the Jewish speculation which finds an anticipation of Daniel in Ezekiel, and identifies his living creatures with the four empires, the Persian having the face of a man because it dealt favourably with Israel. Both in Ezekiel and in the Revelation we must assume that the living creatures are perfectly pure and holy.

Assuming the living creatures to be personal creatures and servants of God, the highest of His creatures, the most honoured of His servants, it becomes less important to determine what is meant by their several forms, though it be admitted that they are symbolical. We need form no exclusive theory of what suggested them or of what they were intended to suggest. Certainly the view that they represent creation will not bear pressing, even in the sense that they are manifested in forms borrowed from all creation, to shew that they act not only for themselves, but for all living creatures upon earth. It is not convincing in itself: the classification of creatures into men, wild beasts, tame beasts and birds, looks arbitrary not to say false, whether judged logically, zoologically, or in reference to the Biblical account of creation: if it were certain that the Jewish explanation of Ezekiel represented a settled tradition older than St John, it would of course tell in favour of applying it with most modern critics to the Revelation, but it does not seem to be older than the conjecture (quite inapplicable to the Revelation) that the four living creatures correspond to the standards of the fourfold host of Israel in the wilderness.

On the other hand there is no doubt that the view which regards the living creatures as symbolical of the Gospels is traditional in the best sense. It is at least as old as St Irenaeus, and it has been handed down ever since. It is true that there is no traditional agreement as to which living creature represents which Gospel. The tradition which ruled medieval and modern art does not go back beyond St Victorinus. According to him St Mark who begins with the voice crying in the wilderness is the roaring lion, St Matthew who begins with the descent of the Lord after the flesh is the man, St Luke who begins with the sacrifice of Zacharias is the ox, St John is the high flying eagle. St Augustin (who does not seem to know the view of St Victorinus), without committing himself to either thinks those more likely to be right who make Matthew the lion, Mark the man, Luke the calf, John the eagle, than those who make Matthew the man, Mark the eagle, and John the lion. This last is the arrangement of St Irenaeus, who like St Victorinus argues from the opening words (instead of as St Augustin thought better from the whole idea of the Gospel[1]); but instead of finding the lion's voice in the opening of St Mark he finds the wings of prophecy, in St John he finds the royalty of the only Begotten of the Father. No one seems to have questioned that the sacrificial calf is the symbol of St Luke (though guessing *a priori* the third of the living creatures seems to symbolise the third evangelist at least as well), and this suggests that the identification rests on a real tradition. The assignment of the eagle to St John is certainly appropriate[2], if we could be sure that his gospel

---

[1] Hence St Matthew is the lion, because his is the Gospel of the Kingdom of the Lion of the tribe of Judah.
[2] See Keble's 'Hymn for St John's Day,' in *Salisbury Hymnal*, reprinted in *Poems*:

> Word supreme before creation,
>   Born of God eternally,
> Who didst will for our salvation
>   To be born on earth, and die;
> Well Thy saints have kept their station,
>   Watching till Thine hour drew nigh.
> Now 'tis come, and faith espies Thee,
>   Like an eaglet in the morn,
> One in steadfast worship eyes Thee,
>   Thy belov'd, Thy latest born:
> In Thy glory he descries Thee
>   Reigning from the tree of scorn.

was written when he saw his vision; and that, if it were, the Four Gospels were as familiar to him as the Twelve Apostles of the Lamb. It might be safer to say that the four forms represent four elements of the highest excellence, which are embodied in Christ's Kingdom, and His Sacrifice, His Humanity and His Union with the Father: if we will we may see in their number a hint at the reason why God's Providence caused His Gospel to be transmitted to us just in four forms respectively devoted to the setting forth of each of these doctrines. As St Irenaeus says, *Cont. Haer.* III. xii., 'the faces of the Cherubim are images of the operation of the Son of God: for the first living creature is like a lion signifying His energy and rule and royalty, the second like a calf manifesting His sacrificial and priestly ministry, the third having a face of a man most clearly describing His coming as Man, the fourth like a flying eagle declaring the gift of the Spirit lighting upon the Church.' The next words are ambiguous; it is not clear whether it is the living creatures or the Gospels, whose voice accords with their nature, that are the throne of Christ. St Jerome is clearer. In his letter to Paullinus he calls the Gospels the chariot of the Lord and the true cherubim. He cannot be said to go too far. Before the Father was revealed in the Son, He made darkness His secret place and shewed Himself to prophets and psalmists wrapt in clouds and riding upon the wings of the wind: it is given to Christians to behold with open face in the fourfold Gospel the Throne of God and the Lamb, Who rides through the world, as St Augustin says, to subdue the nations to His easy yoke and His light burden.

EXCURSUS II.

ON THE HERESIES CONTROVERTED IN THE REVELATION.

THE traditions about St John's life in Asia Minor are unanimous, and the oldest and best authenticated traditions are not least clear or detailed, in the statement that the Apostle was engaged, not only in ordering the Church peaceably, in its internal constitution, but in controversy with heretics, who divided the Church's unity and denied the faith which is its foundation. And in fact, in all St John's Epistles (I. ii. 18—24, iv. 1—6, II. 7, 10, III. 9, 10) we have direct allusions to heretical or schismatical teachers, and St John's own doctrine stated in a more or less controversial form : while large portions of the First Epistle, and some even of the Gospel (e.g. the introduction), become more intelligible if we see in them a tacit reference to the heresies which either denied or perverted the doctrines there stated.

Tradition and internal probability alike lead us to understand these controversies to be particularly concerned with the heresy of the Judaising Gnostic Cerinthus; which, in all probability, did not arise till near the close of St John's life. Not the least of the arguments for referring the Revelation to an earlier date is this, that, while the controversial element in it is at least as large, the doctrines controverted are of a different and, apparently, of an earlier type.

The only sect mentioned by name is the Nicolaitan: and for the characteristics of this, the Apocalypse itself is our only *quite* unimpeachable authority. The Nicolaitans are indeed mentioned by St Irenaeus, and by later writers against heretics who used his works, apparently as still existing: but there is always some uncertainty in statements about the doctrines and practices of these secret and discreditable societies, and we cannot be sure how far St Irenaeus' statements rest on independent evidence, how far on mere inference or conjecture from what is said of them in this Book.

In fact, he says little more than this Book does make plain—that they were one of the Antinomian sects that arose in or beside the early Church, who claimed licence for sensual sin. There are two conceivable grounds on which they may have done so, neither directly supported by the evidence of the Apocalypse, but both intelligible historically, and traceable to causes that were really at work. They may, like the so-called Antinomians of modern times, have pressed St Paul's doctrine of the freedom of Christians from the Law into an assertion of the indifference, to the spiritual, of all outward actions: or they may have argued from the false spiritualism which regarded the flesh as essentially evil, and rejected the attempt to sanctify it.

What traditional evidence we have supports rather the latter view. St Clement of Alexandria—a writer somewhat later than St Irenaeus, and less directly acquainted with the main stream of Johannine tradition in Asia Minor, but early enough to have received genuine traditions, and educated enough to know the difference between tradition and conjecture—describes the sect as deriving their name from Nicolaus or Nicolas the Deacon (Acts vi. 5). He adds, that Nicolas was not really responsible for their excesses, but that they abused in a sensual sense language which he used in an ascetic. Moreover he tells stories of Nicolas' personal life, which do not sound like inventions, but rather like features of a real human character—a man of strong passions and strong principles, willing, in his own words, "to do violence to the flesh," but unable to conceive the higher ideal of "the flesh being subdued to the Spirit."

In fact, there seems no doubt that this representation of the relation of Nicolas and the Nicolaitans is at least ideally true. There were in the later apostolic age—at least as early as the Epistle to the Colossians—ascetic teachers, who preached bodily mortification as the one and the indispensable condition of holiness and spiritual progress, and regarded the indulgence of any bodily appetite as almost necessarily sinful. The characters of such men are often as austere as their theories, and command a half-reluctant respect, which not infrequently commends the theories to aspirants after purity, better than a more willing assent might do. On the other hand, not infrequently even the leaders and teachers, however sincere in their theories and professions, break down in the attempt

"to wind themselves too high
For sinful man beneath the sky,"

and fall into the very carnal sins, for fear of which they have condemned the most innocent carnal indulgences. And if this is not the case with the leaders, it is almost always with their followers, sooner or later. Either their austere theories and practice provoke a reaction, and men boldly assert everything, and do everything, that is most opposed to what they have taught and done: or their followers deduce from their principles (as it is said happened with Nicolas) an indifference to all moral rules. It is said that it is necessarily sinful to indulge the flesh: now human life cannot be sustained without *some* indulgence of the flesh, at least in food and drink. It follows, that fleshly sin is inevitable: if then spiritual perfection is attainable, it must be because fleshly sin is no obstacle to it. Consequently, it ceases to be worth while to minimise fleshly sin, as the ascetics did: the true conclusion (certainly the most agreeable to corrupt human nature) will be, to let the flesh go its own sinful way, while the spirit pursues its own path to what is regarded as perfection.

It thus seems likely enough that the traditions describing the Nicolaitans as teaching the moral indifference of carnal acts are to be trusted; and that the sect grew up without any direct connexion with the controversy about the obligation of the Law upon the consciences of Christians. No doubt, as the Epistle to the Colossians shews, the mystical and ascetic theory of life had an affinity to one side of Judaism, and there were Jewish sects or schools that held it: but it does not appear that St John's controversy with the Nicolaitans was directly connected with the controversies which we hear of in the life of St Paul. It must be remembered that Nicolas the Deacon, if he were in any sense the founder of the sect, was not a Jew by birth. But we seem, in the early chapters of the Apocalypse, to find traces of another controversy, perhaps less vital in its issues, perhaps one of which the danger was over at the date of the vision, which may more probably be identified with that between St Paul and the Judaizers. At Ephesus we hear of them "who say that they are Apostles and are not," and at Smyrna and Philadelphia of "them who say that they are Jews, and are not:" and these designations certainly suggest to our minds men like St Paul's Jewish opponents, "false Apostles," in his own words, "transforming themselves into the Apostles of Christ." And the developement of this party, or some party like them, in the district round Ephesus is foretold by St Paul in Acts xx. 29, and mentioned historically in 2 Tim. i. 15: now if the Apocalypse was written only five or six years after the last, it is likely enough that in the Church of Ephesus, particularly, their memory would be fresh, yet the immediate danger from them be over, in the way implied in the Apocalypse.

And no doubt, what is said of the false Jews at Philadelphia, and perhaps at Smyrna, does suggest that the contrast is between the true Jews who saw the Law fulfilled in the Gospel, and owned all believers in the Gospel as brethren, and those who lost their right to the name of Jews by insisting on the exclusive rights of the old Judaism. So far, St John (or He Whose words he reports) condemns the same spirit as St Paul, though it is doubtful how far the controversy is with Judaism as something external to Christianity, how far with Jewish pretensions within the Christian Church. But while the false Apostles at Ephesus were plainly professing Christians, we learn nothing as to the nature of their false teaching or the ground of their false claims. They *may* just as well have been antinomians as Judaizers: and, as they seem plainly distinguished from the Nicolaitans, their antinomianism *may* have rested on ultra-Pauline rather than on dualistic reasoning.

This possibility is the utmost that can reasonably be conceded towards the view propounded by Baur and his school, and retained and popularized by Renan, that most of the controversy in the Apocalypse is directed against St Paul himself. Not only is he himself the false Apostle whom the Church at Ephesus is praised for rejecting, but his followers are identified at once with the false Jews and with the Nicolaitans, and he or his doctrine or his school with the Jezebel of Thyatira. Arbitrary as this theory is, no less than shocking to our feelings of Christian reverence, it seems necessary to refute what has been advocated with such confidence, and by writers of such reputation. The one point common to St Paul with "Jezebel" and the Nicolaitans is, that while they "taught and seduced Christ's servants to eat things offered to idols, and to commit fornication," St Paul did not teach that it was absolutely and in all cases unlawful to eat meat that might possibly have formed part of an idol sacrifice: and that he regarded marriages between a Christian and a heathen as lawful, at least in some cases. Now it is quite possible, that some Christian teachers in St Paul's day might (on the former point at least) have held more rigorous views than his: in fact, more rigorous views did practically prevail in the Church after the Apostolic age: but it is absurd to imagine that any one could charge him with extreme laxity on either point. On the former, he not only taught that the liberty secured by the knowledge "that an idol is nothing in the world," and "that nothing is unclean in itself," was not to be exercised without regard to the prejudices or scruples of others (1 Cor. viii. 9—13, x. 28 sq.; Rom. xiv. 14 &c.); but also, that to "sit at meat in the idol's temple," at the actual sacrificial feast, was a real act of "communion with devils" (1 Cor. viii. 10, x. 14—22). It might be superstition to think that an idol was a real devil: but the "weak brother" who thought so was right on the practical point, that idol-worship was devil-worship, and that sharing in a sacrificial feast was an act of worship, whether the feast and the worship were Jewish, Christian, or heathen. Moreover, in his discussion of the question he refers (1 Cor. x. 8), as St John does, to the sin into which Israel was led by Balaam.

And if on this point it might be thought that some would have desired a more categorical prohibition than St Paul gave, as to fornication no one could desiderate more definite language than his. And it is absurd to suppose that the word is used in different senses. When the thing itself was so common as everyone knows it to have been in that age—when it was so hard as St Paul found it to keep the infant Church pure from it—it is incredible that St John, or the Church of Jerusalem (Acts xv. 20, 29), should have wasted their indignation on lawful and honourable marriages, even if not such as they altogether approved. St Paul himself, while recognising marriage with a heathen as valid and sacred, when already contracted before the conversion of one party

(1 Cor. vii. 13, 14), and as binding on the Christian so long as respected by the other, did not approve of a Christian contracting a fresh one (ib. 39, 2 Cor. vi. 14).

Unlike as the Apocalypse is to St Paul's writings in style and manner, we shall find in it not infrequent occurrence of ideas supposed to be characteristically Pauline, and one or two probable references (see notes on xviii. 20, xx. 4) to St Paul himself. These are worthy of study, not for controversial purposes only. But to the school of critics who suppose St Paul's dispute with St Peter (Gal. ii. 11 sqq.) to have been bitter and lifelong, and the former to have been repudiated by the Twelve and by the main body of the Church, it is a sufficient reply to ask, "If Christ were divided against Himself, how did His Kingdom stand?"

EXCURSUS III.

ON THE SUPPOSED JEWISH ORIGIN OF THE REVELATION OF ST JOHN.

PERHAPS it is most candid to begin with the confession, that I approached the study of Vischer's theory of the origin of the Apocalypse with a strong prejudice against it, and a conscious reluctance to admit its truth. Such a prejudice, in fact, is likely to be very general, for two reasons. Professor Harnack confesses, that he himself felt one—that, when commentators have laboured over a book for 17 centuries, it is *a priori* unlikely that their labours will be superseded, and the whole subject cleared up, by a single hint throwing a new light on the problem: and, to state the same thing from a lower point of view, when a man has himself laboured for years or decades on the subject, he is not willing to suppose all that labour to be superseded by the happy intuition of a young divinity student.

But there is another ground for reluctance to accept the theory, which one may feel more hesitation in sweeping aside as unworthy. The Revelation of St John as it stands is a sublime work, a work of high inspiration, whether its inspiration be understood in the strictly Christian or supernatural sense, or in the lax sense in which we apply the term to works of human genius. On purely literary grounds, we have the same prejudice against supposing that such a work can have grown by progressive additions and interpolations, that we have to the theory that the *Iliad* was made "by mere fortuitous concourse of old songs:" and the literary prejudice may very well be reinforced by a theological one, if we believe that the writer was not simply a writer of genius, but was, or at all events believed himself to be, a seer, the recipient of a God-given revelation of Jesus Christ.

And just as Mr Gladstone, or any other "conservative" writer on the Homeric question, is able to put his prejudice into the form of an argument, and shew, more or less convincingly, that the traditional view accounts for phenomena which are incredible on the revolutionary view, so here it would be easy to start from this prejudice as a basis for argument: to shew various characteristics that mark the Revelation as a real vision, not a free composition, or to argue that the differences of tone between various parts of it are due, not to differences in the human temper of the author or authors, but to the divine many-sidedness that comprehends at once all the aspects of everything.

I do not say that such an argument would be worthless: but it would be difficult to appreciate its value. What lies at the base of it is what those who share it will call an instinct, and those who do not a prejudice: the arguments that grow out of this will seem convincing to those who use them, even though they prove unconvincing to those to whom they are addressed. Their main strength lies, not in that which can be put in the shape of a formal argument, but in what cannot: and though there may be clear cases, where the instinct is so clearly sound that the statement of its verdict is convincing, I do not venture to think that the case of the Apocalypse is thus clear.

The real evidence in favour of Vischer's view is this, that there are large sections of the Apocalypse where no distinctively Christian elements appear: that some of these, while in harmony with non-Christian Jewish opinions and hopes, are difficult to adjust with a Christian point of view: that the visions, as they stand in the present form of the book, do not present a continuously progressive story: and that a considerable number, both of the visions and of the isolated expressions which interrupt the narrative, are just the passages (sometimes the only passages in their neighbourhood) which are distinctively Christian. This last argument is one that Vischer seems to press rather too universally and rigorously: but there are at least a remarkable number of coincidences between the passages which the theory is obliged to mark as interpolations because they are Christian, and those which might independently be guessed to be so as out of harmony with their context. I do not, however, give very much weight to this last argument. If we suppose the whole Revelation to be a record of a vision really seen in ecstasy—possibly written, in part at least[1], during the ecstasy—it is quite credible that the seer should have written a sentence like xvi. 15 when he heard or seemed to hear the words, though their connexion with what he is describing be remote and subjective: it is really harder to imagine a transcriber or translator interpolating them in the course of his narrative, even if he believed them to be a revelation made to him.

But it will really be best, in judging what weight is to be given to these considerations, or what conclusions are to be drawn from them, to examine the structure of the Revelation itself; not attending to the arguments of Vischer or any other theorist in detail or for their own sake, but using them when they throw any light on the possible source or structure of the work, and accepting or rejecting them if the work in its turn throws a decisive light on their true worth and character.

The first three chapters, it is admitted on all hands, are in some sense separable from the rest, though not really independent of them. On the one hand, the work as we have it is the production of one writer:

---

[1] This is implied, or at least suggested, in x. 4 as well as xiv. 13 and other passages ascribed by Vischer to the Christian redactor.

the peculiar style, language never wanting in vigour, subject to laws of its own, but those utterly different from the laws of ordinary Greek grammar, even in its most Hellenistic modification, are decisive proofs of this. But though the book is the work of one person, and forms a more or less harmonious work of art, there are parts of it that can be separated from the rest, and form in a sense wholes apart from the rest: and this is eminently the case with these chapters. They, it may be said, form a frame for the picture: the picture and the frame suit each other, and we have to decide, substantially, whether this is because the frame was designed by the original artist for the picture, or because the picture has been retouched to harmonise with the frame. The way to determine this will be, to confine our attention to the picture, and see if it shews signs of retouching.

Thus it will suffice for us to begin our examination of the book with the fourth chapter. From this point onwards, we have a series of visions *prima facie* successive, and symbolic of a series of events in chronological succession. We shall see whether this *prima facie* view is tenable: and if not, whether it breaks down in consequence of the various visions being independent of one another, or because they are designed to represent parallel and not successive series of events.

The introduction to this series of visions occupies the fourth and fifth chapters: and this introduction, the sublimest part of the whole book, and the most familiar to the Christian mind, seems to me absolutely to resist the disintegrating forces applied to it by Harnack and Vischer. Like Micaiah, Isaiah, Ezekiel, and the author of the seventh chapter of Daniel, the Seer sees the Lord sitting on His Throne: as in Ezekiel's vision, the throne is supported and surrounded[1] by four living creatures, each one having six wings like Isaiah's Seraphim, and like them repeating incessantly the Trisagion in praise of the Everlasting Lord of the Ineffable Name. Of course, this is all Old Testament imagery, and does not go beyond the range of Jewish ideas: but why should it? No Christian before Gnosticism had made some progress ever doubted that the Father of his Lord Jesus Christ was the eternal Lord God of Israel, Who had revealed Himself to Moses and the Prophets.

But in the next chapter we have distinctive Christian doctrine, indicated by imagery from which it is really impossible to eliminate the Christian element. Vischer admits that here (and, he says, here only) it is impossible to strike out a single sentence or paragraph, and leave the remaining passage to stand in continuous integrity when freed from interpolation. I go further, and venture to say that it is as arbitrary to attempt to eliminate the figure of the Lamb as it is impossible to exclude His action in the next chapter. Vischer and Harnack agree that, if this work be Jewish, "a Lamb standing as it had been slain," can have

---

[1] So I understand ἐν μέσῳ τοῦ θρόνου καὶ κύκλῳ τοῦ θρόνου. Their hinder parts are under the throne, reaching to its centre: their faces appear outside and beyond it—probably at the four corners. The Lamb, when He appears, is ἐν μέσῳ τοῦ θρόνου καὶ τῶν τεσσάρων ζώων—i.e. proceeding from between the feet of Him That sitteth upon the throne, in the midst of the front of it. ἐν μέσῳ τῶν πρεσβυτέρων, in the centre of the circle (or semicircle) of the elders, is coordinate with this clause, not with either of its two members.

had no original place in it: it can symbolise nothing or no one except "Him that liveth and was dead." But they say it is impossible to do more than guess what stood originally in the Lamb's place: they offer two guesses, but do not pretend that either is convincing. To me it seems absurd that either a lion or a human figure should be introduced with the attributes that the Lamb has here. The seven eyes are of course, like the rest of the imagery, taken from the Old Testament.—from the seven "eyes of the Lord" mentioned in Zechariah: and I admit that it would take a skilful artist so to represent them as not to be grotesque. But they can be imagined without a shock to reverence: and I do not think a lion—still less a man—with seven horns can. Of course the Beast with seven heads and ten horns is grotesque enough, but no reverence is due to him. Our author—be he Prophet, visionary, or compiler—has too sound instincts, both literary and religious, to set a monster like either of these in the midst of the Throne of God.

A further question that appears worth asking is, what, on the view that we have here a work of Jewish origin, does the Opener of the seals symbolise? Apparently, still the Messiah: but what Messiah? The divinely sent but human Son of David is not yet born: if, therefore, the visions symbolise events in their chronological order (and on this assumption the theory largely rests), He Who opens the seals must be the *pre-existent* Messiah—who thereby comes very near to the Messiah of Christian, even of Johannine or catholic, belief. I do not say that there is no possibility of explaining the figure by some conception within the range of Jewish thought. I am not prepared to say that no non-Christian Jew ever conceived the Messiah as pre-existing before His manifestation on earth. Still less do I know—I am not sure if it can be known—whether the conception of the Metatron, whose name is readily suggested by the description of "the Lamb in the midst of the Throne"—was a conception already formulated in a Jewish school within the first century of the Christian era. We must leave these questions to specialists: only it must be said that these ideas, if they ever were entertained by Jews uninfluenced by Christianity, are ideas common to them with Christians. He Who opens the Book that lay in the hand of God is, substantially, identical with the eternal Son of God of Christian belief: the only Christian doctrine which can be blotted out of the picture without destroying it altogether is, that this eternal Son of God is the slain yet living Redeemer of mankind. And the doctrine of His Redemption is even harder to eliminate than that of His Death. We might cut out the two words ὡς ἐσφαγμένον, though there is no reason that the Lion of the Tribe of Judah should appear as a Lamb, except for the purpose of suffering a sacrificial, perhaps distinctively a paschal, death: but how are we to cut out the hymns that form the climax of the chapter? Before He has done anything that it will be news to the readers of this Apocalypse to hear of, He Who is in the midst of the Throne has already proved Himself "worthy" to do what He now does: He is already adorable, and adored by them that have their tabernacle in heaven. For if not, *what?* Here we have the climax of this inspired and inspiring work of art (to call it nothing higher): is it credible that the crowning stroke, the central feature, was put to it by the after-thought of an interpolator, in pursuance of a dogmatic purpose? I have tried to avoid treating the matter on mere grounds of taste or feeling: but it is impossible to believe the incredible. I can believe that the *Iliad* once ended without the burial of Hector, and once did not end with it: but I cannot believe that the Seer who described the hymn of the Living Creatures and the Elders to the Creator left it for a successor, and found a successor, to describe the hymn wherein the Redeemer and Revealer appears as coequal with Him. At least if it was so, St John's inspiration was indeed miraculous.

Here we have the sublimest moment of the vision, its highest point as a mere work of art: but here we have not, evidently, its designed or even possible end. The exalted Lamb must now proceed to do the work which He has undertaken, " to open the book and the seven seals thereof:" the sixth chapter, and something like or in the place of the seventh, are necessary as a sequel to the fourth and fifth. And the sixth chapter is, as has often been pointed out, closely parallel to the Prophecy ascribed by all the Synoptic Gospels to the Lord Jesus, three days before He suffered. Since Vischer, and apparently Harnack, adopt the theory—surely a very paradoxical one—that this is itself a Jewish Apocalypse embodied in Christian tradition, the parallelism is no argument against their view: still it is at least as easily explained on the other. We have no need to explain the details of the vision—to enquire whether the Rider on the white horse is the same Person as He Who has the same attributes in ch. xix., or what meaning the Seer may have attached to the passage in Zechariah which suggested the imagery to him. Neither need we discuss whether the Martyrs whose souls are poured out under the Altar are Jewish or Christian martyrs; the former view has been held by Christian interpreters, and if this proves that Vischer's arguments are not without force, it also proves that their force may be felt without necessitating his conclusion. But when we come to the sixth seal, we have—all admit—an image of the state of things expected just before the consummation of all things, and the Advent of the Messiah to judgement. It may be that here we are still within the range of ideas common to Jews and Christians, it may be that the Seer, if called on to interpret his own vision, would have called the things symbolised "the birth-pangs of the Messiah" rather than "the signs of the Coming" or "of the Appearing of the Lord:" all we need say is, that they fit in exactly with Christian belief, and cannot fit *more* exactly with Jewish.

But when six seals are opened, we have, on any hypothesis, a break in the progress of the narrative. As each of the first four was opened, something happened, and the Lamb went on to the next: the cry "Come!" was heard, and some one came—came forth, apparently, from Heaven, and went out over the earth. With the opening of the next two seals, there follow signs in Heaven, the former anticipating, and the latter producing, certain events on earth: so far, though not closely grouped with the first four seals, the effects of these two are analogous with theirs. But now there is a pause: that is in itself something new.

But the first of the events that fills the pause fits naturally enough into its place. War, scarcity, pestilence, convulsions of nature, have already fallen upon the earth: all men are looking in terror for the revelation of the wrath of God: we are now told, that before it is revealed, the elect remnant of God's own people are to be marked as His, presumably in order to shelter them from that wrath in the day of its revelation. I say presumably, for this object of the sealing is not stated: still it is implied both by the context and by the parallel passage in Ezekiel.

But when the servants of God have been sealed in their foreheads, and we expect the wrath of God to break forth upon the rest of the world, we have instead a vision of God's servants already triumphant: not of "the great tribulation" but of those who come out of it. We need not discuss whether other discrepancies can be reconciled:— whether it is possible that "a great multitude which no man could number, out of all nations and kindreds and people and tongues," can be the same as "144,000 sealed of every tribe of the children of Israel," only regarded from another point of view; or whether, as seems more credible, they be coordinate, and there be among the Elect "of the tribes of Israel a certain number, of all other nations an innumerable multitude." The latter view, I think, would hold well enough if the two visions came later on: but as they stand here, one seems so decidedly to come before and one after the end, that the temptation felt by Vischer to regard the second as an interpolation is very strong. On the other hand, it is very difficult to conceive the second vision as not proceeding from the author of the fourth and fifth chapters: the picture of the white-robed multitude, the words of their hymn, the paradox of the Lamb Who is the Shepherd, as there He was the Lion—all these seem to shew that the thought, as well as the expression, is that of the original author.

But let us pass over these nine verses. They can be omitted altogether as an interpolation: we may, perhaps more plausibly, because a test is harder to apply, regard them not as an interpolation but as themselves interpolated: but in no case are they either more or less than an interruption to the course of the main action. After them, the Lamb who had opened the sixth seal opens the seventh; the main action is resumed just where it had left off—and, I would observe, the fact that the *name* of the Lamb is not repeated, but that the verb stands without a subject, is some presumption that the parenthesis had not been very long: cf. xvi. 17, true text, and contrast ix. 1, 13, xi. 15.

But nowhere have we yet had the winds blowing, as we expected, on the earth, the sea, and the trees: the four angels who appeared at the beginning of ch. vii. are heard of no more. "When He had opened the seventh seal"—when *either* the expected wrath of God should break forth, *or* the indignation should have ceased, and His anger, in their destruction,—instead of God's anger appearing either before or after the opening, "there was silence in Heaven about the space of half an hour." Everything has worked up to a climax: and nothing comes of it. Can this be the consummation intended by the original author? It is conceivable, no doubt, that the preceding episode, which we felt to be out of place, has displaced what we feel to be wanting—that when God's servants had been sealed, the earth and sea were smitten, and that then, and then only, there followed the *initium quietis aeternae*. But if this be so, still all difficulty does not vanish. The seven seals of the book are now unloosed: why do we not hear of its being opened, perhaps read? Why is not that done, which the Seer "wept much" to think that none could do?

I can think of no answer, if the Apocalypse be regarded as a self-conscious work of art, deliberately conceived: but if we regard it as a *bona fide* vision, the phenomenon seems natural enough. None of us, probably, have experience of visions which we could by the wildest enthusiasm regard as divine revelations, even in a lower degree than this Book claims to be: but our experience of ordinary dreams, or possibly of delirium, may suggest analogies to the psychological processes at work here, though not to their subject-matter. The seer has much more self-control and self-possession than an ordinary dreamer; he knows as a rule what to look for and what to look at, and sees what is shewn to him: but every now and then there is a transition: "a change comes o'er the spirit of his dream," and he loses the thread of the story that he has been telling.—One point in which there seems a constant uncertainty, is this: is his point of view from earth or heaven? More will depend on this when we come to the twelfth chapter. Here it is enough to say, that the Lamb's opening of the book looks like a magnificent torso, with the limbs perfect, and the head wanting. Under these circumstances it is *a priori* unlikely that the shoulders should have undergone restoration. On the other hand, the thread of narrative that is once lost is, always or almost always, resumed again sooner or later. We hear nothing here of the Lamb opening the book of which He has opened the seals: but further on we hear again and again of the Lamb having a book, the Book of Life: and at last in ch. xx. a book *is* opened, "which is the Book of Life:" and this, I believe, is the book whose seals have been opened in this portion of the vision. I have failed to find authority among commentators for this view, and therefore submit it with all diffidence; but it seems to me less arbitrary, with more support in the Revelation itself, than any of the many theories that have been advanced as to what this book can be.

And again without going into matter so remote or so disputable, though we do not hear of the four angels letting loose the four winds upon the earth before the seventh seal or immediately after it, we do, very soon after it[1], hear of four angels by whose ministry the earth, the sea, and the trees are hurt (viz. those who sound the first four trumpets): and then of a woe on those who have not the seal of God in their foreheads. The vision of the seven seals has, it seems, ended without an end: but if it had received its only adequate ending, how could anything more have followed? As it is, the seven trumpets do follow, and partly, though only partly, supply what seems wanting to

---

[1] We need not pause over the incense-offering angel who is interposed between the seals and the trumpets, nor enquire if "the seven angels who stand before God" have anything to do with "the seven spirits that are before His Throne."

the seven seals. The new series is not independent of the former—it arises out of it.

In fact, we have here a characteristic of the book, which has I think been more clearly insisted on by Renan than by most other commentators. We have a series of events which lead us to expect the end of all things: but instead of an end, we find the beginning of a new series. But every series, or nearly every one, refers backward if not forward to another, and proves that it belongs in its actual place. The phenomenon seems to admit of only two explanations. Either these commentators are right who, from St Victorinus to Alford, have held the different series of visions to be successive only in appearance, and events signified to be not successive but parallel: or else we have one point in which the "continuous historical scheme" of interpretation actually holds good. Again and again, from the Apostles' time to our own, the predicted signs of the Lord's coming have multiplied: men have looked, in hope or fear, for the end of the world: but the world has not come to an end, it has taken a fresh lease of life, and gone on just as before, with judgement and salvation as remote or as imperfect as ever.

We need not discuss what happens on the blowing of the first six trumpets, as here we plainly have no break in the sequence of the narrative, no doubt of its original unity. I should only like to point out, that in the 9th chapter we have one of the dream-like inconsequences, closely resembling that already noted in ch. vii. Again we hear of four angels being let loose, apparently for a work of vengeance: but instead of vengeance being executed by four angels, there appears a countless army of terrible horsemen. And just as, after the sixth seal was opened, instead of the dreaded revelation of the great day of God's wrath, there came the pause and the gathering of the Elect, so after the sixth trumpet—before even "the second woe is past"—there is a pause in which a mighty angel descends, and the Seer receives a new commission.

And here follows the passage whereon Vischer's theory originally rests. "There was given to" the Seer "a reed like unto a staff, saying"—who says it? does the reed itself speak? probably the unnamed, perhaps unseen, giver of it says,—"Arise, and measure the Temple [Sanctuary] of God, and the Altar, and them that worship therein. And the court that is without the Temple cast outward, and measure it not, because it was given to the Gentiles, and the Holy City they shall trample 42 months." It is assumed that this means, that the Gentiles, who at the time of the vision are besieging the Holy City, will capture it, trample it under foot as far as the outer Court of the Temple, perhaps even as far as the Court of Israel: but the Altar and the Sanctuary, the Temple in the narrowest sense, will remain inviolable, and those worshippers who are found in this sacred refuge will be secure. This, I say, is assumed to be the meaning: I cannot think that it is proved. The Seer is bidden to measure the Temple and Altar, and not to measure the outer court: but by what token does that mean that the one is to be destroyed or at least profaned, and the other not? In one passage of Zechariah, the command not to measure Jerusalem means that she shall grow to immeasurable greatness; in Old Testament imagery generally, to measure may be for destruction as well as for preservation. No doubt, here a contrast is intended between the fate of the Sanctuary and of the outer court: but it is not clear what the contrast is, nor which fate is the better. The outer court was, we are told, given to the Gentiles: when and by whom was it so given? Perhaps by Titus: but it is at least as easy to say, by Herod or Zerubbabel whichever built it: he may, designedly or otherwise, have enlarged Solomon's Temple to be, as Isaiah said it should be, "a house of prayer for all nations." I do not say that this *is* the seer's meaning, but it is a quite possible one,—that the outer court of the Lord's Temple only realised its destiny when it was occupied by Gentiles, who used it for prayer, not by Jews who regarded "the mountain of the House" as only useful for "a house of merchandise" or even "a den of thieves;" and that when the "line of confusion and the stones of emptiness" shall pass over the site of the Temple, this outer court shall remain a holy place, a world-wide not a national sanctuary. A Christian of the first century might possibly anticipate this; certainly a Christian of the fifth, perhaps a very tolerant theist of the 19th, might say that it has actually been fulfilled.

I do not myself believe this to be certainly—hardly probably—the true interpretation; I only say that it is one suggested by the words of the text, and that it ascribes no absurdity to the seer's conception. The Judaic meaning ascribed to him is, I venture to think, utterly absurd. It would be credible to a devout Jew, that the Lord would defend His Holy City as in Hezekiah's day—that though the Land of Israel might be overrun by the heathen, City and Temple should be safe. It would be credible even, at least to a fanatical Jew, that when the City was taken, when even the outer court of the Temple was stormed, the Lord would at last arise and break forth upon His enemies, or would be a wall of fire round about His Sanctuary. Such was, we are told, the actual hope of the fanatic defenders of the Temple, at the last moment before its fall. But could the craziest fanatic suppose, that the Lord would maintain a purely passive defence in His last Citadel? that He would allow the hitherto victorious enemy to hold, for three and a half years, everything up to the Temple wall, while the Temple-worship should go on undisturbed and unprofaned, in their midst but out of their reach or sight? What the worshippers are to live on—how sacrifices are to be provided for the Altar—is unexplained. This, if I understand it, is the popular rationalistic view of what the seer meant: the seer was no rationalist, but I do not think he was so irrational as that.

Perhaps the most reasonable view of the meaning of the passage is, that "the Temple" spoken of is not that in the earthly Jerusalem, but its heavenly Archetype, of which we unquestionably read in xi. 19, xv. 5, &c. What then is meant by the different fortune of the Temple proper and the outer court, what by the measuring of one and non-measuring of the other, seems very obscure. Timidly I would ask, can the earthly Temple be regarded as the outer-court of the heavenly; but, if this will not stand, to give no explanation seems better than to give an absurd one. The purely Judaic interpretation of this passage is, I venture to say, utterly absurd; one is tempted to say that any other will be better than this; but it will be enough to say that this has no right to be assumed as an axiom, whereon the true theory of the book's origin or meaning is to be founded.

To proceed to the prediction, rather than vision, that follows: that the two Witnesses are Moses, or a Prophet like unto Moses, and Elias is, I think, almost certain. Their coming as precursors of the Messiah is no doubt quite in harmony with Jewish doctrine, as represented to us at least by the Fourth Gospel. Only as it has (with or without the substitution of Enoch for Moses) been the ordinary belief of Christendom, we cannot deny that it harmonises with Christian doctrine quite as well. That they smite their enemies with plagues after the manner of the historic Moses and Elias, instead of suffering meekly like those who know that they are of another manner of spirit, is hardly a fatal objection to the Christian origin of the passage. It may give a sort of presumption that the tone of the prophecy is not above that of the Old Testament: but when two Christian Apostles delivered offenders to Satan for the destruction of the flesh, it would need a high spiritual discernment to be sure of it. We are on more certain ground, when we note the inconsequent character of the narrative here. The seer does not, in the first instance, see the two Witnesses: the same voice, whosesoever it be, that bade him measure the Temple, tells him what they will do, during 1260 days, presumably the same period as the 42 months of the Gentiles trampling the Holy City. But by degrees the hearing of the description passes into vision—the futures gradually give place, first to presents and then to aorists, just as happens, on a smaller scale, in xx. 7—9. Here, from *v.* 11 or 12 onwards, we are back in the ordinary course of vision. At last, the series of the seven trumpets is resumed: we are told that the second woe is past—did it include the plagues inflicted by the two Witnesses, as well as that of the terrible horsemen of ch. x.?—and the seventh trumpet sounds.

And its sounding is not so purely negative, or at least undefined, in its effect as the opening of the seventh seal. It is declared that the Kingdom of the world has passed into the hands of God and His Anointed: it seems that the promise of the mighty angel is fulfilled, and the mystery of God finished. But its completion is not seen. The divine Kingdom is proclaimed, the Lord Who is and was is no longer spoken of as "to come" (though I doubt if this be significant), and is praised for His assumption of power and execution of judgement: but no judgement is visibly executed. Instead of the consummation of all things, we have again a new beginning, a new series of visions, whose developement extends, with certain interruptions, throughout the remainder of the book.

One commentator has tried to make this series of visions more closely parallel with the others, by representing it as consisting of "seven mystical figures"—meaning, I suppose (he did not make it quite clear), the Woman, the Man Child, the Dragon, the two Beasts, the Lamb, and the Son of Man upon the cloud. But when the seer himself says nothing of this enumeration, it is hardly likely that he was conscious of it: and if not, no light is thrown by it upon the genesis of the work. The symmetry would only be important, if we could use it to prove that this series of visions belongs to its place—that it is not an originally independent apocalypse, embodied with other elements in the work that we have. We are not yet in a position to discuss whether this is so: we will pursue our examination of the sequence of the visions as we find them.

First of all, there appears another great sign in Heaven: the Daughter of Zion, whom Micah described as in travail, now brings forth her Son: Who is, unquestionably, the Messiah, the Hope of Israel. That here the point of view is Judaic need not be questioned: to concede this does not involve the concession of Vischer's theory. Christians have never felt any difficulty in understanding the description here given as applying to the birth of their Christ; though their anti-Judaic feelings have led them to miss the identification of His ideal Mother. They have, as a rule, conceived her as "the Church;" and then there is a little confusion in the image, when afterwards the Church appears as "the Bride, the Lamb's Wife." Regard the vision as that of a Jewish Christian, or at all events a Christian of the days before Jewish and Christian sentiments were hopelessly embittered against one another, and all is clear. Christ is conceived as the Son of the Church of the Old Covenant, the Bridegroom of the Church of the New: we may add, that the Jewish Christian Seer need not have been surprised, though he would have been disappointed, to learn what became plain in the course of the next century, that the Bridegroom had to forsake His Mother, in order to cleave to His Wife.

But while I admit that the crown of twelve stars, and still more the reminiscences of Micah, mark the travailing Woman as being the Daughter of Zion, I do not deny that in other aspects her figure may have other meanings. It seems by no means arbitrary to parallel this passage with the so-called Protevangelium of Gen. iii.—with the legitimacy of which as exegesis, of course, we are not concerned. Here as there, we have the Woman, the Seed of the Woman, and the Serpent— "the old Serpent" is a manifest reference to his action in Eden: here the enmity between the Serpent and the Woman and her Seed is seen at work: and the victory of her Seed over him, though not described under the exact figure of bruising the head, is the main subject of the remainder of the book.

The Woman is then conceived quite as much as being a second Eve, as she is as being the Daughter of Zion. Is she also, in any sense, to be identified with the historical Mother of Jesus? I believe that she is: the language of the Martyrs of Lyons about "the Virgin Mother," and some other fragments of what seemed to be pure Johannine traditions, seem to suggest, not perhaps an exaltation of the personal Mary to a position such as that of the Woman here, but a recognition of an ideal Mother of Christ, into whose glory the historical Mary was admitted, and in whom her personality was lost sight of. But this is rather a theological question than an exegetical; at any rate, it is one which criticism cannot touch and may safely pass by.

The pictures given us in this twelfth chapter are grander than any that we have met with since the seventh, perhaps even since the fifth: yet there is a certain vagueness about them—they seem to shift like a dissolving view. The Woman and the Dragon each appear, in the first instance, "in Heaven;" and there is nothing inconsistent with this in the Child being "caught"—it is not said "caught *up*"—"to God and to His Throne," for the Throne of God is only seen in one definite place, in the midst of Heaven. But, even before the Dragon is cast into the earth, "the Woman fled into the wilderness"—surely there are no wildernesses in Heaven: and when he is cast down, he finds her on earth within seeming reach of his persecution. She flees, we are again told, into the wilderness, and now at least we cannot doubt an earthly one: the earth itself interposes, to protect her flight. And now we find that she who has brought forth one glorious Son—surely, one would think, her First-born—has on earth others of her seed, against whom the Dragon can make war. These are they "who keep the commandments of God, and have the testimony of Jesus." It is utterly arbitrary to excise the last word; even if it were possible to restore the rhythm by substituting a neutral phrase like that in vi. 9, we still could hardly make the doctrine of the passage agree as well with Jewish notions as it now does with Christian, and especially Johannine. "The Firstborn among many brethren"—"I ascend to My Father and your Father"—sayings like these make plain the relations here presupposed: there is nothing inconsistent even with developements like that which St Augustine adopted from Tichonius about the Head and the Members, or even like that of a modern Catholic sermon on "Behold thy Mother."

Vischer's theory seems therefore to pass over the real difficulty of the chapter—the transition from heaven to earth as the scene of action—while he brings forward another, to which this transition affords some sort of explanation. When we read "The Accuser of our brethren is cast down, which accuseth them before our God day and night: and they overcame him"—we surely naturally think of a victory not military (such as was, apparently, gained by Michael and his angels just before), but forensic; and the contradiction between *vv*. 7 and 11 vanishes. We therefore have no need to expunge from the latter the words that tell us how or why the victory was gained. (I say *how* or *why:* for one cannot be sure that this writer knew as well as the author of the Epistle to the Hebrews the classical or philosophical distinction between τὸ δι' οὗ and τὸ δι ὅ.) Still, *v*. 11 does rather break the continuity of the sense; it is difficult to see how the Saints on earth, who suffered even to death in the contest with the Dragon, can be said to have already gained over him, even a forensic victory. But we see that in *v*. 6 we have had a proleptic mention of the flight of the Woman, the detailed explanation of which did not come till *v*. 14: it seems therefore possible that the strife between the Dragon and the Saints on earth mentioned in *v*. 17 is that whose end in the victory of the Saints is celebrated proleptically in *v*. 11.

In fact, the "war" of the Dragon against the Saints on earth, the Seed of the Woman, is not carried on by open force, such as Merodach or perhaps even Michael may have used. The Dragon keeps himself out of sight, and enthrones the Beast, as we are told in ch. xiii., as his regent and champion. Of this Beast we have heard already in ch. xi., and we can hardly doubt that the "war" that he then waged against the two Witnesses is identical with this against the remnant of the Seed of the Woman. It lasts for the same period, Daniel's "time, times, and half a time," otherwise defined as 42 months or 1260 days. If these periods be not coincident, the only plausible view is that one immediately succeeds the other—that they are the first and the second halves of a week of years. But the mention of the Beast as the chief belligerent in both seems to prove their identity: the Woman is placed in safety for just the time that the oppression of her children is to last.

On the details of the oppression we need not dwell, nor on the second Beast, or the enigmatical number. But immediately after the description of the force and fraud exercised by them follows that of the Lamb with His 144,000 redeemed virgins, reminding us, not more by the details of its imagery than by its beauty, both moral and artistic, of the fifth and seventh chapters. How far is it legitimate to regard this passage as out of place where it stands? It certainly interrupts the course of events: but the interruption is of the nature of a relief. From the picture of the triumphant persecuting monster, of the superstitious degradation of the world, we turn away to the spotless holiness and the unapproachable harmony of the Saviour and the saved. The effect is something like that of the doxology in Rom. i. 25, as explained by St Chrysostom—an expression of the sense that the divine blessedness remains unimpaired by human corruption.

However, the five first verses of ch. xiv. are separable from the main narrative: and so, still more, are *vv.* 12, 13. So, most of all, are *vv.* 14 —20: if one might venture to wish to discard as an interpolation any part of the attested text of the Apocalypse, it would be this passage. How can it be understood of anything but the final judgement? yet it comes here as anything but final: the last plagues, the completion of the wrath of God, are still to come. The harvest and the vintage of the earth are gathered, but no harvest home is celebrated, and the earth goes on just as before. How is it, that God's wrath is *not* finished in the treading of the great wine-press, from which blood comes forth? and what horses are they whose bridles are reached by the blood that comes out of the wine-press?

On the other hand, except their coming after this image of the final judgement, there is nothing to surprise us in the succession of the seven last plagues. Like as their imagery is to that of the earlier trumpets, there is a real ethical difference and progress: what is still more important, they fit into the place where they stand. We have had first the wrath of the Dragon, then the enthronement and tyranny of the Beast; then the angels warn mankind of the judgement coming on his worshippers and on Babylon: and then come these plagues, the last which God will send in the character of disciplinary chastisement, leaving room (which mankind do not avail themselves of) for repentance. Then, when these plagues have been sent in vain, the fall of Babylon and the overthrow of the Beast will follow as predicted.

But before Babylon does fall, she is set before us as she was in her prosperity. And this episode, though when the Book is finished we see that it has a certain propriety, is certainly felt as an interruption to the narrative here. The Harlot sits on a Beast having seven heads and ten horns—the fact that such a Beast has been already introduced being ignored. Here he appears as a mere Beast of burden, while before he was enthroned as sovereign of the world. Here he is in scarlet, while there he was like unto a leopard, and presumably the colour of one. I do not wish to speak disrespectfully of the theories of this book that have been built upon one passage in this chapter. As theories of apocalyptic interpretation go, they are at least plausible. But I am afraid that these theories, widely received as they are, may be endangered when we recognise that this chapter is one that can most easily, nay advantageously, be spared, if once we call in question the unity and integrity of the book.

The eighteenth chapter fits on almost equally well with what precedes, whether the seventeenth be retained or no. In either case, there is no description of the fall of Babylon[1], and there is a variation in the tenses, as though the writer were not sure whether it is predicted or commemorated: but we learn, from this and the early part of the next, that the great Harlot City is overthrown, amid the selfish lamentations of earth and the righteous exultations of Heaven. Then "the Son of God goes forth to war," against the Kings of the Earth who, at the outpouring of the sixth vial, had been mustered in the service of the Beast, and who (according to the seventeenth chapter) have dethroned and destroyed the Beast's harlot mistress. The Beast and the False Prophet (who is usually and no doubt rightly identified with the second Beast, or rather perhaps is substituted for him by one of the "dissolving views" of the Book) are overthrown, and the Dragon imprisoned: and the millennial reign of Christ and His Saints follows.

Then comes a prediction, passing gradually (as in ch. xi.) into a description, of the final overthrow of the world. The Dragon, the Devil, repeats in his own person what he had before done through the agency of the Beast: and he, like him, is overthrown, only more by directly divine agency, with even less appearance of a human conqueror. Then follows the final judgement, executed by God in person, Christ not being here named either as His representative or assessor. But the Book of Life is opened, as a kind of check on the other books which contained the record of the good or evil deeds of those who are to be judged: and if we remember how, in other passages, the Book of Life is connected with the Lamb, we have here a hint of almost Pauline doctrine— salvation by the grace of Christ apart from works, and condemnation of those who are judged by works only. There is nothing inconsistent with this in the suggestion, that those who are acquitted will have good works standing to their credit in the other books; these serve, as Alford says, as vouchers for the Book of Life. The concluding vision of

---

[1] One thing I should like to notice in passing: that whether the predictions of this chapter have been fulfilled or no, its ancient interpreters have been unusually happy in predictions that are in a fair way to be so. St Hippolytus gathered from it, though it is hard to see on what grounds, that the kingdoms of the Diadochi of the Caesars will pass into democracies: and St Benedict, from the absence of any description of the actual fall of Babylon, gathered that it will be effected by natural convulsions, not by human enemies. We know what he did not, that *si Albani montes lapides dejecerint*, Rome "might easily share the fate of Pompeii."

the New Jerusalem does not need detailed examination. We need not dispute with Vischer, that the distinctively Christian element in it is confined to a few easily separable phrases: on the other hand, the picture is equally in place as the culmination of a Jewish ideal and of a Christian ideal conceived in Jewish forms. That the gates of the City bear the names of the twelve Tribes of Israel is no evidence that salvation, that the highest salvation, is confined to Israelites: on the other hand, the way that "the Nations" are mentioned is real evidence of a Jewish belief in their necessarily and eternally inferior position in the Kingdom of God. But this is not decisive evidence of an exclusively Jewish point of view; for if, on other grounds, we regard the whole book as Christian, we shall be able to regard the privileged citizens of the heavenly metropolis as being St Paul's "Israel of God," the 144,000 of the seventh chapter interpreted by the fourteenth: a divine aristocracy indeed, but elected on spiritual not on carnal principles.

But there is one point where this concluding vision throws light on the question of the integrity of the book. It can hardly be undesigned, that the same angel, or an angel of the same rank and company, is the revealer of the new Babylon and of the New Jerusalem: it marks a suggestive contrast between the two figures of the Bride and the Harlot. While we saw that ch. xvii. delays and rather embarrasses the progress of the action, we are thus led to believe that it forms an integral part of the designed form of the work.

No one will quarrel with Vischer for marking off the last 16 verses, or nearly all of them, as a conclusion, more or less separable from the central series of visions. We have therefore completed our examination of the course of events described in the Apocalypse, and have only to sum up and tabulate our analysis of the work, regarded as a continuous story, and setting aside the passages that are certainly or probably interruptions to its course.

Chh. iv. v. Description of the throne of God and of the Lamb, in the midst of the Host of Heaven.

vi.—viii. 1. The Lamb opens the seven seals of the Book (of life). [Between the sixth and seventh, the servants of God are sealed.]

viii. 2—xi. Seven trumpets sounded by angels. [Between the sixth and seventh, seven thunders utter what may not be written: and a great angel delivers a new commission to the seer: and (he or another) foretells the prophecy of the two Witnesses, their martyrdom before the Beast, resurrection, and triumph.]

vii. 9—17. Vision of the Saints in triumph seems out of place at this stage of events. Compare however xiv. 1—5, xv. 2—4.

xii. War begun in Heaven, and transferred to earth, between the Dragon and the Woman and her Seed.
xiii.—xix. War between the Beast as the Dragon's vicegerent, and the Saints of God.

[xii. 11 somewhat interrupts the context.]
[xiii. 9, 10, though at a natural pause in the narrative resembles passages that interrupt the context.]
xiv. 1—5 is episodical, but not necessarily irrelevant.
[12, 13 seem irrelevant, and 14—20 utterly inappropriate to this place.]
xv, xvi. are episodical, but relevant.
[xvi. 15 is at best parenthetical, interrupting a continuous narrative.]
[xvii. can be omitted with a gain to clearness.]

xx. 1—6. Partial and temporary establishment of the Kingdom of the Saints.
7—10. Rebellion of the Dragon.
11—15. Divine judgement.
xxi. 1—xxii. 5. Final and universal establishment of the Kingdom of God and Christ.

I think this analysis, though drawn up with Vischer before me, and with the object of looking for illustrations of his hypothesis, really lends it no support. If it points to any hypothesis at all inconsistent with the unity of the book, it would be one more akin to Völter's.

[He analyses the book as follows:

A

The original Apocalypse written by St John the Apostle, i. 4—6 [greeting to the seven *unnamed* Churches of Asia]. iv. 1—v. 10 [omitting the seven horns and seven eyes of the Lamb, iv. 6, because the seven Spirits of God cannot be represented at the same moment by the seven Lamps before the Throne and by the seven eyes]. vi. 1—17 [omitting the wrath of the Lamb, vi. 16, which comes in strangely before 17, where we read, 'the great day of His (i.e. God's) wrath is come.'] vii. 1—8, viii. 1—13, ix. 1—21, xi. 14—19—leaving out 'and of His Christ' in xi. 15, because in the next clause the best attested reading is '*He* shall reign,' and [the time] 'of the dead to be judged' as the destroyers of the earth must be destroyed before, not after, the general judgement. xiv. 1—3, omitting [His Name and], in xiv. 1, as the servants of God are sealed with His Name. xiv. 6, 7, xviii. 1—24, xix. 1—4, xiv. 14—20, xix. 5—10, without the last words 'for the testimony of Jesus is the spirit of prophecy,' which

APPENDIX.

are treated as a later addition, because throughout the original Apocalypse the seer receives his revelations through angels, and the seven Spirits are in no special relation to the Lamb. This work is assigned to 65 or 66 A.D. on the ground that the events of the time more or less suggest what follows in the vision on the opening of the first five seals. A Roman army surrendered to the Parthians in 62. Much of Nero's unpopularity was due to scarcity and high prices. There was a pestilence in the autumn of 65. The wholesale execution of Christians in 66 might suggest the souls crying under the altar.

B

The additions made by the author, x. 1—xi. 13. The angel with the little book (who swears that everything shall be accomplished in the day of the sounding of the Seventh Trumpet, and informs the seer that he has to prophesy *again*) and the Two Witnesses. The section interrupts the connexion. In ix. 21 we have clearly the close of the second woe, and the passing of the second and the coming of the third is announced xi. 14. This passage is assigned to 68 or 69 A.D. on the ground that the seer, after the outbreak of the Jewish War, expects that all Jerusalem except the Temple will be taken and held by the heathen for three years and a half.

If the writer be acquainted with the vision of the Beast out of the Abyss in xvii. 1—18 [when the vision of the seven 'vials' had been inserted before this chapter, the writer of that vision or another would naturally think that the angel who shews the Woman on the Scarlet Beast is one of the seven who had the 'vials'] this vision must be of the same date or earlier. If so Galba, not Vespasian, is meant by the sixth head of the Beast. It is supposed that xiv. 8, the second angel who proclaims the fall of Babylon, was added when xvii. 1—18 was inserted between xiv. 7 and xviii. 1.

C

The episode of the Woman and the Dragon, xii. 1—17. [xii. 11 is assigned to the author of xii. 18—xiii. sqq. and has the look of an afterthought. A year later Völter was convinced by Weiszacker that xii. 13—17 are not by the writer of xii. 1—12; it is hard to see how 6 and 13 could be written by the same man at the same time.] The sequel xix. 11—xxi. 8 [here 'His name is called the Word of God' is omitted as inconsistent with His Name being unknown save to Himself, and again all the mentions of the False Prophet and the mark of the Beast in xix. 20, 21, xxii. 10, are ascribed to the author of xii. 18, xiii. &c.]. xii. is not the sequel of the vision of the Seals and Trumpets which carries us further into the future, still less is it the sequel of xi.; the 42 months in which the Woman is nourished in the Wilderness, and the 1260 days in which the Witnesses prophesy in sackcloth, are two independent representations of the times in which Jerusalem is trodden under foot of the Gentiles. The sequel of xii. in xix. 11—xxi. 8, in which the Man Child fulfils His Mission of ruling with a rod of iron, is plainly independent both of what goes before and what follows it. The thousand years' reign begins and ends without a word of the Marriage Supper of the Lamb announced, xix. 9. The date of the section is made to depend on the Dragon going to make war with the remnant of the seed of the Woman, which is explained of the systematic persecution of Christianity begun, according to Dr Völter, by Trajan, as no systematic regulations for the punishment of Christians can be traced older than his letter to Pliny. A secondary (and more plausible) sense of these words is found in the insurrection of the Jews of the dispersion. The words 'and his Christ', xi. 15, and 'time of the dead to be judged', xi 18, are supposed to have been inserted with this section.

D

The Beast which rises from the sea in xiii. appears to be described by someone already familiar with the description of the beast in xvii. The ten horns, which in xvii. represent ten kings who have received no kingdom as yet, are crowned in xiii. The worship of the beast and the false prophet are recurring topics throughout the description of the seven 'vials' in xv., xvi. The detailed description of the New Jerusalem, xxi. 9—xxii. 5, has the appearance of being added quite independently of the short announcement, quite complete in itself, in xxi. 5. The original close of this addition is to be found in the parts of xxii. 6—21, where the angel is the speaker, not the Lord.

The date of this addition is made to depend partly on that of C, to which it is certainly posterior, partly on the fact that Trajanus Hadrianus, when accurately transliterated into Hebrew, yields both 666 and 616. The Sibylline books give some plausibility to the conjecture that he is meant by the beast out of the sea: he greatly encouraged the worship of the emperors: so did Herodes Atticus when he was acting as imperial commissioner in Asia Minor, when Hadrian paid his second visit there in 129 A.D. No evidence is available to prove that Herodes Atticus used magic for the purposes of his propaganda, or that the worship was enforced by penalties. The writer of this section, which [more certainly than C] was intended to be incorporated with the rest of the revelation, is supposed to have made the following additions, v. 11—14 (an amplification of the praise of the Lamb), the mention of the wrath of the Lamb in vi. 16, vii. 9—17, the great multitude of the redeemed, the mention of the Lamb's name in xiv. 1, xiv. 4, 5, which imply that the 144,000 are the firstfruits, not the whole body of the redeemed, xiv. 9—12 (the third angel who proclaims judgement on the worshippers of the beast), and the mention of the false prophet in xix. 20, 21, xx. 9, 10.

E

Lastly, the Seven Epistles to the Churches were added, and at the same time i. 1—3, i. 7, 8; the mention of the seven spirits in v. 6; xiv. 13, the blessing on the dead that die in the Lord, xvi. 15 'behold I come as a thief' &c. xix. 10, 13 (the mention of The Word); and all in xxii. 7—21 which is spoken by the Lord.

This section is assigned to 140 A.D. on the grounds that the angels of the Churches are bishops and that bishops cannot have been established long before, and that the Nicolaitans are a name for the followers of Carpocrates.

* * * * * *

It will be seen that the analysis is independent of the dates, and that the growth of the book as sketched shews a steady approximation to the doctrines of the Fourth Gospel. It is not surprising that Vischer, by excluding everything distinctly Christian, often arrives at the results which Völter reaches by analysis.

I do not mean that we can, by mere analysis of the story, discover as he claims to have done the exact portions due to different authors, still less that we can assign the date of each. But if the Apocalypse is to be divided into different independent works, I think one of them should be conceived to consist of the Prologue in Heaven, with the series of seven seals, seven trumpets, and seven vials, culminating in the Advent of the Son of Man, the harvest and the vintage: and the other of the vision of the mighty angel, the war between the Dragon and the Seed of the Woman; the victory, first of the Messiah over the Beast, and then of God over the Devil; the Judgement by God in person, and the establishment of the New Jerusalem. In each of these we should have to recognise various episodes, of which some may or may not be interpolations; as well as touches supplied in each to unite them with the other. It would be a little less arbitrary than some of Vischer's excisions, if we suppose the mention of "the Lamb" in the second work to be of this character: and then it might be supposed that this was a Jewish Apocalypse while the other was a Christian.

If I may venture to give an opinion, it is in this form that the hypothesis of the partly Jewish origin of the work is most plausible, and if presented in this form it would require serious attention. But to formulate this hypothesis fairly, and propose it for discussion, would require that one should believe it: and this I cannot say that I do. The unity of style throughout the book seems absolutely fatal to a plurality of authors such as is supposed by Völter. It is more consistent with Vischer's theory, that the Christian redactor and interpolator is the translator of all of which he is not the author: but whether even this would account for the unity of style is more doubtful. The Son of Sirach writes quite differently in his Prologue from his translation: and the presumption would have been that the Son of Zebedee (if it be he) would have written the same fair Hellenistic Greek as other New Testament writers, if it had been only the influence of a Hebrew original that made the grammar of the Apocalypse so peculiar.

On the whole, I think the phenomena are best accounted for by what one may call with Vischer the psychological conditions of the case, which are—as he almost admits—much more intelligible on the view of unity in the work. The two series of visions are presented, in part successively and in part alternately, to the mind of the seer: he writes down what he sees or hears, in part when he sees or hears it, or at any rate as he remembers it: when he hears a divine word, he records it either at once, in the midst of his narrative of visions, or at the first

APPENDIX.

convenient pause therein. Possibly, indeed, there is a sort of middle term between unity and plurality of authorship: the Revelation may have been written as the well-known tradition says that the Gospel was. St John had a vision: he records it, and the messages to the Churches, in a work drawn up by him after his return from the exile in which he had seen the main vision, but under inspiration cognate with that in which he saw it: and so, whether by voice or pen, he pours forth the tide of prophecy. But "if anything is revealed to another that sitteth by, the first holds his peace:" and so inspired utterances, similar to and suggested by the main vision, but not forming part of its orderly course, find a place in it.

THE CAMBRIDGE BIBLE FOR SCHOOLS AND COLLEGES.

GENERAL EDITOR, THE VERY REV. J. J. S. PEROWNE, DEAN OF PETERBOROUGH.

Opinions of the Press.

"*It is difficult to commend too highly this excellent series.*"—Guardian.

"*The modesty of the general title of this series has, we believe, led many to misunderstand its character and underrate its value. The books are well suited for study in the upper forms of our best schools, but not the less are they adapted to the wants of all Bible students who are not specialists. We doubt, indeed, whether any of the numerous popular commentaries recently issued in this country will be found more serviceable for general use.*"—Academy.

"*One of the most popular and useful literary enterprises of the nineteenth century.*"—Baptist Magazine.

"*Of great value. The whole series of comments for schools is highly esteemed by students capable of forming a judgment. The books are scholarly without being pretentious: and information is so given as to be easily understood.*"—Sword and Trowel.

"*The value of the work as an aid to Biblical study, not merely in schools but among people of all classes who are desirous to have intelligent knowledge of the Scriptures, cannot easily be over-estimated.*"—The Scotsman.

The Book of Judges. J. J. LIAS, M.A. "His introduction is clear and concise, full of the information which young students require, and indicating the lines on which the various problems suggested by the Book of Judges may be solved."—*Baptist Magazine.*

1 Samuel, by A. F. KIRKPATRICK. "Remembering the interest with which we read the *Books of the Kingdom* when they were appointed as a subject for school work in our boyhood, we have looked with some eagerness into Mr Kirkpatrick's volume, which contains the first instalment of them. We are struck with the great improvement in character, and variety in the materials, with which schools are now supplied. A clear map inserted in each volume, notes suiting the convenience of the scholar and the difficulty of the passage, and not merely dictated by the fancy of the commentator, were luxuries which a quarter of a century ago the Biblical student could not buy."—*Church Quarterly Review.*

"To the valuable series of Scriptural expositions and elementary commentaries which is being issued at the Cambridge University Press, under the title 'The Cambridge Bible for Schools,' has been added **The First Book of Samuel** by the Rev. A. F. KIRKPATRICK. Like other volumes of the series, it contains a carefully written historical and critical introduction, while the text is profusely illustrated and explained by notes."—*The Scotsman.*

II. Samuel. A. F. KIRKPATRICK, M.A. "Small as this work is in mere dimensions, it is every way the best on its subject and for its purpose that we know of. The opening sections at once prove the thorough competence of the writer for dealing with questions of criticism in an earnest, faithful and devout spirit; and the appendices discuss a few special difficulties with a full knowledge of the data, and a judicial reserve, which contrast most favourably with the superficial dogmatism which has too often made the exegesis of the Old Testament a field for the play of unlimited paradox and the ostentation of personal infallibility. The notes are always clear and suggestive; never trifling or irrelevant; and they everywhere demonstrate the great difference in value between the work of a commentator who is also a Hebraist, and that of one who has to depend for his Hebrew upon secondhand sources."—*Academy*.

"The Rev. A. F. KIRKPATRICK has now completed his commentary on the two books of Samuel. This second volume, like the first, is furnished with a scholarly and carefully prepared critical and historical introduction, and the notes supply everything necessary to enable the merely English scholar—so far as is possible for one ignorant of the original language—to gather up the precise meaning of the text. Even Hebrew scholars may consult this small volume with profit."—*Scotsman*.

I. Kings and Ephesians. "With great heartiness we commend these most valuable little commentaries. We had rather purchase these than nine out of ten of the big blown up expositions. Quality is far better than quantity, and we have it here."—*Sword and Trowel*.

I. Kings. "This is really admirably well done, and from first to last there is nothing but commendation to give to such honest work."—*Bookseller*.

II. Kings. "The Introduction is scholarly and wholly admirable, while the notes must be of incalculable value to students."—*Glasgow Herald*.

"It is equipped with a valuable introduction and commentary, and makes an admirable text book for Bible-classes."—*Scotsman*.

"It would be difficult to find a commentary better suited for general use."—*Academy*.

The Book of Job. "Able and scholarly as the Introduction is, it is far surpassed by the detailed exegesis of the book. In this Dr DAVIDSON's strength is at its greatest. His linguistic knowledge, his artistic habit, his scientific insight, and his literary power have full scope when he comes to exegesis.... The book is worthy of the reputation of Dr Davidson; it represents the results of many years of labour, and it will greatly help to the right understanding of one of the greatest works in the literature of the world."—*The Spectator*.

"In the course of a long introduction, Dr DAVIDSON has presented us with a very able and very interesting criticism of this wonderful book. Its contents, the nature of its composition, its idea and purpose, its integrity, and its age are all exhaustively treated of.... We have not space to examine fully the text and notes before us, but we can, and do heartily, recommend the book, not only for the upper forms in schools, but to Bible students and teachers generally. As we wrote of a previous volume in the same series, this one leaves nothing to be desired. The notes are full and suggestive, without being too long, and, in itself, the introduction forms a valuable addition to modern Bible literature."—*The Educational Times.*

"Already we have frequently called attention to this exceedingly valuable work as its volumes have successively appeared. But we have never done so with greater pleasure, very seldom with so great pleasure, as we now refer to the last published volume, that on the **Book of Job**, by Dr DAVIDSON, of Edinburgh....We cordially commend the volume to all our readers. The least instructed will understand and enjoy it; and mature scholars will learn from it."—*Methodist Recorder.*

Job—Hosea. "It is difficult to commend too highly this excellent series, the volumes of which are now becoming numerous. The two books before us, small as they are in size, comprise almost everything that the young student can reasonably expect to find in the way of helps towards such general knowledge of their subjects as may be gained without an attempt to grapple with the Hebrew; and even the learned scholar can hardly read without interest and benefit the very able introductory matter which both these commentators have prefixed to their volumes. It is not too much to say that these works have brought within the reach of the ordinary reader resources which were until lately quite unknown for understanding some of the most difficult and obscure portions of Old Testament literature."—*Guardian.*

Ecclesiastes; or, the Preacher.—"Of the Notes, it is sufficient to say that they are in every respect worthy of Dr PLUMPTRE's high reputation as a scholar and a critic, being at once learned, sensible, and practical.... An appendix, in which it is clearly proved that the author of *Ecclesiastes* anticipated Shakspeare and Tennyson in some of their finest thoughts and reflections, will be read with interest by students both of Hebrew and of English literature. Commentaries are seldom attractive reading. This little volume is a notable exception."— *The Scotsman.*

"In short, this little book is of far greater value than most of the larger and more elaborate commentaries on this Scripture. Indispensable to the scholar, it will render real and large help to all who have to expound the dramatic utterances of **The Preacher** whether in the Church or in the School."—*The Expositor.*

"The '*ideal* biography' of the author is one of the most exquisite and fascinating pieces of writing we have met with, and, granting its starting-point, throws wonderful light on many problems connected with the book. The notes illustrating the text are full of delicate criticism, fine glowing insight, and apt historical allusion. An abler volume than Professor PLUMPTRE's we could not desire."—*Baptist Magazine.*

Jeremiah, by A. W. STREANE. "The arrangement of the book is well treated on pp. xxx., 396, and the question of Baruch's relations with its composition on pp. xxvii., xxxiv., 317. The illustrations from English literature, history, monuments, works on botany, topography, etc., are good and plentiful, as indeed they are in other volumes of this series."—*Church Quarterly Review,* April, 1881.

"Mr STREANE'S **Jeremiah** consists of a series of admirable and wellnigh exhaustive notes on the text, with introduction and appendices, drawing the life, times, and character of the prophet, the style, contents, and arrangement of his prophecies, the traditions relating to Jeremiah, meant as a type of Christ (a most remarkable chapter), and other prophecies relating to Jeremiah."—*The English Churchman and Clerical Journal.*

Obadiah and Jonah. "This number of the admirable series of Scriptural expositions issued by the Syndics of the Cambridge University Press is well up to the mark. The numerous notes are excellent. No difficulty is shirked, and much light is thrown on the contents both of Obadiah and Jonah. Scholars and students of to-day are to be congratulated on having so large an amount of information on Biblical subjects, so clearly and ably put together, placed within their reach in such small bulk. To all Biblical students the series will be acceptable, and for the use of Sabbath-school teachers will prove invaluable."—*North British Daily Mail.*

"It is a very useful and sensible exposition of these two Minor Prophets, and deals very thoroughly and honestly with the immense difficulties of the later-named of the two, from the orthodox point of view."—*Expositor.*

"**Haggai and Zechariah.** This interesting little volume is of great value. It is one of the best books in that well-known series of scholarly and popular commentaries, 'the Cambridge Bible for Schools and Colleges' of which Dean Perowne is the General Editor. In the expositions of Archdeacon Perowne we are always sure to notice learning, ability, judgment and reverence.... The notes are terse and pointed, but full and reliable."—*Churchman.*

"**The Gospel according to St Matthew**, by the Rev. A. CARR. The introduction is able, scholarly, and eminently practical, as it bears on the authorship and contents of the Gospel, and the original form in which it is supposed to have been written. It is well illustrated by two excellent maps of the Holy Land and of the Sea of Galilee."—*English Churchman.*

"**St Matthew**, edited by A. CARR, M.A. **The Book of Joshua**, edited by G. F. MACLEAR, D.D. **The General Epistle of St James**, edited by E. H. PLUMPTRE, D.D. The introductions and notes are scholarly, and generally such as young readers need and can appreciate. The maps in both Joshua and Matthew are very good, and all matters of editing are faultless. Professor Plumptre's notes on 'The Epistle of St James' are models of terse, exact, and elegant renderings of the original, which is too often obscured in the authorised version."—*Nonconformist.*

"**St Mark**, with Notes by the Rev. G. F. MACLEAR, D.D. Into this small volume Dr Maclear, besides a clear and able Introduction to the Gospel, and the text of St Mark, has compressed many hundreds of valuable and helpful notes. In short, he has given us a capital manual of the kind required—containing all that is needed to illustrate the text, i.e. all that can be drawn from the history, geography, customs, and manners of the time. But as a handbook, giving in a clear and succinct form the information which a lad requires in order to stand an examination in the Gospel, it is admirable......I can very heartily commend it, not only to the senior boys and girls in our High Schools, but also to Sunday-school teachers, who may get from it the very kind of knowledge they often find it hardest to get."—*Expositor.*

"With the help of a book like this, an intelligent teacher may make 'Divinity' as interesting a lesson as any in the school course. The notes are of a kind that will be, for the most part, intelligible to boys of the lower forms of our public schools; but they may be read with greater profit by the fifth and sixth, in conjunction with the original text."—*The Academy.*

"St Luke. Canon FARRAR has supplied students of the Gospel with an admirable manual in this volume. It has all that copious variety of illustration, ingenuity of suggestion, and general soundness of interpretation which readers are accustomed to expect from the learned and eloquent editor. Any one who has been accustomed to associate the idea of 'dryness' with a commentary, should go to Canon Farrar's St Luke for a more correct impression. He will find that a commentary may be made interesting in the highest degree, and that without losing anything of its solid value. . . . But, so to speak, it is *too good* for some of the readers for whom it is intended."—*The Spectator.*

"Canon FARRAR's contribution to The Cambridge School Bible is one of the most valuable yet made. His annotations on **The Gospel according to St Luke**, while they display a scholarship at least as sound, and an erudition at least as wide and varied as those of the editors of St Matthew and St Mark, are rendered telling and attractive by a more lively imagination, a keener intellectual and spiritual insight, a more incisive and picturesque style. His *St Luke* is worthy to be ranked with Professor Plumptre's *St James*, than which no higher commendation can well be given."—*The Expositor.*

"St Luke. Edited by Canon FARRAR, D.D. We have received with pleasure this edition of the Gospel by St Luke, by Canon Farrar. It is another instalment of the best school commentary of the Bible we possess. Of the expository part of the work we cannot speak too highly. It is admirable in every way, and contains just the sort of information needed for Students of the English text unable to make use of the original Greek for themselves."—*The Nonconformist and Independent.*

"As a handbook to the third gospel, this small work is invaluable. The author has compressed into little space a vast mass of scholarly information. . . The notes are pithy, vigorous, and suggestive, abounding in pertinent illustrations from general literature, and aiding the youngest reader to an intelligent appreciation of the text. A finer contribution to 'The Cambridge Bible for Schools' has not yet been made."—*Baptist Magazine.*

"We were quite prepared to find in Canon FARRAR'S St Luke a masterpiece of Biblical criticism and comment, and we are not disappointed by our examination of the volume before us. It reflects very faithfully the learning and critical insight of the Canon's greatest works, his 'Life of Christ' and his 'Life of St Paul', but differs widely from both in the terseness and condensation of its style. What Canon Farrar has evidently aimed at is to place before students as much information as possible within the limits of the smallest possible space, and in this aim he has hit the mark to perfection."—*The Examiner.*

The Gospel according to St John. "Of the notes we can say with confidence that they are useful, necessary, learned, and brief. To Divinity students, to teachers, and for private use, this compact Commentary will be found a valuable aid to the better understanding of the Sacred Text."—*School Guardian.*

"The new volume of the 'Cambridge Bible for Schools'—the **Gospel according to St John**, by the Rev. A. PLUMMER—shows as careful and thorough work as either of its predecessors. The introduction concisely yet fully describes the life of St John, the authenticity of the Gospel, its characteristics, its relation to the Synoptic Gospels, and to the Apostle's First Epistle, and the usual subjects referred to in an 'introduction'."—*The Christian Church.*

"The notes are extremely scholarly and valuable, and in most cases exhaustive, bringing to the elucidation of the text all that is best in commentaries, ancient and modern."—*The English Churchman and Clerical Journal.*

"(1) **The Acts of the Apostles.** By J. RAWSON LUMBY, D.D. (2) **The Second Epistle of the Corinthians**, edited by Professor LIAS. The introduction is pithy, and contains a mass of carefully-selected information on the authorship of the Acts, its designs, and its sources. ...... The Second Epistle of the Corinthians is a manual beyond all praise, for the excellence of its pithy and pointed annotations, its analysis of the contents, and the fulness and value of its introduction."—*Examiner.*

"The concluding portion of the **Acts of the Apostles**, under the very competent editorship of Dr LUMBY, is a valuable addition to our school-books on that subject. Detailed criticism is impossible within the space at our command, but we may say that the ample notes touch with much exactness the very points on which most readers of the text desire information. Due reference is made, where necessary, to the Revised Version; the maps are excellent; and we do not know of any other volume where so much help is given to the complete understanding of one of the most important and, in many respects, difficult books of the New Testament."—*School Guardian.*

"The Rev. H. C. G. MOULE, M.A., has made a valuable addition to THE CAMBRIDGE BIBLE FOR SCHOOLS in his brief commentary on the **Epistle to the Romans**. The 'Notes' are very good, and lean, as the notes of a School Bible should, to the most commonly accepted and orthodox view of the inspired author's meaning; while the Introduction, and especially the Sketch of the Life of St Paul, is a model of condensation. It is as lively and pleasant to read as if two or three facts had not been crowded into well-nigh every sentence."—*Expositor.*

"**The Epistle to the Romans.** It is seldom we have met with a work so remarkable for the compression and condensation of all that is valuable in the smallest possible space as in the volume before us. Within its limited pages we have 'a sketch of the Life of St Paul,' we have further a critical account of the date of the Epistle to the Romans, of its language, and of its genuineness. The notes are numerous, full of matter, to the point, and leave no real difficulty or obscurity unexplained."—*The Examiner.*

OPINIONS OF THE PRESS.

"**The First Epistle to the Corinthians.** Edited by Professor LIAS. Every fresh instalment of this annotated edition of the Bible for Schools confirms the favourable opinion we formed of its value from the examination of its first number. The origin and plan of the Epistle are discussed with its character and genuineness."—*The Nonconformist.*

"**The Second Epistle to the Corinthians.** By Professor LIAS. **The General Epistles of St Peter and St Jude.** By E. H. PLUMPTRE, D.D. We welcome these additions to the valuable series of the Cambridge Bible. We have nothing to add to the commendation which we have from the first publication given to this edition of the Bible. It is enough to say that Professor Lias has completed his work on the two Epistles to the Corinthians in the same admirable manner as at first. Dr Plumptre has also completed the Catholic Epistles."—*Nonconformist.*

The Epistle to the Ephesians. By Rev. H. C. G. MOULE, M.A. "It seems to us the model of a School and College Commentary— comprehensive, but not cumbersome; scholarly, but not pedantic."— *Baptist Magazine.*

The Epistle to the Philippians. "There are few series more valued by theological students than 'The Cambridge Bible for Schools and Colleges,' and there will be no number of it more esteemed than that by Mr H. C. G. MOULE on the *Epistle to the Philippians.*"—*Record.*

"Another capital volume of 'The Cambridge Bible for Schools and Colleges.' The notes are a model of scholarly, lucid, and compact criticism."—*Baptist Magazine.*

Hebrews. "Like his (Canon Farrar's) commentary on Luke it possesses all the best characteristics of his writing. It is a work not only of an accomplished scholar, but of a skilled teacher."—*Baptist Magazine.*

"We heartily commend this volume of this excellent work."— *Sunday School Chronicle.*

"**The General Epistle of St James,** by Professor PLUMPTRE, D.D. Nevertheless it is, so far as I know, by far the best exposition of the Epistle of St James in the English language. Not Schoolboys or Students going in for an examination alone, but Ministers and Preachers of the Word, may get more real help from it than from the most costly and elaborate commentaries."—*Expositor.*

The Epistles of St John. By the Rev. A. PLUMMER, M.A., D.D. "This forms an admirable companion to the 'Commentary on the Gospel according to St John,' which was reviewed in *The Churchman* as soon as it appeared. Dr Plummer has some of the highest qualifications for such a task; and these two volumes, their size being considered, will bear comparison with the best Commentaries of the time."—*The Churchman.*

"Dr PLUMMER's edition of **the Epistles of St John** is worthy of its companions in the 'Cambridge Bible for Schools' Series. The subject, though not apparently extensive, is really one not easy to treat, and requiring to be treated at length, owing to the constant reference to obscure heresies in the Johannine writings. Dr Plummer has done his exegetical task well."—*The Saturday Review.*

THE CAMBRIDGE GREEK TESTAMENT
FOR SCHOOLS AND COLLEGES

with a Revised Text, based on the most recent critical authorities, and English Notes, prepared under the direction of the General Editor, THE VERY REVEREND J. J. S. PEROWNE, D.D.

"*Has achieved an excellence which puts it above criticism.*"—Expositor.

St Matthew. "Copious illustrations, gathered from a great variety of sources, make his notes a very valuable aid to the student. They are indeed remarkably interesting, while all explanations on meanings, applications, and the like are distinguished by their lucidity and good sense."—*Pall Mall Gazette*.

St Mark. "The Cambridge Greek Testament of which Dr MACLEAR'S edition of the Gospel according to St Mark is a volume, certainly supplies a want. Without pretending to compete with the leading commentaries, or to embody very much original research, it forms a most satisfactory introduction to the study of the New Testament in the original....Dr Maclear's introduction contains all that is known of St Mark's life; an account of the circumstances in which the Gospel was composed, with an estimate of the influence of St Peter's teaching upon St Mark; an excellent sketch of the special characteristics of this Gospel; an analysis, and a chapter on the text of the New Testament generally."—*Saturday Review*.

St Luke. "Of this second series we have a new volume by Archdeacon FARRAR on *St Luke*, completing the four Gospels....It gives us in clear and beautiful language the best results of modern scholarship. We have a most attractive *Introduction*. Then follows a sort of composite Greek text, representing fairly and in very beautiful type the consensus of modern textual critics. At the beginning of the exposition of each chapter of the Gospel are a few short critical notes giving the manuscript evidence for such various readings as seem to deserve mention. The expository notes are short, but clear and helpful. For young students and those who are not disposed to buy or to study the much more costly work of Godet, this seems to us to be the best book on the Greek Text of the Third Gospel."—*Methodist Recorder*.

St John. "We take this opportunity of recommending to ministers on probation, the very excellent volume of the same series on this part of the New Testament. We hope that most or all of our young ministers will prefer to study the volume in the *Cambridge Greek Testament for Schools*."—*Methodist Recorder*.

The Acts of the Apostles. "Professor LUMBY has performed his laborious task well, and supplied us with a commentary the fulness and freshness of which Bible students will not be slow to appreciate. The volume is enriched with the usual copious indexes and four coloured maps."—*Glasgow Herald*.

I. Corinthians. "Mr LIAS is no novice in New Testament exposition, and the present series of essays and notes is an able and helpful addition to the existing books."—*Guardian*.

The Epistles of St John. "In the very useful and well annotated series of the Cambridge Greek Testament the volume on the Epistles of St John must hold a high position... The notes are brief, well informed and intelligent."—*Scotsman*.

CAMBRIDGE: PRINTED BY C. J. CLAY, M.A. AND SONS, AT THE UNIVERSITY PRESS.

CAMBRIDGE UNIVERSITY PRESS.

THE PITT PRESS SERIES.

* *Many of the books in this list can be had in two volumes, Text and Notes separately.*

I. GREEK.

Aristophanes. Aves—Plutus—Ranæ. By W. C. GREEN, M.A., late Assistant Master at Rugby School. 3s. 6d. each.
Aristotle. Outlines of the Philosophy of. By EDWIN WALLACE, M.A., LL.D. Third Edition, Enlarged. 4s. 6d.
Euripides. Heracleidae. By E. A. BECK, M.A. 3s. 6d.
—— **Hercules Furens.** By A. GRAY, M.A., and J. T. HUTCHINSON, M.A. New Edit. 2s.
—— **Hippolytus.** By W. S. HADLEY, M.A. 2s.
—— **Iphigeneia in Aulis.** By C. E. S. HEADLAM, B.A. 2s. 6d.
Herodotus, Book V. By E. S. SHUCKBURGH, M.A. 3s.
—— **Book VI.** By the same Editor. 4s.
—— **Book VIII., Chaps. 1—90.** By the same Editor. 3s. 6d.
—— **Book IX., Chaps. 1—89.** By the same Editor. 3s. 6d.
Homer. Odyssey, Books IX., X. By G. M. EDWARDS, M.A. 2s. 6d. each.
—— —— **Book XXI.** By the same Editor. 2s.
—— **Iliad. Books XXII., XXIII.** By the same Editor. [*Nearly ready.*]
Lucian. Somnium Charon Piscator et De Luctu. By W. E. HEITLAND, M.A., Fellow of St John's College, Cambridge. 3s. 6d.
—— **Menippus and Timon.** By E. C. MACKIE, M.A. [*Nearly ready.*]
Platonis Apologia Socratis. By J. ADAM, M.A. 3s. 6d.
—— **Crito.** By the same Editor. 2s. 6d.
—— **Euthyphro.** By the same Editor. 2s. 6d.
Plutarch. Lives of the Gracchi. By Rev. H. A. HOLDEN, M.A., LL.D. 6s.
—— **Life of Nicias.** By the same Editor. 5s.
—— **Life of Sulla.** By the same Editor. 6s.
—— **Life of Timoleon.** By the same Editor. 6s.
Sophocles. Oedipus Tyrannus. School Edition. By R. C. JEBB, Litt.D., LL.D. 4s. 6d.
Thucydides. Book VII. By Rev. H. A. HOLDEN, M.A., LL.D. [*Nearly ready.*]
Xenophon. Agesilaus. By H. HAILSTONE, M.A. 2s. 6d.
—— **Anabasis.** By A. PRETOR, M.A. Two vols. 7s. 6d.
—— **Books I. III. IV. and V.** By the same. 2s. each.
—— **Books II. VI. and VII.** By the same. 2s. 6d. each.
Xenophon. Cyropaedeia. Books I. II. By Rev. H. A. HOLDEN, M.A., LL.D. 2 vols. 6s.
—— —— **Books III. IV. and V.** By the same Editor. 5s.
—— —— **Books VI. VII. VIII.** By the same Editor. [*Nearly ready.*]

London: Cambridge Warehouse, Ave Maria Lane.

20/10/90

II. LATIN.

Beda's Ecclesiastical History, Books III., IV. By J. E. B. MAYOR, M.A., and J. R. LUMBY, D.D. Revised Edition. 7s. 6d.

—— **Books I. II.** By the same Editors. [*In the Press.*

Caesar. De Bello Gallico, Comment. I. By A. G. PESKETT, M.A., Fellow of Magdalene College, Cambridge. 1s. 6d. COMMENT. II. III. 2s. COMMENT. I. II. III. 3s. COMMENT. IV. and V., COMMENT. VII. 2s. each. COMMENT. VI. and COMMENT. VIII. 1s. 6d. each.

—— **De Bello Civili, Comment. I.** By the same Editor.

Cicero. De Amicitia.—De Senectute. By J. S. REID, Litt.D., Fellow of Gonville and Caius College. 3s. 6d. each.

—— **In Gaium Verrem Actio Prima.** By H. COWIE, M.A. 1s. 6d.

—— **In Q. Caecilium Divinatio et in C. Verrem Actio.** By W. E. HEITLAND, M.A., and H. COWIE, M.A. 3s.

—— **Philippica Secunda.** By A. G. PESKETT, M.A. 3s. 6d.

—— **Oratio pro Archia Poeta.** By J. S. REID, Litt.D. 2s.

—— **Pro L. Cornelio Balbo Oratio.** By the same. 1s. 6d.

—— **Oratio pro Tito Annio Milone.** By JOHN SMYTH PURTON, B.D. 2s. 6d.

—— **Oratio pro L. Murena.** By W. E. HEITLAND, M.A. 3s.

—— **Pro Cn. Plancio Oratio,** by H. A. HOLDEN, LL.D. 4s. 6d.

—— **Pro P. Cornelio Sulla.** By J. S. REID, Litt.D. 3s. 6d.

—— **Somnium Scipionis.** By W. D. PEARMAN, M.A. 2s.

Horace. Epistles, Book I. By E. S. SHUCKBURGH, M.A., late Fellow of Emmanuel College. 2s. 6d.

Livy. Book IV. By H. M. STEPHENSON, M.A. 2s. 6d.

—— **Book V.** By L. WHIBLEY, M.A. 2s. 6d.

—— **Books XXI., XXII.** By M. S. DIMSDALE, M.A., Fellow of King's College. 2s. 6d. each.

—— **Book XXVII.** By Rev. H. M. STEPHENSON, M.A. [*Nearly ready.*

Lucan. Pharsaliae Liber Primus. By W. E. HEITLAND, M.A., and C. E. HASKINS, M.A. 1s. 6d.

Lucretius, Book V. By J. D. DUFF, M.A. 2s.

Ovidii Nasonis Fastorum Liber VI. By A. SIDGWICK, M.A., Tutor of Corpus Christi College, Oxford. 1s. 6d.

Quintus Curtius. A Portion of the History (Alexander in India). By W. E. HEITLAND, M.A., and T. E. RAVEN, B.A. With Two Maps. 3s. 6d.

Vergili Maronis Aeneidos Libri I.—XII. By A. SIDGWICK, M.A. 1s. 6d. each.

—— **Bucolica.** By the same Editor. 1s. 6d.

—— **Georgicon Libri I. II.** By the same Editor. 2s.

—— —— **Libri III. IV.** By the same Editor. 2s.

—— **The Complete Works.** By the same Editor. Two vols. Vol. I. containing the Introduction and Text. 3s. 6d. Vol. II. The Notes. 4s. 6d.

London: Cambridge Warehouse, Ave Maria Lane.

III. FRENCH.

Corneille. La Suite du Menteur. A Comedy in Five Acts.
By the late G. MASSON, B.A. 2*s*.

De Bonnechose. Lazare Hoche. By C. COLBECK, M.A.
Revised Edition. Four Maps. 2*s*.

D'Harleville. Le Vieux Célibataire. By G. MASSON, B.A. 2*s*.

De Lamartine. Jeanne D'Arc. By Rev. A. C. CLAPIN,
M.A., St John's College, Cambridge. 2*s*.

De Vigny. La Canne de Jonc. By Rev. H. A. BULL,
M.A., late Master at Wellington College. 2*s*.

Erckmann-Chatrian. La Guerre. By Rev. A. C. CLAPIN,
M.A. 3*s*.

La Baronne de Staël-Holstein. Le Directoire. (Considérations sur la Révolution Française. Troisième et quatrième parties.) Revised and enlarged. By G. MASSON, B.A., and G. W. PROTHERO, M.A. 2*s*.

────── ────── **Dix Années d'Exil. Livre II. Chapitres 1—8.**
By the same Editors. New Edition, enlarged. 2*s*.

Lemercier. Fredegonde et Brunehaut. A Tragedy in Five
Acts. By GUSTAVE MASSON, B.A. 2*s*.

Molière. Le Bourgeois Gentilhomme, Comédie-Ballet en
Cinq Actes. (1670.) By Rev. A. C. CLAPIN, M.A. Revised Edition. 1*s*. 6*d*.

────── **L'École des Femmes.** By G. SAINTSBURY, M.A. 2*s*. 6*d*.

────── **Les Précieuses Ridicules.** By E. G. W. BRAUNHOLTZ,
M.A., Ph.D. 2*s*.

────── ────── **Abridged Edition.** 1*s*.

Piron. La Métromanie. A Comedy. By G. MASSON, B.A. 2*s*.

Racine. Les Plaideurs. By E. G. W. BRAUNHOLTZ, M.A. 2*s*.

────── ────── **Abridged Edition.** 1*s*.

Sainte-Beuve. M. Daru (Causeries du Lundi, Vol. IX.).
By G. MASSON, B.A. 2*s*.

Saintine. Picciola. By Rev. A. C. CLAPIN, M.A. 2*s*.

Scribe and Legouvé. Bataille de Dames. By Rev. H. A.
BULL, M.A. 2*s*.

Scribe. Le Verre d'Eau. By C. COLBECK, M.A. 2*s*.

Sédaine. Le Philosophe sans le savoir. By Rev. H. A.
BULL, M.A. 2*s*.

Thierry. Lettres sur l'histoire de France (XIII.—XXIV.).
By G. MASSON, B.A., and G. W. PROTHERO, M.A. 2*s*. 6*d*.

────── **Récits des Temps Mérovingiens I.—III.** By GUSTAVE
MASSON, B.A. Univ. Gallic., and A. R. ROPES, M.A. With Map. 3*s*.

Villemain. Lascaris ou Les Grecs du XVe Siècle, Nouvelle
Historique. By G. MASSON, B.A. 2*s*.

**Voltaire. Histoire du Siècle de Louis XIV. Chaps. I.—
XIII.** By G. MASSON, B.A., and G. W. PROTHERO, M.A. 2*s*. 6*d*. PART II.
CHAPS. XIV.—XXIV. 2*s*. 6*d*. PART III. CHAPS. XXV. to end. 2*s*. 6*d*.

Xavier de Maistre. La Jeune Sibérienne. Le Lépreux de
la Cité D'Aoste. By G. MASSON, B.A. 1*s*. 6*d*.

London: Cambridge Warehouse, Ave Maria Lane.

IV. GERMAN.

Ballads on German History. By W. WAGNER, Ph.D. 2s.
Benedix. Doctor Wespe. Lustspiel in fünf Aufzügen. By KARL HERMANN BREUL, M.A., Ph.D. 3s.
Freytag. Der Staat Friedrichs des Grossen. By WILHELM WAGNER, Ph.D. 2s.
German Dactylic Poetry. By WILHELM WAGNER, Ph.D. 3s.
Goethe's Knabenjahre. (1749—1759.) By W. WAGNER, Ph.D. 2s.
—— **Hermann und Dorothea.** By WILHELM WAGNER, Ph.D. Revised edition by J. W. CARTMELL, M.A. 3s. 6d.
Gutzkow. Zopf und Schwert. Lustspiel in fünf Aufzügen. By H. J. WOLSTENHOLME, B.A. (Lond.). 3s. 6d.
Hauff. Das Bild des Kaisers. By KARL HERMANN BREUL, M.A., Ph.D., University Lecturer in German. 3s.
—— **Das Wirthshaus im Spessart.** By A. SCHLOTTMANN, Ph.D. 3s. 6d.
—— **Die Karavane.** By A. SCHLOTTMANN, Ph.D. 3s. 6d.
Immermann. Der Oberhof. A Tale of Westphalian Life, by WILHELM WAGNER, Ph.D. 3s.
Kohlrausch. Das Jahr 1813. By WILHELM WAGNER, Ph.D. 2s.
Lessing and Gellert. Selected Fables. By KARL HERMANN BREUL, M.A., Ph.D. 3s.
Mendelssohn's Letters. Selections from. By J. SIME, M.A. 3s.
Raumer. Der erste Kreuzzug (1095—1099). By WILHELM WAGNER, Ph.D. 2s.
Riehl. Culturgeschichtliche Novellen. By H. J. WOLSTENHOLME, B.A. (Lond.). 3s. 6d.
Schiller. Wilhelm Tell. By KARL HERMANN BREUL, M.A., Ph.D. 2s. 6d.
—— —— Abridged Edition. 1s. 6d.
Uhland. Ernst, Herzog von Schwaben. By H. J. WOLSTENHOLME, B.A. 3s. 6d.

V. ENGLISH.

Ancient Philosophy from Thales to Cicero, A Sketch of. By JOSEPH B. MAYOR, M.A. 3s. 6d.
An Apologie for Poetrie by Sir PHILIP SIDNEY. By E. S. SHUCKBURGH, M.A. The Text is a revision of that of the first edition of 1595. [*Nearly ready.*
Bacon's History of the Reign of King Henry VII. By the Rev. Professor LUMBY, D.D. 3s.
Cowley's Essays. By the Rev. Professor LUMBY, D.D. 4s.

London: Cambridge Warehouse, Ave Maria Lane.

Milton's Comus and Arcades. By A. W. VERITY, M.A., sometime Scholar of Trinity College. [*Nearly ready.*

More's History of King Richard III. By J. RAWSON LUMBY, D.D. 3s. 6d.

More's Utopia. By Rev. Prof. LUMBY, D.D. 3s. 6d.

The Two Noble Kinsmen. By the Rev. Professor SKEAT, Litt.D. 3s. 6d.

VI. EDUCATIONAL SCIENCE.

Comenius, John Amos, Bishop of the Moravians. His Life and Educational Works, by S. S. LAURIE, A.M., F.R.S.E. 3s. 6d.

Education, Three Lectures on the Practice of. I. On Marking, by H. W. EVE, M.A. II. On Stimulus, by A. SIDGWICK, M.A. III. On the Teaching of Latin Verse Composition, by E. A. ABBOTT, D.D. 2s.

Stimulus. A Lecture delivered for the Teachers' Training Syndicate, May, 1882, by A. SIDGWICK, M.A. 1s.

Locke on Education. By the Rev. R. H. QUICK, M.A. 3s. 6d.

Milton's Tractate on Education. A facsimile reprint from the Edition of 1673. By O. BROWNING, M.A. 2s.

Modern Languages, Lectures on the Teaching of. By C. COLBECK, M.A. 2s.

Teacher, General Aims of the, and Form Management. Two Lectures delivered in the University of Cambridge in the Lent Term, 1883, by F. W. FARRAR, D.D., and R. B. POOLE, B.D. 1s. 6d.

Teaching, Theory and Practice of. By the Rev. E. THRING, M.A., late Head Master of Uppingham School. New Edition. 4s. 6d.

British India, a Short History of. By E. S. CARLOS, M.A., late Head Master of Exeter Grammar School. 1s.

Geography, Elementary Commercial. A Sketch of the Commodities and the Countries of the World. By H. R. MILL, D.Sc., F.R.S.E. 1s.

Geography, an Atlas of Commercial. (A Companion to the above.) By J. G. BARTHOLOMEW, F.R.G.S. With an Introduction by HUGH ROBERT MILL, D.Sc. 3s.

VII. MATHEMATICS.

Euclid's Elements of Geometry. Books I. and II. By H. M. TAYLOR, M.A., Fellow and late Tutor of Trinity College, Cambridge. 1s. 6d.

—— —— Books III. and IV. By the same Editor.
[*Nearly ready.*

Elementary Algebra (with Answers to the Examples). By W. W. ROUSE BALL, M.A. 4s. 6d.

Other Volumes are in preparation.

London: *Cambridge Warehouse, Ave Maria Lane.*

The Cambridge Bible for Schools and Colleges.

GENERAL EDITOR: J. J. S. PEROWNE, D.D.,
DEAN OF PETERBOROUGH.

"*It is difficult to commend too highly this excellent series.*—Guardian.

"*The modesty of the general title of this series has, we believe, led many to misunderstand its character and underrate its value. The books are well suited for study in the upper forms of our best schools, but not the less are they adapted to the wants of all Bible students who are not specialists. We doubt, indeed, whether any of the numerous popular commentaries recently issued in this country will be found more serviceable for general use.*"—Academy.

Now Ready. Cloth, Extra Fcap. 8vo. With Maps.

Book of Joshua. By Rev. G. F. MACLEAR, D.D. 2s. 6d.
Book of Judges. By Rev. J. J. LIAS, M.A. 3s. 6d.
First Book of Samuel. By Rev. Prof. KIRKPATRICK, B.D. 3s. 6d.
Second Book of Samuel. By Rev. Prof. KIRKPATRICK, B.D. 3s. 6d.
First Book of Kings. By Rev. Prof. LUMBY, D.D. 3s. 6d.
Second Book of Kings. By Rev. Prof. LUMBY, D.D. 3s. 6d.
Book of Job. By Rev. A. B. DAVIDSON, D.D. 5s.
Book of Ecclesiastes. By Very Rev. E. H. PLUMPTRE, D.D. 5s.
Book of Jeremiah. By Rev. A. W. STREANE, M.A. 4s. 6d.
Book of Hosea. By Rev. T. K. CHEYNE, M.A., D.D. 3s.
Books of Obadiah & Jonah. By Archdeacon PEROWNE. 2s. 6d.
Book of Micah. By Rev. T. K. CHEYNE, M.A., D.D. 1s. 6d.
Haggai, Zechariah & Malachi. By Arch. PEROWNE. 3s. 6d.
Book of Malachi. By Archdeacon PEROWNE. 1s.
Gospel according to St Matthew. By Rev. A. CARR, M.A. 2s. 6d.
Gospel according to St Mark. By Rev. G. F. MACLEAR, D.D. 2s. 6d.
Gospel according to St Luke. By Arch. FARRAR, D.D. 4s. 6d.
Gospel according to St John. By Rev. A. PLUMMER, D.D. 4s. 6d.
Acts of the Apostles. By Rev. Prof. LUMBY, D.D. 4s. 6d.
Epistle to the Romans. By Rev. H. C. G. MOULE, M.A. 3s. 6d.
First Corinthians. By Rev. J. J. LIAS, M.A. With Map. 2s.
Second Corinthians. By Rev. J. J. LIAS, M.A. With Map. 2s.

London: Cambridge Warehouse, Ave Maria Lane.

Epistle to the Galatians. By Rev. E. H. PEROWNE, D.D. 1s. 6d.
Epistle to the Ephesians. By Rev. H. C. G. MOULE, M.A. 2s. 6d.
Epistle to the Philippians. By Rev. H. C. G. MOULE, M.A. 2s. 6d.
Epistle to the Hebrews. By Arch. FARRAR, D.D. 3s. 6d.
General Epistle of St James. By Very Rev. E. H. PLUMPTRE, D.D. 1s. 6d.
Epistles of St Peter and St Jude. By Very Rev. E. H. PLUMPTRE, D.D. 2s. 6d.
Epistles of St John. By Rev. A. PLUMMER, M.A., D.D. 3s. 6d.
Book of Revelation. By Rev. W. H. SIMCOX, M.A. 3s.

Preparing.

Book of Genesis. By Very Rev. the Dean of Peterborough.
Books of Exodus, Numbers and Deuteronomy. By Rev. C. D. GINSBURG, LL.D.
Books of Ezra and Nehemiah. By Rev. Prof. RYLE, M.A.
Book of Psalms. Part I. By Rev. Prof. KIRKPATRICK, B.D.
Book of Isaiah. By Prof. W. ROBERTSON SMITH, M.A.
Book of Ezekiel. By Rev. A. B. DAVIDSON, D.D.
Epistles to the Colossians and Philemon. By Rev. H. C. G. MOULE, M.A.
Epistles to the Thessalonians. By Rev. G. G. FINDLAY, M.A.
Epistles to Timothy & Titus. By Rev. A. E. HUMPHREYS, M.A.

The Smaller Cambridge Bible for Schools.

The Smaller Cambridge Bible for Schools *will form an entirely new series of commentaries on some selected books of the Bible. It is expected that they will be prepared for the most part by the Editors of the larger series (The Cambridge Bible for Schools and Colleges). The volumes will be issued at a low price, and will be suitable to the requirements of preparatory and elementary schools.*

Now ready.

First and Second Books of Samuel. By Rev. Prof. KIRKPATRICK, B.D. 1s. each.
Gospel according to St Matthew. By Rev. A. CARR, M.A. 1s.
Gospel according to St Mark. By Rev. G. F. MACLEAR, D.D. 1s.
Gospel according to St Luke. By Archdeacon FARRAR. 1s.
Acts of the Apostles. By Rev. Prof. LUMBY, D.D.
[*Nearly ready.*]

London: Cambridge Warehouse, Ave Maria Lane.

The Cambridge Greek Testament for Schools and Colleges,

with a Revised Text, based on the most recent critical authorities, and English Notes, prepared under the direction of the General Editor,

The Very Reverend J. J. S. PEROWNE, D.D.,
DEAN OF PETERBOROUGH.

Gospel according to St Matthew. By Rev. A. CARR, M.A.
With 4 Maps. 4s. 6d.

Gospel according to St Mark. By Rev. G. F. MACLEAR, D.D.
With 3 Maps. 4s. 6d.

Gospel according to St Luke. By Archdeacon FARRAR.
With 4 Maps. 6s.

Gospel according to St John. By Rev. A. PLUMMER, D.D.
With 4 Maps. 6s.

Acts of the Apostles. By Rev. Professor LUMBY, D.D.
With 4 Maps. 6s.

First Epistle to the Corinthians. By Rev. J. J. LIAS, M.A. 3s.

Second Epistle to the Corinthians. By Rev. J. J. LIAS, M.A.
[In the Press.

Epistle to the Hebrews. By Archdeacon FARRAR, D.D. 3s. 6d.

Epistle of St James. By Very Rev. E. H. PLUMPTRE, D.D.
[Preparing.

Epistles of St John. By Rev. A. PLUMMER, M.A., D.D. 4s.

London: C. J. CLAY AND SONS,
CAMBRIDGE WAREHOUSE, AVE MARIA LANE.
Glasgow: 263, ARGYLE STREET.
Cambridge: DEIGHTON, BELL AND CO.
Leipzig: F. A. BROCKHAUS.

www.ingramcontent.com/pod-product-compliance
Lightning Source LLC
Chambersburg PA
CBHW020758230426
43666CB00007B/757